Using Motif with C++

ADVANCES IN OBJECT TECHNOLOGY SERIES

Dr. Richard S. Wiener
Series Editor

Editor
Journal of Object-Oriented Programming
Report on Object Analysis and Design
SIGS Publications, Inc.
New York, New York

and

Department of Computer Science
University of Colorado
Colorado Springs, Colorado

Additional Volumes in Preparation

Using Motif with C++

Daniel J. Bernstein
Computer Science Services Group
Wichita, Kansas

SIGS
BOOKS
New York

Daniel J. Bernstein is a partner at Computer Science Services Group, LLC, and offers various training and consulting services related to object oriented analysis, design and programming, as well as Motif and OpenLook. For more information, contact the author at CSS Group, LLC, PO Box 544, Wichita, KS 67201 or call (316) 652-7700.

Electronic versions of the source code fragments and examples presented in this book are available via anonymous FTP. To obtain the distribution, login to ftp.sigs.com as anonymous (use the password <your email address>). The distribution can be found in the /pub/sigs/bernstein directory. After downloading the distribution, see the file "README" for more information.

Athena is a trademark of Massachusetts Institute of Technology; g++ is a trademark of the Free Software Foundation; Gnu is a trademark of the Free Software Foundation; Motif is a registered trademark of the Open Software Foundation; OpenLook is a registered trademark of Sun Microsystems, Inc.; Rose is a registered trademark of Rational, Inc.; Solaris is a registered trademark of Sun Microsystems, Inc.; Unix is a trademark of X/Open; X Toolkit is a trademark of Massachusetts Institute of Technology; X Window is a trademark of Massachusetts Institute of Technology

Library of Congress Cataloging-in-Publication Data

Bernstein, Daniel, 1965–
    Using Motif with C++ / Daniel Bernstein.
      p. cm. -- (Advances in object technology : 5)
    Includes bibliographical references and index.
    ISBN 1–884842–06–2 (pbk. : acid-free paper)
    1. Motif (Computer file) 2. X Window System (Computer system)
    3. C++ (Computer program language) I. Title. II. Series.
    QA76.76.W56B475   1995
    005.2--dc20   94–44611
                                      CIP

PUBLISHED BY
SIGS Books
71 W. 23rd Street, Third Floor
New York, New York 10010

SIGS Books ISBN 1–884842–06–2
Prentice Hall ISBN 0–13–207390–0

Printed in the United States of America
99 98 97 96 95   10 9 8 7 6 5 4 3 2 1
First Printing March 1995

To my mother, who raised me,
and my wife, who keeps me . . .

About
the Author

Daniel J. Bernstein is Partner and Principal Software Engineer at Computer Science Services Group, LLC, Wichita, Kansas, a firm specializing in object-oriented software development, consulting, and training. Previously, as Project Manager at One Call Concepts, Inc., Wichita, the author designed and managed a project for a mapping software library (MSL), which was written in the C++ programming language with strict adherence to object-oriented development principles. This project was recognized as one of the top 19 object oriented projects in a contest held by the Object World 1992 Conference, Computerworld magazine, and the Object Management Group (OMG). The author also held the position of Software Engineer at Link Flight Simulation Corporation, Sunnyvale, California, where he designed and developed flight simulation software in Ada for a large military project that involved converting Defense Mapping Agency satellite data for real-time 3-D flight simulation display. As Engineer at HRB Systems, Inc., State College, Pennsylvania, Bernstein wrote quality control and analysis software to develop a world map database for military applications. Other accomplishments at HRB Systems include leading a team in the design and development of an in-house Computer Aided Software Engineering environment that increased overall productivity, and designing a successful man-machine interface for an in-house Software Reuse tool Ada on a VAX/VMS platform. In the Computer Science Department at Wichita State University, the author instructed classes in various areas such as Introduction to Software Engineering, and Programming in Ada. Bernstein also held the position of Research Programmer at Carnegie Mellon University where he developed software to translate waveforms generated by a YM2151 FM Synthesizer chip to MIDI and RS232 signals. Bernstein graduated from the prestigious Bronx High School of Science, Bronx, New York, received the B.S. in Applied Mathematics/Computer Science (1987) from Carnegie Mellon University, Pittsburgh, Pennsylvania, and the M.S. in Computer Science (1994) from Wichita State University, Wichita, Kansas.

Series
Introduction

The *Advances in Object Technology* series seeks to present readers with books that provide incisive and timely information relating to object-oriented programming and programming languages, object-oriented requirements, object-oriented domain analysis, and object-oriented design. In addition, testing, metrics, formal methods and applications of object technology to areas including object-oriented databases, real-time systems, emergent computation, neural networks, and object-oriented distributed systems will be featured. The books are aimed at practicing software development professionals, programmers, educators, and students in computer-related disciplines.

It is a pleasure to introduce Daniel Bernstein's important book, *Using Motif with C++*. This intermediate-to-advanced book will take you "under the hood" and explain in detail the C++ programming protocols required to design and implement useful graphical user interfaces using Motif. The book contains many well-crafted C++ examples that I believe will provide great benefit. I hope you find this book an important addition to your technical library.

Richard S. Wiener
Series Editor

Foreword

Whenever I teach people about software programming, I always emphasize a few fundamentals that will help produce good working code as well as good performing code. The most important fundamental is, "abstract and generalize your work." One possible method is by using C++ with the Motif toolkit, both of which provide an abstraction layer that can be generalized for reusability, and which happens to be the topic of this book. This always applies more to GUI programming than any other kind, mostly because the user interface typically involves reusing a lot of code in different contexts. If you write a segment of code that you find you can use somewhere else in your application, you should break out that code into a function and call it from the places in the code that need to use it. Sound simple? Well, that's only half the perspective. Another fundamental is, "don't take that other rule too seriously." Let me explain.

Long ago, every UNIX vendor had its own proprietary windowing system and API to the graphical layer, so in order to appeal to the largest possible audience, software programmers had to choose the workstation that was used more than any other for a particular market. Those that used CAD software may have chosen one UNIX vendor, and those that used financial software would choose another. And so it would go until all 30 UNIX vendors were considered. Because of the proprietary nature of different vendors' workstations, it would have been too costly to support too many systems. This was a major problem for software programmers, vendors, and customers alike since most applications were not available across enough platforms and the UNIX market was too fragmented for any one vendor to dominate the entire market. Thus, one fundamental goal was shared by the designers of these workstations and their application developers: design code that is highly portable (among various UNIX implementations) to make it as easy as possible to make the software more widely available. This objective helped popularize another growing trend: object-oriented programming (OOP).

OOP was nice in that it generalized many "methods" of implementing common tasks, and proceduralized different classes of methodologies. That way, the programmer could write relatively few lines of code and accomplish many complex (yet common) tasks. Unfortunately, without empirical experience across many platforms, products, and windowing systems (and other library layers), the methods of OOP had a long way to go. There were OOP languages, but they were not suitable for commercial products usually because of poor performance. Thus, OOP's stigma had to be overcome, and people learned that the way to do it was to bypass the "object layer" and write code fragments that took advantage of the lower layers of the system.

One of the best examples of where this has been successful is with the X Window System. As most readers of this text know by now, X is a protocol that is exchanged between two processes: a client(typically an end-user application) and an X server that drives the keyboard/mouse devices and renders imagines on the screen. For example, an application can send a request to draw a circle, and the receiving application (the X server) would then "implement" that instruction by calling the appropriate system level API necessary to draw a circle. That may be a proprietary command for any given computer, but the X programmer needn't be bothered by those details. As long as the programmer sends the instruction using X protocol, the user will see the correct thing on the screen, regardless of the computer he's using.

Because the X protocol requires knowledge about networking and other inconvenient (and irrelevant) layers normally associated with GUI programming, a library called Xlib, was derived as the primary and most direct way (short of writing impractical networking code) to interface with the X Window System. However, Xlib can be rather verbose, so to simplify things, a new library layer was written on top of Xlib, called the X Toolkit (Xt). Xt provided a number of different features that ultimately encapsulated a number of different Xlib functions into a much smaller set of commands. For example, if you wanted to create a window that said "Hello World" in it, Xt makes this possible using much fewer calls than it would to get the same result in Xlib. However, because Xt generalized a number of different methods for performing X Window activities, most of the better programmers learn that there are times when you simply have to bypass Xt to get the right job done, or done "faster", and go directly to Xlib.

Motif is the next step beyond Xt in that it has further abstracted and generalized the task of writing even more specific, fundamental user interface code. The Motif toolkit, written in C by the Open Software Foundation, has similar characteristics to any other software toolkit: it has a number of features, bugs, workarounds and blatant omissions that the programmer should know about, so he can work around them (or take advantage of them) as necessary. In this case, there are plenty of bugs in Motif that may require the programmer to bypass Motif and go directly to Xt (or Xlib in some cases) to get the right job done (or the job done right). And, for completeness, the same is true for C++ and its relationship to C. Why is this significant? Because knowledge about why things evolved will help the programmer understand the constraints about their designs. Having specific knowledge about how X works will not only help you understand the best way to program something, but it will also help you diagnose a problem in case something doesn't work. The same can be said about Xlib, Xt, and even C. This knowledge may also provide insight as to more efficient ways of doing something.

This book is about writing applications using C++ and the Motif toolkit, both of which are the highest level toolkits in the totum pole of APIs. And, like anything else (and everything else) from which they are built, you should use these layers when they work to your advantage, and you should avoid them when they don't. That is, don't take Motif too seriously—it has its problems—and rest assured, you are going to have to lift the hood and tinker with the components inside (bypass the toolkit) to get the right thing done. Accordingly, it is not advisable to learn about Motif without a good fundamental understanding of Xt, and if you don't already know how X works, then you should start there. If you don't know C very well, learning C++ will only help you in very superficial ways. Don't be afraid to learn the prerequisites, and don't take the higher level APIs too seriously. It's great that you are now using higher level tools such as C++ and Motif, but learning the basics will only help your understanding and it will definitely help the software you ultimately write.

Dan Heller
President
Internezzo, Inc.

Preface

With the recent popularization of both object-oriented (OO) development and the graphical user interface (GUI), it has become imperative for those of us in the software industry to become experts in one or both of these fields if we wish to do such things as buy food or pay rent. In addition to considering the economic aspects of writing interfaces under the OO paradigm, many of us have come to realize something even more important—it's just plain fun!

Any way you look at it, writing a GUI library designed to be used and reused by others is a daunting task. The reason I wrote this book is to share some of the experience I have gained in writing a comprehensive GUI library that is being used by "real" applications around the country and around the world. I hope that this will help you avoid some of the pitfalls and frustrations involved in undertaking such a major project.

If you are an experienced C++ programmer who is just beginning to work with Motif, you should find this book to be extremely useful. I should emphasize that the book is not merely an instruction manual on how to write "wrapper" classes for Motif widgets but a comprehensive guide to structuring a GUI library; automating initialization for X and the X Toolkit; designing portable, usable, and consistent interfaces; designing complex interface elements not directly provided by Motif; and, making your GUI work with "real" applications.

My goal is to provide you with the tools to implement a portable, reusable GUI library using the OO paradigm. Therefore, you should read this book from start to finish, especially if you have never worked with a Motif-like programming interface before. To summarize, Chapter 1 provides a brief introduction to some of the conventions, notations, methods and typographical elements used in the remainder of the book. Chapter 2 contains a detailed introduction to the fundamental concepts required to use the Motif C language interface, including the event driven input model, callbacks, event handlers, and widgets. Chapter 3 is a discussion of design issues germane to maintaining portability and consistency between different versions of Motif and between Motif and other GUI platforms, while Chapter 4 contains an overview of some of the ancillary data types and classes used in the remaining chapters to build the GUI library. Chapter 5 describes the overall structure of a typical Motif-based GUI library, including the base class for the entire library. Chapter 6 contains a description of the subtree of classes which encapsulate Motif widgets, giving special attention to the root class of the subtree. And, Chapter 7 consists of a description of classes which encapsulate some useful, representative Motif widgets. Chapter 8 contains a description of classes which encapsulate some useful, advanced Motif widgets. And finally, Chapter 9 contains a discussion on integrating a GUI library into applications. If you are an experienced Motif programmer with solid OO development skills, Chapters 2 and 3 may be skipped entirely, and the rest of the book may be used as a reference guide. Chapters 7 and 8 contain descriptions of classes written for particular Motif widgets, and are specially organized for quick reference.

On a final note, I do not claim that the classes and techniques presented in this book are by any means perfect for all situations. However, I believe that this book will provide you with a general framework for using Motif in the context of C++ when designing your own GUI library.

Acknowledgments

Many people contributed to the content and circumstances that allowed me to write this book. First of all, I would like to express appreciation to my colleagues, Robert Zembowicz and Don Stearns for not complaining about the amount of time and effort I put into this book when I should have been working on other tasks. I would also like to thank Mohammad Jafar for the many years of intellectual stimulation he provided during graduate school and beyond.

Randy Peterson, Tom Hoff, Susan Volkman, Jim Anacker and my other cohorts at One Call Concepts, Inc. deserve a hearty thanks as well. Fortunately for me, these folks have the vision and motivation to keep moving into the future. The concepts described in this book have their foundation in the technology developed by OCC.

I must also acknowledge those professors and mentors I have encountered over the years who motivated me by their instruction and example, even when I didn't want to be motivated. These include Roger Dannenberg and Jim Tomayko of Carnegie Mellon University, and Marek Suchenek, Mahesh Rathi, and Raj Sunderraman of Wichita State University.

Finally, I would like to express my love and thanks to my wife Christine, my mother Jane, and my brother Matt for supporting and encouraging me over the years.

Contents

## CHAPTER 1

Introduction

Welcome to the wonderful world of graphical user interface (GUI) programming. If you have never programmed a GUI before, you are in for a treat. GUI programming is different from all other types of programming because of the instant gratification you get from seeing the results of your efforts immediately. GUI programming is one of the few fields in which you have the potential to truly dazzle people (even end users). If you do everything correctly, your sense of accomplishment will grow immeasurably. If you do something wrong, believe me, you will know instantly.

1.1 What You Should Know

This book is intended for use by professional C++ programmers who are just getting their feet wet in X Window/Motif user interface programming. The author does not assume that you have much experience using the Motif C language interface. However, it is expected that you have programmed extensively in the C++ language. Thus, advanced C++ concepts and constructs will not be explicated here.

While this book specifically uses the Motif C language interface for the sake of discussion, the concepts introduced and explained here could easily be applied to other widget sets such as Athena or OpenLook or even to GUI packages that have nothing to do with the X Window system. A similar point should be made about the C++ programming language. While it seems that C++ is the current language of choice for developing object oriented (OO) software, the concepts explained in this book can be easily extended to any programming language that supports the OO paradigm. It is assumed that you are already somewhat familiar with the OO development paradigm.

1.2 Versions and Revisions

The source code examples in this book were compiled using the Gnu g++ v2.6.0 C++ language compiler, distributed by the Free Software Foundation. All source code examples in this book were compiled on the Sun Solaris 2.3 operating system (a Unix SVr4 variant). This book uses X Window X11R5 and Motif v1.2 for the purposes of all discussion and examples regarding X Windows, the X Toolkit, and Motif. All of the graphically depicted object hierarchies that appear in this book were drawn using the *Rational Rose* object oriented analysis program. These hierarchies are in Booch notation (see Booch, 1994).

1.3 Conventions and Notations

This book contains some special notation, which assists in differentiating between normal text and discussion items such as source code elements and special terminology. The term *end user* is used to refer to someone who will be using our GUI end product via some application. A *user* is someone who will be using some component in our GUI library to develop GUIs for specific applications. This book uses the terms *user*, *developer*, and *programmer* interchangeably.

A source code element mentioned in the text will appear in `teletype` print. This will highlight the difference between a word used in normal discussion, such as "class," and a C++ language reserved word or identifier, such as `class`. Furthermore, this book uses empty parentheses to distinguish between functions or methods and other source code elements mentioned in the text, regardless of the function or method parameters. For example, a function named "foo" will appear in the text as `foo()`. An exception to this rule occurs when we need to distinguish between two functions or methods with the same name, but different signatures. In this case we will use ellipses with the signature difference between the parentheses. For example, we might distinguish between two versions of function `foo()` by writing `foo(...int...)` and `foo(...double...)`.

The following devices are used to differentiate special text from normal text:

Italic type is used to introduce new terminology.

Underlined text or **bold text** is used for emphasis.

SMALL CAPITAL letters are used to denote document or software titles.

<ANGLE BRACKETS> are used to refer to keyboard keys.

By convention, any sample source code listing should be considered as a fragment, unless explicitly designated otherwise. These fragments will usually contain just the right amount of detail to get the point across. This means that for most examples, you may be required to provide the implementation details, or other source code elements, to get the fragment to compile.

## CHAPTER 2

Motif

The Motif toolkit is a C language library that allows the development of sophisticated GUI front ends for all kinds of applications. Motif is developed and distributed by the Open Software Foundation (OSF), a foundation created by a consortium of computer companies to promote the development and use of open platforms.

Motif is implemented on top of the X Toolkit Intrinsics (Xt), which is a standard toolkit provided with all X Window distributions. Xt is primarily a collection of interface elements called *widgets* and *gadgets* together with some functions to operate on these elements. These widgets and gadgets are used by Motif to create more complicated widgets and gadgets. In fact, the typical Motif programmer works exclusively with Motif widgets and almost never encounters Xt widgets. Hereafter, Xt will only be discussed as it pertains to Motif.

Xt also provides some general functions common to all widgets, such as registering *callback functions* and *event handlers* (more on these later). Xt itself is implemented on top of the basic X Window toolkit (X). X provides elementary window and graphics manipulation services, such as creating and destroying windows and pixel maps, changing colors, and so on.

2.1 What's a Widget?

So, what exactly is a *widget*? A widget is a window or group of windows that has been assigned a special purpose in the user interface. For example, a menu widget is a window that contains push button widgets. In turn, push-button widgets are windows, each containing a label widget, and so on. A *gadget* is a widget implemented without windows. Gadgets are used to conserve memory for widgets that are small and numerous, such as push buttons. For the purposes of this book, we will concentrate only on widgets. Both widgets and gadgets are opaque data structures. This means that widget and gadget developers can manipulate the internals of these objects only through Motif and Xt functions.

When we use widgets instead of windows, we are guaranteed by Motif that the windows in question will take on a certain appearance and behavior, depending on the purpose of the widget. Furthermore, widgets can be constructed from other widgets. This minimizes the work we need to do when building our interface. To illustrate this, consider the push button widgets previously mentioned. In addition to using push button widgets as part of a menu, we may need to use a push button widget as a "stand-alone" widget or as part of some other widget. Therefore push button widgets are self-contained, regardless of the context in which they are used. This helps us to avoid perceiving push buttons as menu buttons, command panel buttons, menu bar buttons, etc.

In addition to being used by widgets, widget types may actually be derived from other widget types! Even though it provides a C language interface, Motif is quite object oriented. Each widget type can be viewed as a class of objects, possibly derived from other classes. Going back to our push button example, we can see that a push button is actually a label that can be visually "pressed." In this case, the push button class of widgets is actually derived from the label widget class and inherits all of the attributes of the label class in addition to defining some of its own.

The Motif widget class derivation tree is given in Figure 2.1. Even though Motif is written in the C language, it is still quite object oriented. Therefore, this hierarchy has been drawn using the Booch object notation (see White, 1994) for class hierarchies. While a complete discussion of Booch notation is beyond the scope of this book, it is necessary to present a brief discussion of the elements of the notation used in this book.

In Figure 2.1, there are two types of enclosed areas: empty and shaded. An empty area, enclosed by a dashed border, represents a single class denoted by

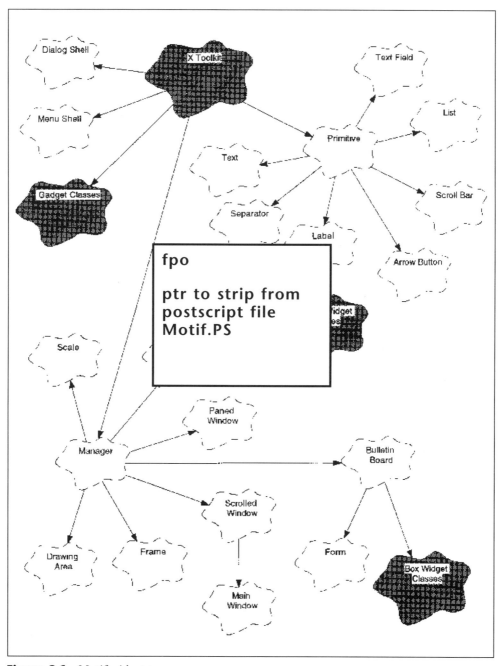

Figure 2.1. Motif widget tree.

the label within the enclosed area. A shaded area represents a *metaclass*. A metaclass is an aggregate of classes that have something in common. For example, in Figure 2.1, the shaded area labeled "Button Widget Classes" represents a metaclass for all widgets pressed by an end user. The arrows between the enclosed areas represent derivation, with the head of the arrow directed toward the child in the derivation relationship.

Because of space limitations, not every Motif widget class is used in this book. Actually, it is not necessary to cover every single widget class. Some widget classes, such as the shell widget family, are very similar to one another, and examples concerning one class can be applied to the other similar classes. We will take an in-depth look at the most representative Motif widget classes, with the knowledge that the discussion and examples are extensible.

2.2   Shell Widgets

A *shell* widget is an "invisible" widget that controls the geometry (i.e., size and position) of other widgets. A shell widget is invisible because it is precisely the same size and shape as the widget it controls. It is useful to think of a shell widget as being "shrink-wrapped" around the widget that it controls.

It is the shell widgets that are responsible for communicating widget geometry information to and from the window manager and other shell widgets. Every widget is the descendant of some shell widget in the GUI.

For example, assume that there is a message box widget that is used to inform end users of various application-dependent information. This widget contains some message text and an "OK" button, which the end user presses when he or she is through reading the message. In order to "pop up" the message box inside of a dialog, we must put the message box under the control of a dialog shell, thereby creating a new entity called a message dialog widget. Placing a widget under the control of another widget is called *parenting*. The shell object allows the message dialog to be treated as a stand-alone popup window, with a window manager title bar. The shell also allows the developer to control exactly where the dialog pops up.

Without shell widgets, an application could never be sure of where and how big its widgets actually are. The window manager would know all of this information, but it would be inaccessible (or at least hard to get to) via the application.

2.3   Simple Types

Before discussing how to create and use Motif widgets, it is useful to discuss some of the more basic X, Xt, and Motif types.

Motif uses the type name `Cardinal` to denote (unsigned) counting types. For example, `Cardinal` is the type used for variables and parameters that store the number of elements in some program structure, such as argument counts, number of push buttons, and the like. Similarly, Motif uses the type name `Position` to denote positional types. For example, `Position` is the type used for variables and parameters that store the position of some graphical element, such as a window or pixel map. Motif also uses the type name `Dimension` for dimensional variables and parameters. For example, `Dimension` is the type used for variables and parameters used to store the width and height of any graphical element. Values for variables or parameters of either the `Cardinal` or `Dimension` type must be unsigned. Values for `Position` variables or parameters may be negative, as they might indicate a relative position.

Motif aliases the `char *` type with the type name `String`. These types may be freely intermingled. The Xt type `XtPointer` is a type that can hold the largest of `char *`, `int *`, a function pointer, a structure pointer, or a `long int`. The X type name `Window` is used to provide *handles* to the opaque structures representing windows. A handle is a type name that is used to refer to some structure or other type frequently referenced in an application. A similar situation exists with the Xt type `Widget`, which is used to provide handles to the opaque structures representing widgets.

2.4   Creating and Destroying Widgets

Widget instances can be created and destroyed using "generic" Xt functions. Alternatively, Motif provides many functions (`XmCreate*()`) to create specialized widgets. In either case, the following information is needed in order to create a widget:

- **widget name:** Widget names are alphanumeric character strings that are usually unique to a widget. Widget names should give an indication of the widget function (e.g., `"zoomInButton"`).

- **widget class:** Motif provides a unique class identifier for each widget class. For example, the identifier for the push-button widget class is `xmPushButtonWidgetClass`. The type for Motif class identifiers is `WidgetClass`.
- **parent:** Every widget has a parent widget except for the top-level widget in the run-time hierarchy (more on top-level widgets later).

Optionally, the user can assign some initial values to the attributes of the widget upon creation, such as color, size, position, and so on.

Once a developer has the above information, he or she can use the Xt function `XtVaCreateWidget()` to actually create a widget. The prototype for this function is as follows:

```
Widget XtVaCreateWidget(String name,
                        WidgetClass class,
                        Widget parent,
                        ...,
                        NULL) ;
```

Here, the ellipsis ("...") represents variable arguments, which are discussed in detail below. What follows is a widget creation example involving `XtVaCreateWidget()`.

```
// Create compound string for button label
XmString xmStr = XmStringCreateSimple("Zoom In") ;

// Create push button widget
Widget pushButton = XtVaCreateWidget("zoomInButton",
                                     xmPushButtonWidgetClass,
                                     topLevel,
                                     XmNx,      0,
                                     XmNy,      0,
                                     XmNlabel, xmStr,
                                     NULL) ;

// Destroy compound string
XmStringFree(xmStr) ;
```

In the preceding code fragment, a number of things are going on. First, we create a *compound string* to store the label that will be displayed on the face of the button. A compound string is a Motif structure that holds a character string along with some additional information about string direction (i.e., right-to-left or left-to-right) and the character set used to display the string. For our purposes we will always assume a left-to-right string direction and the default character set (XmSTRING_DEFAULT_CHARSET): hence the use of the function XmStringCreateSimple(). There are many other Motif functions that manipulate compound strings. However, these are beyond the scope of this book.

Second, we create the widget pushButton using the Xt function XtVa-CreateWidget(). This function takes the developer-defined name of the widget as its first argument. Note that this name is not the same as the label, which is displayed on the face of the button. The name is used by Xt and Motif to track the widget and to identify any exceptions arising from run-time use of the widget. The second argument is the Motif widget class identifier, as discussed above. The third argument is the parent widget for pushButton, which in this case is the top-level widget for the application, topLevel. All remaining arguments to XtVaCreateWidget() are name/value pairs indicating some initial settings for widget attributes (or resources). XtVaCreateWidget() takes a variable number of these pairs, terminated with NULL, hence the Va in the function name. All resources for Motif widgets have a unique identifier prefixed with XmN. The first two name/value pairs indicate the desired positioning of the widget (0, 0), relative to the parent. The third name/value pair is the displayed button label.

Finally, we destroy the compound string, so as not to lose track of the associated memory. As an alternative to using XtVaCreateWidget(), Motif provides its own specialized widget creation functions, XmCreate*(). The * in the function name represents the name of any Motif widget. In fact, some of these functions create multiple widgets and return a handle to the widget of interest. An example of this is XmCreateMessageDialog(), which creates a DialogShell widget with a MessageBox widget as its child. It then returns the MessageBox widget, which is usually the widget of interest to any developer creating such a dialog. The prototype for this function is given below. All Motif widget creation functions have this same general prototype.

```
typedef struct
{
  String    name ;
  XtArgVal  value ;
} Arg, *ArgList ;

Widget XmCreateMessageDialog(Widget    parent,
                            String    name,
                            ArgList   argv,
                            Cardinal  argc) ;
```

This prototype is quite similar to the one for XtVaCreateWidget(), except for the method it uses to obtain the variable number of optional name/value pairs used to set the initial resources of the widget. This method is to pass an array of structures holding name/value pairs along with the count of the number of elements in the array. The typedef for Arg is the structure used for the name/value pairs, with XtArgVal being a type that is large enough to hold any resource value.

In addition to the functions already described, other Xt functions can create widgets. These include XtCreateWidget(), which is analogous to XtVaCreateWidget(), except that it takes as arguments an argument list and count instead of a variable list of name/value pairs. These functions also include XtCreateManagedWidget() and XtVaCreateManagedWidget(), which create widgets that will be immediately placed on screen. Once again, the Va tells us whether or not the function takes variable arguments.

Table 2.1 gives a summary of all of the various Xt and Motif functions for creating widgets.

Table 2.1. Widget creation functions.

Function	Purpose	Variable Args
XmCreate*()	Creates Motif widget	No
XtCreateWidget()	Creates Xt or Motif Widget	No
XtVaCreateWidget()	Creates Xt or Motif widget	Yes
XtCreateManagedWidget()	Creates Xt or Motif widget and places it on screen	No
XtVaCreateManagedWidget()	Creates Xt or Motif widget and places it on screen	Yes

We must be very careful about which name/value pairs we pass to the Motif widget creation functions. Remember, we may be creating multiple widgets. This means that any resource names that are unique to one of the widgets being created will apply only to that widget. However, any resource names that are shared among widgets being created will affect all of these widgets. For example, consider the following code fragment.

```
...
Arg arg ;

// Create compound strings
XmString msg = XmStringCreateSimple("Hello World") ;
// Set message to display in message box
XtSetArg(arg, XmNmessageString, msg) ;

// Create the widget
Widget msgDialog = XmCreateMessageDialog (topLevel,
                                          "helloDlgName",
                                          &arg,
                                          1) ;

// Clean up
XmStringFree(msg) ;
...
```

In this example, we declare a variable of Xt type `Arg` called `arg`. We then convert the string `"Hello World"` to a Motif compound string and use the Xt function `XtSetArg()` to set the message string resource `XmNmessageString` for the message dialog widget. Next we create the dialog. Note that we do not need a widget class identifier here. The identifier is not needed because Motif already knows the class (or classes) of any widgets created using Motif widget creation functions. The string `"helloDialogName"` is the title of the dialog shell displayed in the title bar by the window manager. Keep in mind that we are setting the resources for two widgets, the dialog shell and the message box, through the use of a single function. Finally, we destroy the compound string.

Destroying widgets is much easier than creating them. A call to `XtDestroyWidget()` destroys the widget in question. The prototype for this function is the following:

```
void XtDestroyWidget(Widget w) ;
```

A call to this function is the only thing necessary to destroy a widget. It is very important to destroy a widget when it is no longer in use in order to preserve memory.

2.5 Displaying Widgets

Just because we have created a widget does not mean that it automatically appears on the screen. In fact, widget creation does not even imply that any windows needed to display the widget are actually created. The windows are not automatically created because some (if not most) widgets, such as dialogs, are displayed conditionally, depending upon the actions of the end user. If the end user never causes a particular widget to be displayed during the course of using an application, why create the windows needed to display it?

Xt provides a pair of methods that create and destroy all of the graphical elements needed to display an existing widget. These functions are `XtRealizeWidget()` and `XtUnrealizeWidget()`, respectively. Each takes a widget argument and creates/destroys graphical elements for the widget. The process of creating the graphical elements is called *realization*, hence the names of these functions.

When a widget is realized, all of its children are realized as well, and all of their children, and so on. This means that realization is recursive. If a widget is realized, all of its descendants are realized also, so if we realize the top-level widget in our application, all widgets in the hierarchy are realized.

Once a widget has been realized, there is one more thing we must do before we can display it: we must place it under the management of its parent widget. This means that the placement of the widget is controlled by the parent widget. For example, a menu bar manages its menu bar buttons as well as the pulldown menus associated with the buttons. In turn, a pulldown menu manages its push buttons, and so on. If a child widget is not managed, then when the parent widget is displayed, the child widget will not be displayed. If a child is placed under management of a realized parent widget, the child will automatically be realized.

By default, `XtVaCreateWidget()` and the `XmCreate*()` functions do not place the created widget under the management of its parent widget. If we want the widget to be managed automatically, then we must use a variant of XtVaCreateWidget() called XtVaCreateManagedWidget(), both of which have the same prototype. Alternatively, we can manage and unmanage widgets explicitly using the Xt utility functions XtManageChild() and XtUnmanageChild(), both of which take the child widget as the only argument.

Strictly speaking, dialogs should be managed and unmanaged by another pair of functions called XtPopup() and XtPopdown(). However, because of a quirk in Motif, XtManageChild() and XtUnmanageChild() have the same effect. From here on, we will only use XtManageChild() and XtUnmanageChild() for the sake of consistency.

2.6   Widget Resource Manipulation

Once a widget has been created, we can obtain and modify most of its *resources* at will. As mentioned in Section 2.4, each resource is a name/value pair representing some attribute of a widget, such as height or color. Xt provides four functions that allow us to obtain and modify resources for a widget: two for obtaining and two for setting the resources.

The pair of functions that allow us to obtain the current values for widget resources are called XtGetValues() and XtVaGetValues(). XtGetValues() takes as arguments a widget, followed by an argument list and count. The value field of each argument should contain the address of a variable used to store the resource value. It then populates the value field of each argument with the requested resource associated with the name field of the argument.

The prototype for XtGetValues() is as follows:

```
XtGetValues(Widget w, ArgList argv, Cardinal argc) ;
```

For example, we can use XtGetValues() to obtain the width and height of a widget, as illustrated in the following code fragment.

```
...
extern Widget      w ;
Arg                argv[2] ;
```

```
Dimension           width, height ;

// Set the name/address pairs
XtSetArg(argv[0], XmNwidth,  &width) ;
XtSetArg(argv[1], XmNheight, &height) ;

// Get the resource values
XtGetValues(w, argv, 2) ;
...
```

Notice that we use XtSetArg() to set the name/address pairs for the argument list.

XtVaGetValues() takes as arguments a widget, followed by a variable list of name/address pairs terminated with a NULL, and populates the values to the indicated addresses directly. This allows us to circumvent using the Xt Arg type altogether.

The prototype for XtVaGetValues() is as follows:

```
XtVaGetValues(Widget w,  ..., NULL) ;
```

Here, the ellipsis represents a list of name/address pairs in which the name of the requested resource is given along with the address of a variable that will store the value for the requested resource.

The following code fragment corresponds to the example above, which uses XtGetValues() to obtain the values of the width and height resources for a widget, except that we now use XtVaGetValues().

```
...
extern Widget   w ;
Dimension           width, height ;

XtVaGetValues(w,
            XmNwidth,  &width,
            XmNheight, &height,
            NULL) ;
...
```

In this text, we will use only XtVaGetValues(), because it is easier to use and provides a better understanding of the purpose of the code in which it appears. This is because it uses the names of the resources we are interested in directly in the invocation.

The pair of functions that allow us to modify the resource values of an existing widget are XtSetValues() and XtVaSetValues(). XtSetValues() takes as arguments a widget, followed by an argument list and count in exactly the same fashion as the XmCreate*() functions do.

The prototype for XtSetValues() is as follows:

```
XtSetValues(Widget w, ArgList argv, Cardinal argc) ;
```

Assume that we must change the dimensions of a particular widget. We can accomplish this by using XtSetValues(), as illustrated in the following code fragment.

```
. . .
extern Widget       w ;
Arg                 argv[2] ;
Dimension           width = 200, height = 200 ;

// Set the name/address pairs
XtSetArg(argv[0], XmNwidth,  width) ;
XtSetArg(argv[1], XmNheight, height) ;

// Get the resource values
XtSetValues(w, argv, 2) ;
. . .
```

Notice that we are no longer using the addresses of the width and height variables; we now use the values of these variables.

XtVaSetValues() takes as arguments a widget, followed by a variable list of name/value pairs, terminated by a NULL, in exactly the same fashion as XtVaGetValues() and XtVaCreateWidget().

The prototype for XtVaSetValues() is as follows:

```
XtVaSetValues(Widget w, ..., NULL) ;
```

We can use `XtVaSetValues()` in place of `XtSetValues()` in the preceding example, as illustrated in the following fragment.

```
...
extern Widget    w ;
Dimension        width = 200, height = 200 ;

XtVaSetValues(w, XmNwidth, width, XmNheight, height, NULL) ;
...
```

While we will not use `XtGetValues()`, we will use both `XtSetValues()` and `XtVaSetValues()` in the remainder of this text.

There are some widget resources that cannot be obtained by the application. Similarly, there are some widget resources that cannot be modified after the widget is created. The reasons for this depend on the widget and resource in question. For example, shells have a Boolean resource called `XmNallow-ShellResize`. This resource determines whether the end user is allowed to resize the shell once it is displayed. It does not make sense to change the value of this resource after the widget has been created, because the end user may get confused.

There are so many ways to obtain and modify widget resource values that we may get confused. To avoid this confusion, all of the different functions that manipulate widget resources are summarized in Table 2.2.

2.7 Event-Driven Programming

Motif uses an *event-driven* user interface paradigm, which views the world as a sequence of any one of a number of *events*, such as mouse pointer motion, mouse button clicks, keyboard key presses, window resizes, and so on. These events are all directly caused by the end user and mean that the end user is trying to alter the state of the application in some way. From the point of view of the interface, these events are generated at random, which means that the composition of the sequence is completely unpredictable.

All such events occur in one or more widgets—usually the widget that currently contains the mouse pointer or has keyboard focus. In order to handle an event meant for a specific widget, we must write a handler function and register it with Motif at run-time. If the widget in which the event occurs does not

Table 2.2. Widget resource manipulation functions.

Function	Purpose	Variable Args
XtGetValues()	Obtains widget resource values	No
XtVaGetValues()	Obtains widget resource values	Yes
XtSetValues()	Modifies widget resource values	No
XtVaSetValues()	Modifies widget resource values	Yes
XmCreate*()	Creates Motif widget, sets resource values	No
XtCreateWidget()	Creates Xt or Motif widget, sets resource values	No
XtVaCreateWidget()	Creates Xt or Motif widget, sets resource values	Yes
XtCreateManagedWidget()	Creates Xt or Motif widget and places it on screen. Sets resource values.	No
XtVaCreateManagedWidget()	Creates Xt or Motif widget and places it on screen. Sets resource values.	Yes

handle the event, it is propagated up to the widget's parent (usually the widget that contains the event widget). If the parent widget does not handle the event, it is propagated up to its parent, and so on. For example, if we select a button from a menu, we will generate an event. If the button has no registered event handler for this event, it will be passed up to the menu.

Event handlers can be registered with Motif using the XtAddEventHandler() function, which is prototyped below.

```
void XtAddEventHandler(Widget        w,
                       long          evMask,
                       Bool          nonMaskableEvents,
                       XtEventHandler handler,
                       XtPointer     udata) ;
```

Event handlers are registered with a particular widget for any event types we are interested in handling, such as key presses or mouse motion. The Widget parameter w takes the particular widget. XtAddEventHandler() adds the event handler to an internal list of handlers for that widget. The specific event types that triggers the handler are given to the second parameter, evMask. These types are created from the bitwise "or" of X-defined masks, such as `KeyPressMask` or `PointerMotionMask`, each representing a particular kind of event. The third parameter provides the capability of handling nonmaskable events, which are beyond the scope of this book. For our purposes, the argument value for this parameter will always be `False`. The final two parameters, `handler` and `udata`, take the event handler and, optionally, some *client data*, which is passed to the event handler when it is triggered. Client data is untyped data that is specific to the implementation of the handler. If there is no client data, we will supply a `NULL` argument value to the last parameter.

It is important to note that we may register multiple event handlers for a single widget and a single kind of event. In this case, when an event of this kind is generated, all of the event handlers for the widget are triggered in the order in which they were registered. This ordered invocation allows us the flexibility to write very small event handlers and then mix and match them at our convenience.

The actual type for an event handler function is `XtEventHandler`, which is given below.

```
typedef void (* XtEventHandler)(Widget      w,
                                XEvent     *event,
                                XtPointer  udata,
                                Bool       *continueDispatch);
```

We may choose to register the same event handler for multiple widgets. In this case, the argument to the first parameter w, of type `Widget`, indicates the precise widget for which the event handler was triggered. Xt passes the event that triggered the handler through the second parameter. The third parameter is passed any client data we may have registered when adding the event handler. The final parameter is the address of a `Bool` variable called `continueDispatch`, which is always passed to the event handler with a value of `True`. If multiple event handlers are registered for widget w, and for this type of event, we may change the value of `continueDispatch` to `False` in any of these handlers to prevent the rest of the handlers from being triggered.

The following code fragment illustrates exactly how to devise and then register an event handler.

```
...
// Zoom in implementation is defined elsewhere
extern void zoomIn(double percent) ;

// The event handler
void zoomInHandler(Widget    w,
                   XEvent    *event,
                   XtPointer udata,
                   Bool      *cd)
{
  zoomIn(*((double *) udata)) ;
}

// Zoom in button creation
Widget createZoomInButton(Widget parent)
{
    // Enlargement percentage for "zoom in" operations
    static double zoomPercent = 0.5 ;

    // Create the button
    Widget ziButton = XmCreatePushButton(parent,
                                         "zoomInButton",
                                         NULL,
                                         0) ;

    // Register event handler
    XtAddEventHandler(ziButton,
                      Button1PressMask,
                      False,
                      zoomInHandler,
                      &zoomPercent) ;
}
...
```

This example shows how we can tie a "zoom-in" function to a push button. Of course, the fragment does not go in to enough detail for us to figure out what exactly we are zooming in on, but that is not relevant. What is important is that some external function named zoomIn() takes some enlargement factor and zooms in on something. Following the declaration for zoomIn(), we see the definition of a function that will act as the event handler, zoomInHandler(). This function calls zoomIn() with the enlargement factor passed through the client data parameter for the event handler. Next we have a function called createZoomInButton(), which creates a push button and registers zoomInHandler() as the push button's event handler for presses of mouse button 1. It is important to note that we register the address of a static function-scoped variable called zoomPercent as the client data for the event handler. This address will be passed to zoomInHandler() through its client data parameter.

In the preceding example, we did not make any use of the event parameter in the event handler. There is good reason for this. Events can occur at two levels: high and low. High-level events tell us what happened, but not how it happened. Low-level events tell us exactly how something happened, but they do not tell us anything about how to handle them. The reason the event handler does not use the event parameter in the above example is that we are only interested in <u>what</u> happened. To illustrate this, let's take another look at push buttons. When we select a push button we are generating a number of low-level events for:

- entering the push-button window
- pointer motion
- mouse button press
- mouse button release

Since every single selection of any push button will generate exactly these same low-level events, in the same order, it would be nice to be able to handle these as a single high-level event. In fact, Motif provides this service, termed a *callback*. For our push button, we can register an *activation* callback handler function with Motif, which is called every time the button is selected. Callbacks tell us nothing about how they were invoked. For example, our push button activation callback can be invoked by clicking the left mouse button within the borders of the button or by somehow giving the button keyboard focus and hitting the <SPACE> key. Motif defines which combinations of events cause certain callbacks to be invoked, but these mappings can be overridden.

The function that we use to register callback handlers is `XtAddCallback()`. The prototype for this function appears as follows:

```
void XtAddCallback(Widget          w,
                   String          callbackName,
                   XtCallbackProc  handler,
                   XtPointer       udata) ;
```

This function takes a widget and registers a callback handler for a particular kind of callback with the widget. Each Motif widget accepts certain kinds of callbacks (possibly none at all), which are defined by Motif. For example, we can register "arming" callback handlers with Motif push button widgets, which are triggered when the button is armed (i.e., the pointer has moved into the widget). We can also register an activation callback handler, as discussed above. In any case, we can also register client data, which is passed to the callback handler when it is triggered. The client data mechanism is exactly the same as for event handlers.

Once again, we may register many different callback handlers for a single widget and kind of callback. When a callback of this kind is generated, the callbacks are triggered in the order in which they were registered.

The callback handler itself is of type `XtCallbackProc`, which is defined as follows:

```
typedef void (* XtCallbackProc)(Widget     w,
                                XtPointer  clientd,
                                XtPointer  calld) ;
```

The first parameter of any function used as a callback handler is the widget for which the callback was triggered. The second parameter, `clientd`, is the client data registered with the callback, just as in event handlers. The third parameter, `calld`, is referred to as *call data*. This is a structure unique to the type of widget passed through the first parameter. The structure contains widget type–dependent details of why the callback was generated. For example, when we register a callback with a push button, the call data will point to a structure of the following type:

```
typedef struct
{
  int          reason ;
  XEvent       *event ;
  int          click_count ;
} XmPushButtonCallbackStruct ;
```

The reason field tells us the precise reason that a callback was triggered. This is necessary when we have registered the same callback handler function for different kinds of callbacks. The event field gives us the final event in the sequence that triggered the callback. This is rarely used for the reasons discussed above. Finally, the click_count field tells us if there were multiple button clicks. This comes in handy if we want to handle a callback only on a double mouse click, for example.

No matter what widget type we are dealing with, we are guaranteed to have the reason and event fields as the first two in the widget type's call data structure. These two fields are captured in a structure typedefed to XmAny-CallbackStruct. This way, regardless of the actual widget type, we can treat the call data structure as an object of this type.

```
typedef struct
{
  int     reason ;
  XEvent *event ;
} XmAnyCallbackStruct ;
```

We are now ready to revisit our "zoom-in" example. However, this time we will use callback handlers instead of event handlers.

```
// Zoom in implementation is defined elsewhere
extern void zoomIn(double percent) ;

// The callback handler
void zoomInCB(Widget w, XtPointer udata, XtPointer cdata)
{
  XmAnyCallbackStruct *cbs = (XmAnyCallbackStruct *) cdata ;

  if (cbs->reason == XmCR_ACTIVATE)
```

```
        zoomIn(*((double *)udata)) ;
}

// Zoom in button creation
Widget createZoomInButton(Widget parent)
{
  // Enlargement percentage for "zoom in" operations
  static double zoomPercent = 0.5 ;

  // Create the button
  Widget ziButton = XmCreatePushButton(parent,
      "zoomInButton", NULL, 0) ;

  // Register callback
  XtAddCallback(ziButton,
               XmNactivateCallback,
               zoomInCB,
               &zoomPercent) ;
}
```

As we can see, the act of registering callbacks is very similar to the act of registering event handlers. However, in the callback handler `zoomInCB()` we are checking the reason for the callback explicitly. This may seem rather point-less, since we have registered the handler for only one kind of callback, but it helps to document why we expect the callback to be triggered. The reason code, `XmCR_ACTIVATE`, is defined by Motif. The callback type string used when registering the callback with `XtAddCallback()`, `XmNactivateCall-back`, is also defined by Motif.

Callbacks are not always desirable. There are times when we must have access to the low-level events. Consider a drawing application, for example. If we wish to provide rubber band drawing operations, we will have to closely monitor each pointer motion event within the drawing area widget. Each time our motion event handler is invoked, it will erase the line segment from the anchor to the old location of the pointer and draw a line from the anchor to the new location of the pointer. We would not be able to do this without access to low-level events.

The only thing left in the discussion of event driven programming is under-standing how events generated by an end user get to a particular event or callback handler. This is accomplished by establishing a driver loop called the *event loop*. Here is a simplified algorithmic description of an event loop:

```
do forever

    wait for next event ;

    if handler is registered for event then
        call handler for event ;
    end if ;

end do ;
```

At the top of the loop, an application blocks until an event is received. Once an event is received, Xt determines whether it wants the event for processing by some kind of handler (callback or event handler). If so, the handler is invoked with the event as an argument. Of course, the actual event loop provided by Xt is much more complicated. However, this description should suffice for now.

To summarize, the gist of event-driven programming is to create a single handler function, which responds to a single event or callback in the context of a single widget. Once we write source code for these handlers for all events our application is going to handle and for all widgets in our application, we have a user interface.

2.8   Style in Motif

It should be stated clearly that Motif is not simply a programming tool. It is also a philosophy. This philosophy can be described in these simple words: the end user is king. The behavior of the entire user interface is governed by this philosophy. It subtly pervades all Motif functions and widgets.

The philosophy has been codified into a document published by the OSF called the MOTIF STYLE GUIDE (see Sun Microsystems, Inc., 1992). This document provides rules and guidelines that govern the "look and feel" of all Motif applications. Because of these rules and guidelines, any good Motif application will look and operate somewhat like any other Motif application, given the differences in applications from highly dissimilar domains. The reader is strongly urged to obtain and read a copy of the MOTIF STYLE GUIDE in order to familiarize himself or herself with Motif GUI development rules and guidelines.

2.9   A Marriage Made in Heaven

As mentioned earlier, Motif has been designed to be used as an object-oriented system. This statement requires a bit more explanation. The fact is, object orientation is ideal for any GUI, because an interface can be naturally decomposed into classes of objects, such as buttons, menus, pictures, lines, and so on. The very reason why GUIs are so popular is that they provide a natural, visual model of a real workspace.

The object-oriented paradigm was devised to provide a better model of the real world than the function-oriented paradigm. An object is better able to simulate the real world by packaging any data used to represent a real world element together with the methods to manipulate the object. A widget does exactly the same thing. As we previously noted, a widget is a window that has a specific purpose. This purpose is represented in software by resources unique to the type of the widget (object data) along with specific functions also unique to the widget's type (object methods). Therefore, a widget is an object.

Taking all of this into account, Motif should fit into the C++ programming language far better than it fits into the C programming language. We will indeed see that it does.

## CHAPTER 3

Design Issues

Before discussing the design and implementation of a good GUI library, it is useful to consider some important factors in making design decisions.

3.1 Design Components

There is a wide range of Motif widgets, which in turn provide a wide range of services to the outside world. There is also a wide range of services provided by X and Xt. Not all of these widgets and services are needed or necessarily desirable. When faced with the decision of which widgets and services to support in a GUI library, we should ask ourselves a few questions:

1. Is this widget/service useful to developers using our GUI library?
2. Is this widget/service cost-effective to provide and maintain in terms of development effort?
3. Is this widget/service worth the resources (memory, disk, etc.) needed to provide and maintain it?
4. Is this widget/service likely to be present in other widget sets?

Depending upon the answers to the first three questions, we will most likely arrive at the most useful set of widgets and widget services to support. Keep in mind that these answers will depend primarily on the kinds of applications we develop. The answer to the fourth question depends on the level of portability we wish to design into our GUI library.

3.2 Designing for Portability

If there is even the slightest possibility that we will someday port our GUI from Motif to another GUI toolkit or from Unix to another operating system, then we should design our GUI for portability from the very outset. Keep in mind, however, that no matter how much portability we design into any system, we should always assume that some changes will have to be made.

There are two goals to strive for when designing for portability:

1. Minimize recompilation caused by dependencies among source files. It is not unusual to have many source code (.C) files (which contain function and class method definitions) depending on a single header (.h) file (which contains class declarations). This is due to the nature of the OO paradigm, in which there are many classes derived from many other classes.

2. Minimize source code changes resulting from a change in the programming environment (e.g., compilers, operating systems, graphical toolkits, etc.).

Fortunately, these goals are complementary. For example, minimizing source code changes to .h files minimizes any recompilation that might be caused by real or structural dependencies.

3.2.1 Dependencies

The distinction between *real* and *structural* dependencies is very important. A real dependency is caused by a class derivation. In the code fragment below, class Y has a real dependency on class X because any changes to the method or data members of X will directly affect Y.

```
// Begin X.h

class X
{
  // ...Class declaration...
} ;

// End X.h

// Begin Y.h

#include "X.h"

class Y : public X
{
  // ...Class declaration...
} ;

// End Y.h
```

There is not much we can do about real dependencies, because we are not about to do without derivation! However, we can do something about structural dependencies. A structural dependency occurs when a .h file for a class contains declarations that are directly referenced only in the class definition. This usually occurs when a class uses an object of another class as a data member or as a parameter type. If these members and parameters are pointers (*) or references (&), the #include directive for the .h file of the class being used can be replaced with a forward declaration. To illustrate this point, let's examine the following code fragment, in which class Z uses class W as both a data member and a parameter type.

```
// Begin W.h

class W
{
  // ...Class declaration...
} ;
```

```
// End W.h

// Begin Z.h

#include "W.h"

class Z
{
  private:

    W *w ;

  public:

    void a(W &w) ;
    void b(W *w) ;
} ;
```

```
// End Z.h
```

If we replace the #include "W.h" directive in Z.h with a forward declaration for class W, we will need to include only W.h in Z.C. We can do this because the compiler would not need the internals of W until the definition of methods a() and b(), or until a dereference of the w data member. This means that any .h file that includes Z.h would no longer have to carry around the extra baggage associated with W, unless required to do so by a real dependency. The following code fragment contains the modified code.

```
// Begin Z.h

class W ;

class Z
{
  private:

    W *w ;
```

```
  public:

    void a(W &w) ;
    void b(W *w) ;
} ;


// End Z.h
```

One of the main disadvantages of using this approach, however, is that it may restrict our use of `inlines`. For example, if we `inlined` methods `a()` and `b()` in the code fragment above, and either method directly dereferenced an object passed through the `W` parameter, we would not be able to use a forward declaration for `W`. Because speed and efficiency are important in any GUI, and the use of `inlines` assists in achieving both, we will sometimes have to choose between designing for speed and efficiency, and designing for portability.

3.2.2   Information Hiding

The conclusion we should draw from the entire discussion of dependencies is that, wherever possible, we should only include `.h` files at the point at which they become absolutely necessary. This applies to all `.h` files, not only the ones containing class declarations. This is called information hiding, and it is essential to the portability of any system.

As discussed in Section 3.2.1, hiding information is important from the standpoint of avoiding unnecessary recompilation. There is an even more important reason to practice information hiding: isolation of code that is sensitive to the programming environment.

In the ideal design for a GUI library, there is a separate library containing environment-independent functions, which are implemented on top of environment-dependent functions. This is done to isolate the changes necessary to accommodate the differences in such things as operating system and graphical toolkit. For example, many operating systems differ on some of the non-ANSI C language functions, such as `pcmp()`, which partially compares character strings. Furthermore, many operating systems differ in the location of these declarations, if they even exist. In the absence of these functions we are forced to implement them for ourselves. However, we may run into linking problems if we do this and they are present. The solution is to create a new function such as `partialCompare()`, which is named differently and calls whatever ANSI functions are available to perform this task. These new, environment-independent functions are collected into our system isolation library, and are called everywhere else in the code in place of the non-ANSI function that they mimic.

If we ever plan to migrate our GUI to another graphical toolkit, such as Microsoft Windows, or a different widget set, such as OpenLook, it is essential to practice information hiding with regard to X, Xt, and Motif. The least painful way to accomplish this is to prevent any inclusion of X-, Xt-, or Motif-specific `.h` files in our GUI library `.h` files.

If we are relatively sure that we will never be porting our library to a new programming environment, it may not be cost-effective to take such drastic measures, but it is certainly worth considering. In the design of our GUI library, we will discuss portability issues and suggest techniques for maintaining portability.

3.3 Designing for Consistency

Consistency is one of the most important attributes of any GUI. Two kinds of consistency will concern us: *internal* and *external*.

3.3.1 External Consistency

Any end user who may use our interface has probably already encountered a GUI at some point. Therefore, it is important to provide support for mechanisms and concepts with which the end user is already familiar. This will minimize the learning curve that the end user will experience when trying to learn our interface. We will term this type of consistency *external* consistency.

For example, most GUIs change the pointer shape to the shape of a watch or hourglass to indicate that the end user must wait for a long operation to be completed before proceeding. We should also support this feedback mechanism in our GUI. If we were to use, for instance, a hand shape instead of a watch to indicate long operations, the end user will probably not realize what is happening.

In addition to shapes, we must attempt to keep many aspects of our GUI consistent with other GUIs. These include, but are not limited to, the following items.

- Relative location of graphical elements (i.e., widgets). For example, control panels usually appear on the extreme right or left side of most GUIs.
- Relative size of graphical elements. For example, the relative size of a scrollbar should be much less than the size of the display area to which it is attached.
- Functionality of graphical elements. For example, clicking the mouse on the top arrow of a vertical scroll bar usually causes data above the top border of the display area to be moved into the display area.
- Color of graphical elements. For example, red is usually used to indicate that an exceptional situation has arisen.
- Naming of functions and modes. For example, a "zoom-in" function should enlarge the viewed data with respect to the display area.

There is a very practical reason to maintain external consistency among GUIs. In a commercial environment, training costs can be a disincentive for managers to try to use new software. We can significantly reduce these costs by allowing users in training to concentrate on application domain concepts instead of user-interface mechanisms. This way, if an end user has used any application that has a GUI, he or she will recognize say, 80% of the mechanisms present in any GUI. By increasing the incentive for managers to purchase new software, we keep ourselves employed!

3.3.2 Internal Consistency

Consistency among the elements of a GUI for a single application is termed *internal* consistency. The internal consistency of a GUI will determine whether it is usable or not. If we do not provide this type of consistency for our GUI, end users will never know what to expect. Take as an example a "hot" key, such as <ESCAPE>, for a specific GUI mode that allows end users to cancel a mode. If we assign this key to some other function in a different mode, the end user will undoubtedly become confused. He or she will attempt to hit the key to cancel a mode when the key does not currently perform that function.

In addition to keystrokes, we must provide consistency between other aspects of a single GUI, such as:

- **mouse buttons:** We can make a case analogous to the one for the <ESCAPE> key if we allow the right mouse button to cancel a mode.

- **popup window placement:** We might decide that the first time any dialog is popped up, it will always be centered in the display area.
- **devices:** We might decide to allow all number-changing operations to take place via a slide bar. Alternatively, we might decide to always force the end user to type in the number. However, these devices should not be haphazard.
- **invalid input handling:** We could decide that we will make graphical elements "insensitive" (i.e., greyed or dimmed) if they cannot be used in the current mode.

Many other aspects of the GUI should be made consistent. We will review these as they are encountered. The important thing is that we must provide support for internal consistency directly into our GUI library.

3.4 Designing for Ease of Use

To become truly outstanding GUI programmers, we must put ourselves in the place of the GUI end user. This means we should possess more than just the tools and know-how to program a GUI. We should develop the ability to assume the psychology of people who will be using it. A GUI can be a great asset to any system, but one that is hard to use can be a great detriment. While this book is mainly concerned with tools and know-how, it is useful to state some guidelines that will help a GUI satisfy the needs of its end users. (Most of the following guidelines are paraphrased from the MOTIF STYLE GUIDE.)

We should always be looking for ways to make it easy for the end user to perform the functions accessed most frequently, with a minimum of mouse clicks and/or keystrokes.

We should always give the end user the ability to choose his or her favorite input method. Some end users prefer to use the keyboard instead of the mouse. Therefore, all GUI functions should have shortcut keys (Motif *accelerators*) that circumvent the mouse. However, there are some activities (such as drawing) for which this may be difficult or even impossible.

We should make our GUI as flexible as possible. It is impossible to predict the psychology of everyone who will use the system. The more flexibility the end user has in assigning his or her own keys, menus and functions, the more satisfied the end user will be.

The use of color is extremely important. This cannot be emphasized enough. Color should be used as a method of communication between the GUI and the end user. As an example, color can be used to indicate a change of modes or to highlight a problem that has occurred. The judicious use of color can make our GUI; the poor use of color can break it.

Our GUI should cooperate with all common window manager functions. For example, if we develop the GUI for a text editor, our GUI should react to a resize event by changing the number of characters per line and the number of rows of text in the text window accordingly. Other common window manager functions that we should handle include iconifying, de-iconifying, raising, lowering, and moving a window.

If these guidelines are consistently followed, our GUI will be widely praised and used. Nothing could be more rewarding to a professional GUI programmer.

## CHAPTER 4

Nongraphical Data Types

I t is nearly impossible to build a good user interface library without the use of classes and types that do not relate directly to user interface building. In fact, we should very carefully consider which auxiliary classes and types we might need before attempting to build any high-level library, whether it is for a user interface or some other purpose. Such auxiliary classes can make or break a library. Therefore, it is worthwhile discussing such types and classes at length.

4.1 The Boolean Type

Of course, every C and C++ program makes use of a `Boolean` type, either implicitly or explicitly. In fact, the X Window C interface library defines two types, `Bool` and `Boolean`, which facilitate passing and testing flags. These types are actually just one type that has been given two different names. This type can be defined as `int`, `char`, or `long`, depending on the operating system we are using. However, many C++ libraries define their own `Boolean` type in order to guarantee consistency among library components. Some actually go so far as to define a `Boolean` class and subsequently overload all needed operators for `Boolean` objects. While this is a bit drastic for our purposes, we will define `Boolean` as the raw type `int` and make explicit casts to the X `Bool` type where appropriate. This will guarantee that our code is correct, regardless of the storage size of elements of the X `Bool` type. The following `#define` directives should do the trick.

```
// "Defines" are as efficient as any other way...

// The type itself
#define Boolean int

// Boolean value definitions
#define TRUE      1
#define FALSE     0
#define true      TRUE
#define false     FALSE

// For readability
#define and    &&
#define or     ||
#define not    !
```

We should be careful about which variants of `TRUE` and `FALSE` we define. The X `Bool` type includes definitions of `True` and `False`, so we will not redefine them here. The definition of `and`, `or`, and `not` is done for purely cosmetic purposes and should not affect the operation of applications in any way.

When the `Boolean` type name appears in code fragments given as examples in this text, it is assumed that it is our `Boolean` type. The `Bool` type name will be used to denote the X `Boolean` type.

4.2 Containers

One of the tasks most crucial to building a GUI library is to design and implement an auxiliary library for some of the more commonly used container classes. A container class is any class that is specially designed to contain other objects. For example, when designing classes for use in a user interface, we often need to create and maintain lists of objects such as buttons. In this case, our list object is a container for button objects. In some cases, we need not only a container, but a container that allows us, for example, to search for contained objects as quickly as possible. This requires the use of more specialized containers, such as sets.

The first thing we notice about containers is that we need them to contain many different kinds of objects. In other words, we need a generic container. This poses a serious problem, because in order to implement a class that contains objects of, say, type `Button`, we need to use the `Button` class methods (such as the assignment or comparison operators) explicitly in the container class. However, such a class would prevent us from containing any object other than a `Button` object or an object derived from `Button`. There are at least four ways to solve this problem:

1. Implement all container classes to contain pointers to objects and use `void *` to point to any contained objects.
2. Write macros to declare and define a container class that takes as an argument the type or class name of the objects to be contained.
3. Define a class called something like `Contained`, from which all objects that can possibly be contained are derived. Implement all container classes to contain objects derived from `Contained`.
4. Use the C++ template mechanism.

Let's take a hard look at each one of these solutions.

4.2.1. Generic Container Alternatives

Void Pointers
The use of void pointers (the C type `void *`) in C++ should be avoided at all costs. C++ is a strongly typed language (at least, a lot more strongly typed than C), and the use of the `void *` mechanism violates this typing philosophy. Furthermore, the use of `void *` can be dangerous, because it is sometimes difficult to tell which class pointer to use when we need to cast the void pointer back to something useful. This is especially true for objects instantiated from virtual classes.

MACROS

This method of defining generic container classes is frequently used. This is because the C++ template mechanism (discussed below) was "unstable" until it was recently reviewed by the ANSI committee formed to oversee standards development for C++. This method also happens to be extremely difficult to debug, as most preprocessors expand macros so that they occupy only one line of source code.

BASE CLASSES

The main advantage of defining a base class (`Contained`) is that this is probably the most simple and straightforward way to solve our problem. It would require only minimal changes to existing code and would be simple to debug. However, the disadvantages are twofold. First, any changes to the `.h` file for the `Contained` class would affect the `.h` files of all classes derived from `Contained`, causing extensive recompilation. Second, any nonstatic data members from `Contained` will be carried around as "extra baggage" in each object belonging to any class derived from `Contained`. Frequently, there may be hundreds or thousands of such objects, each carrying an extra few bytes. This would have a detrimental effect on the amount of memory used by applications.

C++ TEMPLATES

There are certain risks associated with the use of standardized C++ templates, but it is a good technique to use in order to solve our problem. The first risk is that the ANSI committee might change its mind, rendering our templates obsolete. The second risk is present depending upon how our C++ compiler implements templates. If our compiler adds new object code to the application each time we instantiate a template, then this will have a negative impact on the amount of memory used by applications.

Because templates are easy to use and, most importantly, have been standardized, we will use this method to implement generic containers.

4.2.2. What to Contain?

The only decision about generic containers we still haven't made is a subtle but important one: Do our containers contain objects or pointers to objects? The answer really depends on the size of the objects we wish to contain and the techniques we use to write our container classes.

Size is all-important, because the larger an object is, the less we should construct, copy, and destroy it. These operations take time, and because there are likely to be quite a number of contained objects, this time can be significant. If we minimize the construction, copying, and destruction of objects, our application will be more time efficient. Remember, X Windows usually operates on a network shared among many end users, and our objects will make heavy use of X Windows by way of Motif. Any application that hogs network resources will surely raise the ire of these end users. Therefore the application should be time efficient.

If we contain the objects themselves, then the objects should somehow be built into the container. This means that objects outside the container will have to be copied in order to be contained, wasting valuable CPU (and possibly network) time. Furthermore, this prevents us from simultaneously putting a single object into multiple containers. Therefore we will choose to implement containers to contain pointers to objects rather than the objects themselves whenever possible.

Note that there are alternatives other than the ones chosen for use in this book for minimizing construction, copying, and destruction, such as the use of *representation classes* and *reference counts*. These alternatives are beyond the scope of this book.

4.2.3 Container Examples

LISTS

We use lists when we need a container for some objects but are not sure how many objects we need to contain. If we were absolutely certain of the number of objects, we could allocate an array of objects or declare an array of object pointers. Before we give a declaration for the `List` class, we must place some requirements on the objects a list will contain.

1. All objects contained in a list must provide a comparison operator, `operator ==()`, which compares any two objects and returns a `Boolean` value indicating whether they match.
2. All objects contained in a list must provide an assignment operator, `operator =()`, which allows objects to be copied.
3. All objects contained in a list must provide a "copy" constructor, which allows objects to be copied at creation.

The following code fragment is one way to write a template to declare a list of objects.

```
#define ListLoop (l,i) for (l.reset(i); l.inRange(i); \
                            l.advance(i))

template <class T> class ListIndex ;

template <class T> class List
{
    // Implementation details...

  public:

    List(void) ;
        // Constructor

    List(const List &other) ;
        // Copy constructor

    ~List(void) ;
        // Destructor

    List &operator =(const List &other) ;
        // Assignment operator

    Boolean operator ==(const List &other) const ;
    Boolean operator !=(const List &other) const ;
        // Comparison operators

    Boolean isEmpty(void) const ;
        // Predicate for empty list

    long length(void) const ;
        // Obtains length of list

    List &operator +=(const T &item) ;
        // Appends item to list
```

```
List &operator +=(List &other) ;
    // Merges two lists, leaving list argument empty

ListIndex<T> first(void) const ;
ListIndex<T> last(void) const ;
    // First/last list index access

ListIndex<T> find(const T &item) const ;
    // Finds list index of first item match argument

ListIndex<T> next(const ListIndex<T> index) const ;
    // Obtains index following list index argument

void reset(ListIndex<T> &index) const ;
    // Resets list index argument to first list index
    // in list

void advance(ListIndex<T> &index) const ;
    // Sets list index argument to next list index
    // in list

Boolean inRange(const ListIndex<T> index) const ;
    // Determines if list index is valid for list

List &eliminate(ListIndex<T> index) ;
    // Eliminates list item which is at list index
    // argument

List &insertBefore(ListIndex<T> index, const T &item) ;
List &insertAfter (ListIndex<T> index, const T &item) ;
    // Inserts item argument before/after list index
    // argument

    T &operator [](long n) ;
const T &operator [](long n) const ;
    // Accesses item by position sequence number
```

```
     T &operator [](const ListIndex<T> index) ;
const T &operator [](const ListIndex<T> index) const ;
    // Accesses item by list index

List &clear(void) ;
    // Clears list without destroying member items

List &zap(void) ;
    // Clears list and destroys member items
} ;
```

The first thing to notice about this declaration is the use of a template class called ListIndex<T>. This is used to give us access to individual items in the list, based on the type of item. This type is not declared here and is implementation dependent.

The List<T> template provides all of the standard methods necessary to provide fully functional lists. These methods can be grouped into the following categories:

- **constructors and destructors:** These include item insertion and deletion methods. Methods such as insertBefore(), clear(), and operator +=() all fall into this category.
- **access methods:** This category includes methods such as operator [](), reset(), and last(). Note that some methods, such as operator [](), allow access by position (if the implementation of ListIndex<T> is not positional). Also, in some cases, both const and nonconst versions are provided. The version used will depend on if we are changing the item in question or not. The compiler should be able to automatically determine the proper version to use.
- **predicates:** Methods such as operator ==() and isEmpty() fall into this category. All of the methods in this category test whether something is true or false about a list. All of them return a Boolean value.
- **informational methods:** These methods, such as length(), provide some information about the list to the developer.

SETS
The need for sets is much more specific than the need for lists. We use sets when we need to contain a large number of objects on which we have imposed

some linear order. The values used to determine this order are called keys. We will define our set on the assumption that each object to be stored in the set has one and only one key. However, we will allow two or more objects to share the same key. Key values should be elements of a discrete type or range of values. For example, the `int` or `enum` types would be excellent choices for keys, but the `float` type would not. Regardless of the actual type chosen for the key of a specific class of objects, we will define our own type as follows:

```
typedef long KeyType ;
```

We do this for much the same reason that we defined our own `Boolean` type: to guarantee consistency among storage sizes for keys.

Just as for objects contained in lists, we impose some requirements on objects contained in sets. Objects contained in sets must conform to the same requirements for objects contained in lists. However, we will also impose an additional requirement. We will require any class of objects destined for set storage to provide a `nonstatic` method called `getKey()`, which takes no parameters and returns `KeyType`. The following code fragment illustrates the point with a class called `Class`.

```
// Objects of this class are to be stored in sets
class Class
{
  // ...implementation details...

public:

  // ...public methods...

  KeyType getKey(void) const ;
      // Returns key to be used in set searches

  // ...public methods...
} ;
```

You may be asking the question, "When do I use lists, and when do I use sets?" We use sets when the contained objects do not directly permit us to determine their ordering within the domain of all possible values for the object. For example, strings do not permit us to directly impose a simple linear ordering based on the value of each string. Each string must first be "hashed" to a key value before we know its ordering within the range of all possible strings.

We also use sets when the contained objects actually do permit us determine their ordering but the values are expected to have large gaps between successive values. Aggregations with large gaps between successive values are called *sparse*.

Finally, we use sets when we need to quickly find a contained object in better than $O(n)$ (linear) time, where n is the number of objects contained in the set (see Hopcroft et al., 1982, for a discussion of algorithmic time). Sets facilitate very quick searching (logarithmic time) on contained objects. The structures used to represent sets are usually hash tables, binary trees, or B-trees (see Hopcroft et al., 1982), but they are beyond the scope of this book. Whatever structure is ultimately used, we make the assumption that our sets allow for rapid searching and retrieval based on the key value of an object.

The following is a code fragment illustrating one possible way to declare a template for a set of objects.

```
template <class T> class SetIndex ;

template <class T> class Set
{
        // Implementation details...

    public:

        Set(void) ;
            // Constructor

        Set(const Set &other) ;
            // Copy constructor

        ~Set(void) ;
            // Destructor
```

```
size_t count(void) const ;
   // Obtains number of items in set

Boolean isEmpty(void) const ;
   // Predicate for empty set

Boolean insert(const T &item) ;
   // Inserts item into set based on item key

Boolean eliminate(const T &item) ;
   // Removes item from set

Boolean member(const T &item) const ;
   // Tests membership of item in set based on item key

SetIndex<T> first(void) const ;
SetIndex<T> last(void) const ;
   // Obtains first/last set index from set

Set &operator =(const Set &other) ;
   // Assignment operator

Boolean operator ==(const Set &other) const ;
Boolean operator !=(const Set &other) const ;
   // Comparison operators

void reset(SetIndex<T> &index) ;
void reset(SetIndex<T> &index) const ;
   // Resets set index argument to first set index
   // in set

Boolean inRange(SetIndex<T> &index) const ;
   // Determines if set index argument is valid for set

void advance(SetIndex<T> &index) const ;
   // Advances set index argument to next set index
```

```
SetIndex<T> next(SetIndex<T> &index) ;
SetIndex<T> next(SetIndex<T> &index) const ;
    // Obtains set index following set index argument

       T &operator[](SetIndex<T> index) ;
const T &operator[](SetIndex<T> index) const ;
    // Accesses item referred to by set index argument

KeyType getKey(SetIndex<T> index) const ;
    // Obtains key for item referred to by set
    // index argument

void zap(void) ;
    // Clears set and destroys all items

void clear(void) ;
    // Clears set without destroying items

Set &operator -=(const T &item) ;
    // Removes item matching item argument from set

Set &operator +=(const T &item) ;
    // Adds an item argument to the set

Set &operator +=(Set &other) ;
    // Merges two sets, leaving set argument empty

Boolean member(const KeyType k) const ;
    // Determines if set contains an item with this key

SetIndex<T> find(const KeyType k) const ;
    // Finds set index of first item in set which
    // matches key
} ;
```

This template uses a type called SetIndex<T>, which is analogous to the ListIndex<T> type for the list template. There are also analogous categories for the kinds of methods we provide in the set template. However, we also provide some membership and search methods, such as `find()` and `member()`, which are based on the key of a contained item.

4.3 Strings

Another useful auxiliary class that will be used in this book in order to simplify some of the source code examples is the `CString` "character string" class. (We cannot call our class `String` because Motif reserves `String` as a `typedef` for `char *`.) The `CString` class allows us to perform all kinds of string manipulations for character strings without having to worry that we'll overrun the end of a string (causing a segmentation fault or something equally nasty).

The class declaration for `CString` is as follows:

```
class CString
{
    // Implementation details...

  public:

  enum { NOT_FOUND = -1 } ;

  CString(size_t allocSize = 0) ;
  CString(const CString  &source, size_t allocSize  = 0);
  CString(const char     *source, size_t allocSize  = 0);
  CString(char source,            size_t allocSize  = 0);
    // Constructors

  ~CString(void) ;
    // Destructor

  operator const char *(void) const ;
    // Cast to character pointer

  char  operator[](size_t n) const ;
  char &operator[](size_t n) ;
    // Single character access methods
```

```
size_t length(void) const ;
    // Obtains length of string

CString subString(size_t position, size_t count) const ;
    // Obtains substring starting at position

Boolean isBlank(void) const ;
    // Determines whether the string consists only of ANSI
    // whitespace

CString &operator =(const CString &source) ;
    // Assigns another string to string

CString &operator +=(const CString &s) ;
    // Appends another string to this string

CString operator +(const CString &s2) const ;
    // Appends another string to this string, without
    // changing this string

Boolean operator ==(const CString &s2) const ;
Boolean operator !=(const CString &s2) const ;
Boolean operator <=(const CString &s2) const ;
Boolean operator < (const CString &s2) const ;
Boolean operator >=(const CString &s2) const ;
Boolean operator > (const CString &s2) const ;
    // Comparison operators

CString &trim(void) ;
    // Trims blank space from both ends of string

int find (const char *s, size_t position = 0) const ;
int find (char        c, size_t position = 0) const ;
int rfind(const char *s, size_t position = 0) const ;
int rfind(char        c, size_t position = 0) const ;
    // Search methods for character strings/characters.
    // Returns CString::NOT_FOUND if the string/character
```

```
        // was not found.

    friend CString ntos(long          n,
                        int           width      = 0,
                        const char    *flag       = "") ;
    friend CString ntos(double        n,
                        int           width      = 0,
                        int           precision  = 6,
                        const char    *flag       = "") ;
        // Number to string conversion methods.
        // Flags are standard printf flags after '%' and
        // before 'd' or 'f'.

    operator long   (void) const ;
    operator double (void) const ;
        // String to number conversion cast operators

    KeyType getKey(void) const ;
        // Obtains a key value for indexed container storage.
        // Key value is calculated from a hash function on
        // length and contents of string.

    static const CString Empty ;
        // Empty strings are used extensively, why not
        // have a constant?

    friend istream &operator >>(istream &is, CString &string) ;
    friend ostream &operator <<(ostream &os, const CString &string) ;
        //Stream I/O
} ;
```

It is plain to see that we gain many more advantages by implementing a class such as CString than by simply not going past a string terminator. In addition to all of the methods listed, we can use reference counts and representation classes and perform memory management on strings. Most good C++ books discuss these subjects in depth (See Ellis and Stroustrup, 1990; Lippman, 1993).

A good string class is essential to small, readable source code. Believe it or not, we will use almost all of the methods listed in the CString class declaration at some point in this book. A typical application might need even more methods!

## CHAPTER 5

The Graphical Environment

A lthough the main focus of any Motif-based GUI library is on the widgets provided by Motif, it is useful to first discuss what we shall call the *graphical environment*. The graphical environment acts as a toolbox, providing tools to make use of Motif widgets to the maximum extent. The graphical environment tracks information that is global to the entire library and acts as a basis for ancillary classes, which help us to:

- render lines
- manipulate color
- receive and manipulate events
- create and manipulate pixel maps
- change pointer shapes

We use the term *render* to mean the physical drawing to the screen of some set of pixels, such as a line. Some of these tasks have already been discussed in the contexts of feedback to the end user and of event driven programming. First, without the ability to change pointer shapes and colors, we would be severely restricted in providing feedback to the user. Second, because the graphical environment allows us to receive and process events, we would not be able to support event driven programming without it. Finally, if applications based on our library are to perform non-textual graphics operations, such as rendering images or geometric shapes, it is essential to provide support for drawing operations. In this chapter we will look at all of these tasks.

5.1 Variables for X Environment

The graphical environment is not actually implemented on top of Motif, but rather on top of X and Xt. Motif does not provide a lot of the "low-level" graphical manipulation necessary to do such things as rendering lines or images. The underlying implementation, of course, does not matter to the library user, but it is extremely important to maintain the separation during this discussion.

When using X Windows we must maintain a set of global variables, which are used to perform any task of significance through X. Following is a brief summary of all of the variables with which we are concerned.

5.1.1 Display

Almost every function call in X Windows uses a variable of `Display *` type, which is used to store information about the actual connection to the X server.[1] Actually, the fields in the `Display` structure are not important to this discussion. However, it suffices to know that almost every X function call requires that such a structure be passed as the first argument.

5.1.2 Screen Number

To account for future technologies, X is equipped to recognize multiscreen display connections. The screen number is the ordinal number of the screen to be used for a graphics request, where this information is required by X. In current practice, almost all X terminals have only one screen, and therefore a screen number of 0. For the purposes of this book, we will proceed under the

---

[1]Note that in X Windows, the notion of client and server can be counterintuitive. The server is an X Terminal (or console), which "serves" requests for graphics, while the client is the machine to which the end user logs in.

assumption that our library is for use on single screen displays only. However, the examples herein can be easily extended to handle multiscreen displays.

In addition to the number of a screen, it is useful to review some other global information pertaining to screens:

- **width:** The width of a screen in pixels.
- **height:** The height of a screen in pixels.
- **depth:** The number of bit planes of color for a screen. The depth is used for color-manipulation activities. The depth can be thought of as a third dimension for a screen in bits. Each bit belongs to a bit plane, and the planes can be combined to create colors. For example, a screen with a depth of 4 (bits) can provide $2^4 = 16$ colors, while a screen with a depth of 8 can provide $2^8 = 256$ colors.
- **root window:** The root window for a screen on a display connection is the default window that automatically appears on the screen. This window is sometimes referred to as the "desktop."

X must be initialized by *opening* the display (by creating a `Display` variable). Once the display has been opened, we may access information about the screen (or screens) and the root window. While X stores these data in the `Display` structure, we may want to consider storing them directly in the library, since these data will not change during the course of execution of an application.

5.2   Variables for the X Toolkit

The X Toolkit also makes use of some global information necessary to access some of the utilities that it provides. The information with which we are concerned is as follows.

5.2.1   Application Context

Like X, Xt maintains global information, but about the application instead of about the display connection. The application context is a structure (Xt structure `XtApp-Context`), which contains application-specific information, including functions registered as event handlers by an application. While the guts of this structure are not important to this discussion, it suffices to know that such a structure is needed.

5.2.2   Application Class

All Xt widgets make use of configurable resources, such as color and geometry. Values for these resources can be configured by way of text files created and edited by the end user. One of these files is .Xdefaults, which usually resides in the home directory of each end user. Values can be assigned to each resource on a per application basis (by application name) or by the class of an application. The application class is a user label for a group of applications all having similar configuration requirements.

For example, we might formulate an application class for any application based on our GUI library called LibraryApp. That way any application in this class may, for example, be assigned a common geometry, as in the following line from a typical .Xdefaults file:

```
LibraryApp.geometry:              600x600+0+0
```

This line specifies that all applications of class LibraryApp will start execution at the origin of the screen and with a top level window having a shape 600 pixels high and 600 pixels wide.

The precise details of configuration through files such as .Xdefaults and app-defaults are beyond the scope of this book, except where they directly affect the behavior of library classes.

5.2.3   Application Name

The application name is a unique user label assigned to an application to differentiate it from other applications for configuration purposes (see above).

5.2.4   Command Line Arguments

The command line arguments are important for Xt, because Xt defines some standard options that can be used for any Xt-based application. Most of these options are used for configuration purposes and are analogs of configuration directives appearing in standard configuration files such as .Xdefaults. We store the command line arguments in order to pass the arguments to Xt. The precise syntax of the standard Xt options are beyond the scope of this book.

5.3   The Root of the Problem

Given the initialization and global information requirements for both X and Xt, it becomes clear that we need a mechanism to perform these initializations and store the necessary global information. This mechanism is implemented through the root class of our entire GUI library: `GraphicalEnv`.

All classes in our library are derived (directly or indirectly) from `GraphicalEnv`. The declaration of this class is as follows:

```
extern "C"
{
#  include <X11/Intrinsic.h>
}

#include "Boolean.h"
#include "CString.h"

class GraphicalEnv
{
  protected:

    static const CString    appClass ;    // App class
    static CString          appName ;     // App name
    static XtAppContext     appContext ;  // App context
    static Display         *display ;      // Display for X
    static Window           root ;         // Desktop X window
    static int              screen ;       // Screen # for X
    static uint             scrWidth ;     // Width of screen
    static uint             scrHeight ;    // Height of screen
    static int              depth ;        // # of color planes
    static Boolean          debug ;        // Debug graphics?
    static int             *argc ;         // Argument count
    static char           **argv ;         // Command line args
    static Boolean          classInit ;    // Class initialized?

    static void classConstruct(void) ;
        // Class constructor
```

```
    static inline void testConstruct(void)
    { if (not classInit) classConstruct() ; }
        // For convenience

    inline GraphicalEnv(void) { testConstruct() ; }
        // Constructor

public:

    inline ~GraphicalEnv(void) {} // NULL
        // Destructor

    static void setEnvironment(const CString &pname,
                               int          &ac,
                               char         **av,
                               Boolean      dflag = FALSE) ;
        // Sets program name, command line arguments,
        // debugging flag

    static inline const CString &getProgramName(void)
    { return appName ; }
        // Obtains program name

    static void processEvent(void) ;
        // Processes first event in queue for application

    static inline void startApp(void)
    { XtAppMainLoop(appContext) ; }
        // Starts the main app event loop

    inline friend Display *getDisplay(void)
    { return GraphicalEnv::display ; }
        // Provides access to display pointer for X
        // windows

    inline friend Window getRootWindow(void)
    { return GraphicalEnv::root ; }
        // Provides access to root window for X windows
```

```
    inline friend int getDepth(void)
    { return GraphicalEnv::depth ; }
        // Provides access to number of color planes
        // for X windows

    inline friend int getScreenNumber(void)
    { return GraphicalEnv::screen ; }
        // Provides access to screen number for X windows

    inline friend uint screenWidth(void)
    { return GraphicalEnv::scrWidth ; }
    inline friend uint screenHeight(void)
    { reurn GraphicalEnv::scrHeight ; }
        // Returns dimensions of screen
} ;
```

Let's take a close look at each of the members and methods in `Graphi-calEnv`.

5.3.1 Class Members

The first thing we should notice about the members of the `Graphi-calEnv` class is that they are all `static` (in other words, global to the class). This is because they are used to store global information needed for both X and Xt. Because we can obtain this information by making various function calls to X and Xt, storing this information is redundant. We do this for clarity and convenience for the sake of this discussion. Next, we give all members `protected` visibility, so that derived classes can directly reference them.

The `appName` and `appClass` members are used to assign labels to the application and application group, respectively, for configuring widget resources through `.Xdefaults`, for example. Storing these in the `Graphi-calEnv` class is redundant because these values can be retrieved through calls provided by Xt.

Notice that `appClass` is declared constant, while `appName` is not. This is because we "hard code" the application class, while we allow the user to specify a value for `appName`.

The members `display` and `appContext` are used to hold global information essential for X and Xt, respectively. These data are not redundant and <u>must</u> be tracked by the class.

The `screen` and `root` members refer to the screen number of the display connection for X and the root window of the screen. The `scrWidth`, `scrHeight`, and `depth` members hold the dimensions and number of color planes for the screen. All of this information is available from X or Xt through the use of provided functions or macros, but is stored for convenience (and possibly efficiency).

The `debug` member is a flag that indicates if we wish to debug X by synchronizing the graphics requests made by X. This is explained in detail below.

The `argc` and `argv` members represent the count and text of command line arguments to an application. We store these in case we have specialized options for our application. After passing these to Xt, the standard arguments recognized by Xt will be removed. The remaining arguments are special to the application.

Finally, the `classInit` member indicates whether "class construction" has taken place (see Section 5.3.2).

The class members are initialized as follows:

```
const CString   GraphicalEnv::appClass    = "LibraryApp" ;
CString         GraphicalEnv::appName     = "" ;
XtAppContext    GraphicalEnv::appContext  = (XtAppContext) NULL ;
Window          GraphicalEnv::root        = (Window) NULL ;
Display         *GraphicalEnv::display     = NULL ;
int             GraphicalEnv::screen      = 0 ;
uint            GraphicalEnv::scrWidth    = 0 ;
uint            GraphicalEnv::scrHeight   = 0 ;
int             GraphicalEnv::depth       = 0 ;
Boolean         GraphicalEnv::debug       = FALSE ;
int             *GraphicalEnv::argc        = NULL ;
char            **GraphicalEnv::argv       = NULL ;
Boolean         GraphicalEnv::classInit   = FALSE ;
```

5.3.2 Construction

The first method to look at when examining any class is the constructor. Note that the constructor for `GraphicalEnv` is declared `protected`. This is to prevent objects of type GraphicalEnv from being directly instantiated. In other words, GraphicalEnv should act only as a base class. Note that we can also accomplish this by declaring one of the GraphicalEnv methods to be *pure virtual* (see Ellis and Stroustrup, 1990; Lippman, 1993), but there are no likely candidates for this.

There is only one constructor for the GraphicalEnv class.

```
class GraphicalEnv
{
  protected:

    ...
    inline GraphicalEnv(void) { testConstruct() ; }
        // Constructor
    ...
} ;
```

The implementation of the constructor is a call to the class static method testConstruct().

```
class GraphicalEnv
{
  protected:

    ...
    static inline void testConstruct(void)
    { if (not classInit) classConstruct() ; }
        // For convenience
    ...
} ;
```

The GraphicalEnv class contains a static Boolean variable called classInit. At the point of definition, this variable is assigned a value of FALSE. During the proper execution of an application, this assignment will be performed <u>before</u> any methods for any class are invoked. Therefore we are guaranteed that classInit will contain the value FALSE before it is used by any GraphicalEnv method.

After the first construction, we will set `classInit` to TRUE. Therefore, the `static` method `classConstruct()` will be called once and only once in the course of execution for any application. This call will take place upon construction of the first object belonging to a class that is derived from `GraphicalEnv`. For all other invocations, the `testConstruct()` method is essentially a null operation. This means that the `GraphicalEnv` constructor will also be a null operation under these circumstances.

Using the `classInit` variable in this manner is essentially a workaround for an omission in the formulation of the C++ programming language: *class constructors*. While a detailed discussion of flaws in C++ is outside the scope of this book, this particular flaw is a serious one that we will encounter again. C++ does not provide any mechanism for dynamic initialization of class `static` members. Normally, `static` members are initialized in the `.C` file containing the class definition, as in the following `static` initialization:

```
uint  GraphicalEnv::scrWidth = 0 ;
```

However, this is not the final value for `GraphicalEnv::scrWidth`. In fact, at the point of this initialization, we do not know what the correct value is because we have not yet opened a display connection. Ramifications of this include:

1. Any `static` members that would otherwise be declared as constant (such as `scrWidth` in the `GraphicalEnv` class) cannot be declared that way. This is because we need two assignments: one for initialization only and one for the actual value, which occurs inside the `classConstruct()` method. In C++, constants can be assigned once and only once.

2. We must provide our own class construction, as in the `GraphicalEnv` constructor. This requires us to test a flag for each invocation of the constructor, even though the test will succeed only once.

The `classConstruct()` method implements class construction for the `GraphicalEnv` class.

```
extern Boolean  parseAppArguments  (int argc, char **argv) ;
extern void     fatalErrorHandler  (char *errstr) ;
extern void     errorHandler       (char *wrnstr) ;
```

```
extern int    errorHandlerX    (Display *, XErrorEvent *) ;
extern int    ioErrorHandlerX  (Display *) ;

void GraphicalEnv::classConstruct(void)
{
  // Initialize toolkit
  XtToolkitInitialize() ;

  // Get application context
  appContext = XtCreateAppContext() ;

  // Open display
  display = XtOpenDisplay(appContext,
                         NULL,
                         appName,
                         appClass,
                         NULL,
                         0,
                         argc,
                         argv) ;
  if (display == NULL)
  {
    // Report problem and exit...
  }

  // Perform parsing of remaining arguments
  // NOTE: This function is user defined
  parseApplicationArguments(*argc, argv) ;

  // Debug?
  XSynchronize(display, debug) ;

  // Set up error handling
  XSetErrorHandler      (errorHandlerX) ;
  XSetIOErrorHandler    (ioErrorHandlerX) ;
  XtAppSetErrorHandler  (appContext,
                         fatalErrorHandler) ;
```

```
  XtAppSetWarningHandler (appContext, errorHandler) ;

  // Other initialization
  screen    = DefaultScreen   (display) ;
  root      = RootWindow      (display, screen) ;
  depth     = DefaultDepth    (display, screen) ;
  scrHeight = DisplayHeight   (display, screen) ;
  scrWidth  = DisplayWidth    (display, screen) ;

  // Set flag
  classInit = TRUE ;
}
```

The `classConstruct()` method for `GraphicalEnv` allows us to <u>automatically</u> initialize X and Xt the first time an object belonging to a class derived from `GraphicalEnv` is instantiated. This means that the users of our classes do not have to make special required calls to methods that initialize X and Xt. This is important for two reasons:

1. It prevents our implementation from "showing through" (see Section 5.4).
2. It removes an unnecessy burden from the user of the library.

In performing class construction for GraphicalEnv, we call `XtToolkitInitialize()` to initialize Xt internal data structures. If you are already familiar with Xt, you are probably asking why we don't call `XtAppInitialize()` here and save ourselves some trouble. The short answer is that `XtAppInitialize()` returns the top-level widget in the application widget hierarchy, and we wish to create this widget later and store it elsewhere (see the discussion of `GraphicalObject` class construction in Section 6.2).

Actually, `XtAppInitialize()` is a convenience function that calls a number of other Xt initialization functions. What we are doing here is breaking `XtAppInitialize()` into its constituent parts, and calling each part where convenient for <u>us</u>. The next two function calls to `XtCreateAppContext()` and `XtOpenDisplay()` represent calls that would have otherwise been made by `XtAppInitialize()`.

`XtOpenDisplay()` initializes X by calling `XOpenDisplay()` and, if successful, parses the command line arguments to see if any standard Xt options have been specified. You may have noticed that we use the `Graph-icalEnv` members `appName`, `argc`, and `argv` without ostensibly assigning any valid values to these members. This observation is correct in that we give the user an option to initialize these members by calling the `setEn-vironment()` method <u>before</u> constructing any object descended from `GraphicalEnv`. The `setEnvironment()` method sets these members to user-specified values. It may happen that the user does not call `setEnvi-ronment()` before constructing an object descended from `Graphi-calEnv`. This will not be a problem because the static members are initialized to values that will not crash the application (see Section 5.3.1).

```
void GraphicalEnv::setEnvironment(const CString  &pname,
                                  int            &ac,
                                  char           **av,
                                  Boolean        dflag)
{
  appName    = pname ;
  argc       = &ac ;
  argv       = av ;
  debug      = dflag ;
}
```

If `XtOpenDisplay()` returns `NULL`, then X or Xt was not initialized correctly. There are a number of possible causes for this, the most common of which is a bad value for the `DISPLAY` environment variable. X uses the `DISPLAY` environment variable to obtain the name of the display to connect to. In any event, we must report an error and exit from the application if this situation occurs.

Once we have a valid display connection, we can parse any command line arguments specified by the end user. We parse the command line by calling a function, which for lack of a better name we will call `parseAppArgu-ments()`. The implementation of this function depends on the application in question, and therefore is not defined here. We can make an educated guess that the arguments to this function will consist of the command line arguments. These will be modified by our call to `XtOpenDisplay()` such that after the call any remaining arguments are not recognized by Xt.

Following the command line parsing is a call to `XSynchronize()`. Debugging X windows (and therefore Xt and Motif) is made all the more complicated by the fact that the graphics requests made by the client machine are processed asynchronously by the X server. This means that a crash may not occur until long after the offending X function has been called. We can eliminate this problem by telling X to process requests synchronously (i.e., setting `debug` to `TRUE`. However, while this simplifies debugging, it also <u>dramatically</u> decreases performance.

In addition to synchronizing graphics requests, we may also want to trap various error messages sent by X and Xt. One of the advantages of doing this is that it affords the capability of setting a breakpoint in the debugger at the precise moment the error is trapped. The calls to `XSetErrorHandler()` and `XSetIOErrorHandler()` set up error handlers (implemented elsewhere) for X. The calls to `XtAppSetErrorHandler()` and `XtAppSetWarningHandler()` set up the error handlers (implemented elsewhere) for Xt. Please see X and Xt documentation (in particular Flanagan, 1993; Nye, 1993a,b; Nye and O'Reilly, 1992) for further details.

Finally, all that remains is to assign valid values to our other class `static` variables. This is accomplished through various X macro calls. After setting `classInit` to `TRUE`, class construction for `GraphicalEnv` is complete!

5.3.3 Destruction

Destruction is much easier than construction. Like construction, we want the real task of destruction, such as destroying the application context and closing the display connection, to be performed only once. However, how do we determine exactly when to do this? One solution is to count all of the `GraphicalEnv` instances through the use of a class `static` and then perform destruction when no more instances exist. The following fragment illustrates this technique.

```
class GraphicalEnv
{
  ...
  static unsigned int exist ;    // Instance count
  ...
} ;

// No instances to start with
unsigned int GraphicalEnv::exist = 0 ;
```

```
GraphicalEnv::GraphicalEnv(...)
{
  ...
  // An instance is created
  exist++ ;
  ...
}

GraphicalEnv::~GraphicalEnv(void)
{
  ...
  // An instance is destroyed
  exist-- ;

  // Check if there are any more instances
  if (exist == 0)
  {
    // Close display connection, toolkit, etc. ...
  }
  ...
}
```

There is one serious problem with this technique: once there are no more instances, how can we guarantee that another instance will not be created as the application continues? If this situation occurs, we can waste lots of time closing and reopening the display. This will dramatically affect the performance of our library.

We solve this problem by not solving this problem. In other words, we perform no destruction whatsoever. This way, when the execution of the application has finished, the application context will be destroyed and the display connection closed by the operating system. This will occur when the operating system process containing the application is destroyed.

If absolutely necessary, a mechanism for monitoring instances of all classes derived from GraphicalEnv can be designed. However, for the purposes of this book, we will not perform any real destruction for the GraphicalEnv base class. We explicitly define an empty constructor for

`GraphicalEnv` just in case the compiler decides to come up with one of its own, which is often the case.

5.3.4 Managing the Event Loop

In Section 2.7 we discussed some of the details of event-driven programming, including the main "event loop" for an application. In order for an interface to begin working, we must start this event loop.

The `startApp()` method is used to start the Xt event loop:

```
class GraphicalEnv
{
    . . .

  public:

    . . .
    static inline void startApp(void)
    { XtAppMainLoop(appContext) ; }
    . . .
} ;
```

The `startApp()` method should not be called until the following tasks are complete:

- environment initialization
- widget creation
- callback and event handler registration

Sometimes it is necessary to formulate a function or method such that the flow of control remains there until we encounter a particular event. This means that we need a mechanism for processing events locally. This mechanism is provided via the `processEvent()` method:

```
void GraphicalEnv::processEvent(void)
{
  // Tell X to get all events currently in queue
```

```
    XSync(display, FALSE) ;

    // Process an event
    XtAppProcessEvent(appContext, XtIMAll) ;
}
```

The call to XSync() tells the X server to "flush" all events currently queued, that is, to make them available to the application. The second parameter is a flag telling X whether to discard the events. The call to XtAppProcessEvent() tells Xt to process the first event in queue for the application. The second parameter tells Xt that it may process the event whether it is a "normal" event or an "input" or "timer" event. See Xt documentation (in particular Flanagan, 1993; Nye and O'Reilly, 1992) for a detailed description of input and timer events. We will see some examples of how to use this mechanism later on.

5.3.5 Access Methods

All of the other methods in GraphicalEnv are access methods, which allow the user to access various data members.

5.4 Portability Issues

In the class declaration for GraphicalEnv, we allow the X and Xt to "show through" in our include directive,

```
extern "C"
{
# include <X11/Intrinsic.h>
}
```

in class static members,

```
class GraphicalEnv
{
```

```
                              . . .
    static XtAppContext      appContext ;     // App context
    static Display          *display ;         // Display for X
    static Window            root ;            // Desktop X window
                              . . .
} ;
```

and in class methods,

```
class GraphicalEnv
{
                              . . .
    inline friend Display *getDisplay(void)
    { return GraphicalEnv::display ; }
      // Provides access to display pointer for X windows

    inline friend Window getRootWindow(void)
    { return GraphicalEnv::root ; }
      // Provides access to root window for X windows
                              . . .
} ;
```

X and Xt also show through not just by the types visible in the declaration, but by virtue of the fact that we are allowing some implementation detail, such as screen number, to show through. For example,

```
class GraphicalEnv
{
                              . . .
    inline friend int getScreenNumber(void)
    { return GraphicalEnv::screen ; }
      // Provides access to screen number for X windows
                              . . .
} ;
```

Allowing these code elements such high visibility may be undesirable if the library is intended for other graphical platforms, such as Microsoft Windows.

Under ideal circumstances, we want the implementation details encapsulated so that they can be changed locally for global effect.

We allow such visibility in this discussion for the sake of convenience and clarity. But X and Xt code elements can be easily hidden by designing a private class present only when needed for definition of GraphicalEnv methods, which should be placed in .C files. This hypothetical class could hold all of the implementation detail necessary for a particular platform.

We can carry this even further by placing #ifdef directives at the appropriate points in our hypothetical class to adapt the class to the various platforms. This way, the implementation is completely hidden from the user.

The following fragment contains a hypothetical .h file for a declaration of class SystemPart, which illustrates this technique.

```
extern "C"
{
# include <X11/Intrinsic.h>
}

struct SystemPart
{
  static const CString   appClass ;      // Application class
  static CString         appName ;       // Application name
  static XtAppContext    appContext ;    // Application context
  static Display        *display ;       // Display for X
  static Window          root ;          // Desktop X window
  static int             screen ;        // Screen # for X
  static uint            scrWidth ;      // Width of screen
  static uint            scrHeight ;     // Height of screen
  static int             depth ;         // # of color planes

  SystemPart(void) ;
    // Constructor

  inline ~SystemPart(void) {} // NULL
    // Destructor } ;
} ;
```

Notice that this is declared as a `struct` rather than a `class`. This means that by default, all members are public. We must do this so that `GraphicalEnv` has access to the members. We can now hide all system dependent information by rewriting `GraphicalEnv.h` as follows:

```
#include "Boolean.h"
#include "CString.h"

class SystemPart ;

class GraphicalEnv
{
  protected:

    static SystemPart    *sysPart ;  // System dependent info
    static Boolean        debug ;    // Debug graphics?
    static int           *argc ;     // Argument count
    static char          **argv ;    // Command line arguments

    GraphicalEnv(void) ;
        // Constructor

  public:

    inline ~GraphicalEnv(void) {} // NULL
        // Destructor

    static void setEnvironment(const CString    &pname,
                               int               &ac,
                               char              **av,
                               Boolean           dflag = FALSE) ;
        // Sets program name, command line arguments,
        // debugging flag

    static void processEvent(void) ;
        // Processes first event in queue for application
```

```
    static void startApplication(void) ;
        // Starts the main application event loop

    static SystemPart *getSystemPart(void) ;
        // Anybody wishing to call this method must include
        // SystemPart.h
} ;
```

Notice that we have replaced the `#include <X11/Intrinsic.h>` directive with a forward declaration to `SystemPart`. We can use a forward declaration because we make no direct reference to the structure of `SystemPart`. Furthermore, there are no implementation details showing through. Finally, any user of this class can still get to the implementation if absolutely necessary, by including `SystemPart.h` and calling the `getSystemPart()` method.

In the remainder of this book, we will encounter this system dependence problem time and time again. It is left to you, the reader, to generalize this technique and apply it as needed.

5.5 Graphical Environment Classes

Let's take a look at some essential classes that are descended from `GraphicalEnv`.

5.5.1 Color

Color is perhaps the most important and most frequently manipulated element of any graphical user interface. For these reasons we must design our `Color` class so that it is very easy to use.

COLORMAPS

Most GUI toolkits (including X) store colors as a value indicating the intensity of red, green, and blue (RGB) for a given pixel. This technique makes use some kind of lookup table to allow a programmer to look up a RGB value for particular color by providing the name of the color. In X, this lookup table is called a *colormap*. For example, if we wished to find the RGB value for "blue," we could use a colormap to figure out the RGB value (R = 0, G = 0, B = 255) associated with this string.

Actually, X colormaps are slightly more complicated than the above description would seem to indicate. X supports the sharing of colors between applications. Therefore, an X colormap is managed by the X server, and not the application. This means that we cannot simply specify a color name to get the desired color. We must ask X if the color is available and, if so, get the color from X. If the color is not available, we must ask X to place the color in the colormap for us if there is room.

This is complicated even further by the fact that X supports both read-only and read-write colormaps. Color sharing is available only through read-only colormaps or read-only *cells* in read-write colormaps. Read-write cells in read-write colormaps cannot be shared with other applications. These cells can be used to change the color of graphical elements without redrawing these elements. However, if we use such cells, we are "stealing" available colors from other applications, because the number of RGB values that can be stored in a colormap is finite. For this reason, we will use only read-only color cells in our design of the color manipulation mechanism. If this is not sufficient for your needs, see X and Xt documentation (in particular Flanagan, 1993; Nye, 1993a,b; Nye and O'Reilly, 1992) to extend the classes described in this section to support read-write color cells.

COLOR CLASS

We must satisfy two main goals in the design of a color manipulation mechanism: ease-of-use (as discussed above) and efficiency. We accomplish the first goal by allowing color manipulation by name only. This way, a programmer need not be concerned with RGB values. A programmer need only specify a name for a color, such as "yellow" or "maroon" and the mechanism will take care of the rest.

We are fortunate in that the goals of ease-of-use and efficiency for the Color class are complementary. In order to achieve efficiency, we must minimize our calls to X. One such call we will be making frequently is to ask X to look up a color name based on the index for the color in the colormap. If we track these names within the class itself, we can eliminate many of these lookups.

The declaration of the Color class is as follows:

```cpp
#include "GraphicalEnv.h"
#include "Boolean.h"
#include "CString.h"

class Color : public GraphicalEnv
{
  // Class scoped members
  static Boolean   classInit ;  // Class constructed?
  static Visual    *visual ;    // Visual policy for X
  static int       cells ;      // # of colors for X
  static Colormap  cmap ;       // Available colors for X
  static ulong     bgIndex ;    // Foreground pixel
  static ulong     fgIndex ;    // Background pixel
  static CString   *names ;     // All color names in use

  // Instance members
  ulong     index ;      // Index to X color map

  static void classConstruct(void) ;
      // Performs class construction

  static inline void testConstruct(void)
  { if (not classInit) classConstruct() ; }
      // For convenience

  void requestColor(const CString &cname) ;
      // Requests color by name from X

public:

  Color (const CString &cname = CString::Empty) ;
  inline Color (const Color &color) : GraphicalEnv()
  { index = color.index ; }
      // Constructors

  inline ~Color(void) {} // NULL
      // Destructor
```

```
inline const Color &operator = (const Color    &c)
{ index = c.index ; return *this;}
    const Color &operator = (const CString &s) ;
    // Color assignment

inline Boolean operator == (const Color    &c) const
{ return index == c.index ; }
inline Boolean operator == (const CString &s) const
{ return names[index] == s ; }
    // Compares two colors

inline const CString &name(void) const
{ return names[index] ; }
    // Obtains the name of a color

inline operator ulong(void) const { return index ; }
    // Implementation dependent access to
    // system colormap index for color

static inline const CString &defForeName(void)
{ testConstruct() ; return names[fgIndex] ; }
static inline const CString &defBackName(void)
{ testConstruct() ; return names[bgIndex] ; }
    // Obtains name of default fore/background color name

static inline int numColors(void)
{ testConstruct() ; return cells ; }
static inline Colormap getColorMap(void)
{ testConstruct() ; return cmap ; }
static inline Visual *getVisual(void)
{ testConstruct() ; return visual ; }
    // Implementation dependent access to X data
} ;
```

Just like the GraphicalEnv class, the Color class maintains a set of class statics, which must be dynamically assigned values. To do this, we adopt the same class construction mechanism that we designed for the GraphicalEnv class.

Each of these class `statics` has a special purpose within the color handling mechanism:

- `classInit`: This is the flag used to test whether the class `statics` have been dynamically assigned.
- `visual`: This is X data that indicates the color capabilities of the X server, including whether the server supports read-write colormaps. This data is necessary for various system calls involving color. (Also note that we must obtain a `visual` if we wish to extend the class to support read-write colormaps.)
- `cells`: This is a count of the number of colors supported on the X server.
- `cmap`: This is the X colormap.
- `bgIndex`: This is the colormap index for the default background color.
- `fgIndex`: This is the colormap index for the default foreground color.
- `names`: This is a table of color names in use by the application.

The `names` member is array of `CString` objects that is dynamically allocated based on the number of cells in a colormap. We track color names within the `Color` class because X does not provide us with a straightforward mechanism to look up names based on the colormap index. However, depending upon the number of colors available at any one time, this may be a sparse array. For example, if our X server supports 256 colors, it is improbable that any application would use all 256 of them. If the number was even larger, we could also run into the problem of not having enough memory to support this array. An alternative implementation could use a `Set` to store the color names, with the colormap index as the key.

It is also quite possible that a number of different names could refer to the same index within a colormap. For example, "beige" and "tan" may be represented by the same RGB value within a colormap. In our implementation of color manipulation, our name lookup table will contain the last name used for the RGB value. This means that if a user first requests "tan" and then "beige," the lookup table will contain "beige" for the shared RGB value. This is not a major problem, but it does cause a slight inefficiency in that the next time "tan" is requested, the class must ask X for the colormap index value again.

Finally, all of the `static` members in the `Color` class, except `classInit` and `names`, are implementation dependent. We can hide these implementation dependent data members by creating a new class analogous to `SystemPart` for `GraphicalEnv`, as discussed in Section 5.4.

CLASS CONSTRUCTION

Once again, we are forced by C++ to perform our own class construction for the `Color` class. The class statics are dynamically assigned values via the `static` method `classConstruct()`, which is implemented as follows:

```
void Color::classConstruct(void)
{
  // Make sure environment is initialized
  GraphicalEnv::testConstruct() ;

  // Get X visual
  visual = XDefaultVisual(display, screen) ;

  XVisualInfo templ, *visualList ;
  int         matched ;

  // Get visual data
  templ.visualid = XVisualIDFromVisual(visual) ;
  visualList     = XGetVisualInfo(display,
                                  VisualIDMask,
                                  &templ,
                                  &matched) ;

  // Check visual data
  if (matched == 0)
  {
    // Report to end user and terminate...
  }

  // Get number of colors
  cells = visualList[0].colormap_size ;
```

```cpp
  // Get rid of visual list
  XFree(visualList) ;

  // Allocate name table
  names = new CString[cells] ;

  // Get color map
  cmap = DefaultColormap(display, screen) ;

  // Test for 0 black pixel
  if (BlackPixel(display, screen) == 0)
  {
    fgIndex = WhitePixel(display, screen) ;
    names[bgIndex] = "black" ;
    names[fgIndex] = "white" ;
  }

  // Test for 0 white pixel
  else if (WhitePixel(display, screen) == 0)
  {
    fgIndex = BlackPixel(display, screen) ;
    names[bgIndex] = "white" ;
    names[fgIndex] = "black" ;
  }

  // We are in trouble...
  else
  {
    fgIndex = WhitePixel(display, screen) ;
    bgIndex = BlackPixel(display, screen) ;
    names[fgIndex] = "white" ;
    names[bgIndex] = "black" ;

    // Tell end user we do not have the 0 pixel...
  }

  // Set class construction flag
  classInit = TRUE ;
}
```

The first job in class construction is to obtain the default visual data for the display connection. This data contains information about how many cells the default colormap contains. Once we have obtained this information, by assigning it to the `cells` data member we can allocate the lookup table for color names.

The next task is to obtain a reference to the default colormap for the display connection. Since we have already decided that our library will not support read-write colormaps, this should be sufficient (and friendly to other applications). However, if we needed to create a read-write colormap, we would create it here.

Our final job is to find the 0 index into the X colormap. This is important because the 0 index has special properties for rendering. An index to an X colormap actually serves a dual purpose. Not only does it provide access to the correct color cell, but contains `GraphicalEnv::depth` bits. These bits are also used to store the actual RGB value in the index. When we render lines or other graphical elements, X combines the color of the rendered object with the background according to one of various bitwise combinations specified by the user. One of the most important of these is the bitwise "xor" of the bits. This particular combination is important because we can use it to turn a color on and off without redrawing the background, but only if the bits of the background color are 0.

Therefore, we default the `bgIndex` member to 0, as follows:

```
ulong Color::bgIndex = 0 ;
```

This is why there is no assignment to `bgIndex` in the first two branches of the 0 index test.

On most X systems, the "black pixel" in the default colormap is 0. In `classConstruct()`, we are assuming that if the black pixel is not 0, then the white pixel is 0. This is usually the case. For systems on which some other color has a pixel value of 0, we could add code to find the name of the color which has the 0 pixel, but we will not do it here. Finally, note that the "black" or "white" pixel is not necessarily black or white, but just how X describes them.

In addition to the `classConstruct()` method, we provide a `testConstruct()` convenience method, which performs class construction only if the class construction flag `classInit` is clear. This method is used whenever there is a possibility that the user could invoke some other method before `Color` class construction. However, there is a serious flaw in this mechanism. A user could invoke a method such as `defBackName()` before class construction for `GraphicalEnv` or `Color` occurs. In this case, `testConstruct()`, invokes `classConstruct()`, which constructs the `Color` class but not the `GraphicalEnv` class. This is why we call `testConstruct()` for the `GraphicalEnv` class in the `Color` class constructor.

INSTANCE CONSTRUCTION

Now that we have talked about class construction for `Color`, let's see what happens when a `Color` object is instantiated.

There are two flavors of `Color` construction: one that takes a `CString` argument and a copy constructor. Notice that the string constructor also acts as the *default* constructor (i.e., the one with an empty parameter list). This is because the parameter is defaulted to the empty string.

The `CString` flavor of `Color` construction is defined as follows:

```
Color::Color(const CString &cname) : GraphicalEnv()
{
  // Perform class construction, if necessary
  testConstruct() ;

  // See if no color was requested
  if (cname.isBlank()) index = fgIndex ;

  // Request the color
  else requestColor(cname) ;
}
```

First the constructor creates a base instance through the `GraphicalEnv` constructor. Next it performs conditional class construction for the Color class by invoking `testConstruct()`. After this, it tests the validity of the supplied name. A name is valid if it is not blank. If the name is invalid, the constructor assigns the X colormap index of the default foreground color. If the name is valid, it requests the color from X using the private method `requestColor()`. This method is defined as follows:

```
void Color::requestColor(const CString &cname)
{
  XColor exact, approx ;

  if (XAllocNamedColor(display,
                       cmap,
                       (const char *) cname,
                       &approx,
                       &exact))
  {
    index         = approx.pixel ;
    names[index]  = cname ;
  }
  else index = fgIndex ;
}
```

When we invoke XAllocNamedColor() we obtain both an exact match for the color name, if available, and X's best approximation of the color, in case it is not available. If the exact match is available, exact and approx will be identical. In our GUI library we will always use approx, because we will not be overly concerned if we request "peach" and instead get "orange."

One excellent side effect of having a CString constructor for Color is that it allows us to treat colors as strings. We can now use a CString in place of a Color for any function or method that requires an argument of type Color. This is quite convenient for the user of the class.

The copy constructor is implemented as follows:

```
class Color : public GraphicalEnv
{
  ...
  inline Color(const Color &color) { index = other.index ; }
  ...
} ;
```

The copy constructor assigns the index member of the argument to the index member of the newly constructed object. Notice that we do not need to call `testConstruct()` because if this particular constructor is called, we must have previously constructed a `Color` object, which means that we have already constructed the `Color` class.

OTHER METHODS

No destruction is necessary for the `Color` class, because it contains only a single data member, which is a raw type. Class destruction occurs upon termination of the application process within the operating system.

Assignment is overloaded to support assignment of either `CString` objects or `Color` objects. This is analogous to construction. The string assignment operator is quite similar to the string constructor:

```
const Color &Color::operator =(const CString &cname)
{
  // Color found?
  if (cname.isBlank()) index = fgIndex ;
  else requestColor(cname) ;

  return *this ;
}
```

The assignment operator requests the appropriate color from X if the color name is valid. We return `this` object to allow for chained assignment. The color assignment assigns the `index` data member of the argument to the `index` data member of `this` object, as does the copy constructor.

The remaining, undiscussed methods consist of comparison operators and access methods. These should be self-explanatory.

5.5.2   Contexts

X provides a very sophisticated and customizable rendering mechanism by way of a structure called a *graphics context* (GC). This structure contains all of the information necessary to manipulate the color, style, technique, and bit combinations for any rendered or filled element, such as a line, polygon, text string, or pixel map.

Our library supports GCs through a class called `Context`:

```
// Forward declarations
class Color ;
class CString ;
class PixelMap ;

// Includes
#include "GraphicalEnv.h"
#include "Color.h"

class Context : public GraphicalEnv
{
  public:

    // Bitwise combination functions
    enum DrawFunction
    {
      DRAW_FUNC_CLEAR,
      DRAW_FUNC_SET,
      DRAW_FUNC_AND,
      DRAW_FUNC_NAND,
      DRAW_FUNC_COPY,
      DRAW_FUNC_NOOP,
      DRAW_FUNC_XOR,
      DRAW_FUNC_OR,
      DRAW_FUNC_NOR,
      DRAW_FUNC_INVERT
    } ;

    // Line styles
    num LineStyle
    {
      LINE_STYLE_SOLID,
      LINE_STYLE_DASH,
      LINE_STYLE_DOUBLE_DASH
    } ;

    // Fill styles
```

```
    enum FillStyle
    {
      FILL_SOLID,
      FILL_STIPPLE,
      FILL_STIPPLE_OPAQUE,
      FILL_TILE
    } ;

    // Line "widths" for drawing lines 1 pixel wide
    static const uint LW1_FAST ;      // Speed for precision
    static const uint LW1_PRECISE ;  // Precision for speed

private:

    static uint   tileWidth ;    // Optimum width of tile
    static uint   tileHeight ;   // Optimum height of tile
    static uint   stipWidth ;    // Optimum width of stipple
    static uint   stipHeight ;   // Optimum height of stipple

    GC      gc ;     // X representation
    Color fore ;   // Foreground color for rendering
    Color back ;   // Background color for rendering


    static void classConstruct(void) ;
       // Class constructor for initializing class statics

public:

    Context(const Color &fcolor, const Color &bcolor) ;
       // Constructor

    ~Context(void) ;
       // Destructor

    void setForeground(const Color &color) ;
       // Changes foreground color
```

```
void setBackground(const Color &color) ;
   // Changes background color

void toggleReverse(void) ;
   // Flips foreground and background colors

inline const CString &getForeName(void) const
{ return fore.name() ; }
   // Obtains foreground color name

inline const CString &getBackName(void) const
{ return back.name() ; }
   // Obtains background color name

Boolean setFunction(const DrawFunction func) ;
   // Sets Boolean draw function used to combine
   // pixels on draw

Boolean setLineStyle(const LineStyle ls =
                 LINE_STYLE_SOLID) ;
   // Sets line style for draw

void setLineWidth(const uint lw = LW1_FAST) ;
   // Sets line width for draw

Boolean setFillStyle(const FillStyle  fs,
               PixelMap       *pmap  = NULL,
               int            x      = 0,
               int            y      = 0) ;
   // Sets fill style for draw

static uint getTileHeight(void) const
{ return tileHeight ; }
   // Obtains allowed height for any tile
   // for filling

static uint getTileWidth(void)
```

```
    { return tileWidth ; }
      // Obtains allowed width for any tile used
      // for filling

    static uint getStippleHeight(void)
    { return stipHeight ; }
      // Obtains allowed height for any stipple
      // pattern used for filling

    static uint getStippleWidth(void)
    { return stipWidth ; }
      // Obtains allowed width for any stipple pattern
      // used for filling

    inline operator GC(void) const { return gc ; }
      // Cast to system representation
} ;
```

The Context class provides public types which correspond to X types. These types allow us to specify exactly how a drawn element is to be rendered:

- DrawFunction: When elements are drawn to the screen, the foreground pixel value for the element (termed the *source* pixel) is combined bitwise with the pixel values already on screen (*destination* pixels) at the desired location to produce a *final* pixel value. The bitwise combination is done according to a logical combination function specified by the caller. DrawFunction enumerates all of these logical functions. For example, if we set the drawing function to DRAW_FUNC_COPY, the source pixel value "wipes out" the destination values, making the final value equal to the source value. However, specifying DRAW_FUNC_AND results in final values that are the bitwise "and" of the source value and destination values.

- LineStyle: The LineStyle type enumerates all of the ways that we can change the appearance of a line. We can make lines appear solid, dashed, or double-dashed.

- FillStyle: In addition to drawing lines, we will see that our library provides various mechanisms for filling enclosed areas on the screen.

The `FillStyle` type enumerates all of ways we can change the appearance of the filling. We can fill with solid colors, tiles, or stipples (see below).

The `Context` class also provides two `public static` constants for specifying whether to trade speed for precision when drawing lines that are one pixel wide. X chooses a line-rendering algorithm for single-width lines based on these constants. For example, if an application performs a large amount of single-width line drawing and has strict performance requirements (as many do), we can tell X to trade precision for speed by specifying `LW1_FAST` as the line width. X does not provide these alternatives for lines more than one pixel wide.

In addition to these two `static` constants, there are four other `static` members that should be constant but cannot be declared that way because of class construction flaws in C++, as discussed in Section 5.3.2. These members are `tileWidth`, `tileHeight`, `stipWidth`, and `stipHeight`.

As previously mentioned, there are a number of ways to change the appearance of the filling within filled graphic elements. These elements can be filled with a solid color, a tile, or a stipple. For tile filling, we create a pixel map (see Section 5.5.3) of specific dimensions and then fill an element by repeatedly rendering the pixel map, like placing tiles on a bathroom wall. Stipple filling involves creating a pixel map one bit deep (i.e., a bitmap), which acts as a mask used to filter the GC foreground and background. X allows us to perform this filtering with or without the use of the GC background. If we specify `FILL_STIPPLE`, a pixel on the screen is set to the foreground color of the GC if the corresponding stipple bit is set. All other screen pixels remain unchanged. If we specify `FILL_STIPPLE_OPAQUE`, the foreground is rendered if the corresponding stipple bit is set, and the background is rendered if the corresponding stipple bit is clear.

On many X servers, there are optimum dimensions for tiles and stipples. When the tiles or stipples conform to these optimum dimensions they can be rendered a great deal faster. In our implementation of `Context`, we force the user to use these optimum values when performing tile or stipple fills. We store these optimum values in the `*Width`/`*Height` members upon class construction.

The remaining members consist of the system GC representation `gc` and the `Color` objects, `fore` and `back`. Actually, `gc` already stores the colormap index values of its foreground and background colors. We store them redundantly in a `Context` instance for convenience only.

CLASS CONSTRUCTION

Class construction for `Context` entails querying the X server for the optimum dimensions of tiles and stipples for filling purposes. Here is the definition of the `classConstruct()` method:

```
#define REQ_HEIGHT      16
#define REQ_WIDTH       16

uint Context::tileWidth       = 0;
uint Context::tileHeight      = 0;
uint Context::stipWidth       = 0;
uint Context::stipHeight      = 0;

void Context::classConstruct(void)
{
  // Obtain optimum tile/stipple dimensions
  XQueryBestTile          (display, root,
                           REQ_WIDTH, REQ_HEIGHT,
                           &tileWidth, &tileHeight) ;
  XQueryBestStipple       (display, root,
                           REQ_WIDTH, REQ_HEIGHT,
                           &stipWidth, &stipHeight) ;
}
```

We use `REQ_WIDTH` and `REQ_HEIGHT` to tell the X server our preferred dimensions. X returns the closest values that can be used to render tiles and stipples quickly.

Once again, class destruction occurs as a result of the termination of the application process within the operating system.

INSTANCE CONSTRUCTION AND DESTRUCTION

Construction of `Context` instances is fairly straightforward:

```
Context::Context(const Color &fcolor, const Color &bcolor) :
    GraphicalEnv(), fore(fcolor), back(bcolor)
{
  static Boolean classInit = FALSE ;
```

```
  // Initialize class
  if (not classInit)
  {
    classConstruct() ;
    classInit = TRUE ;
  }

  XGCValues      vals ;

  // Create system representation
  vals.foreground        = (ulong) fore ;
  vals.background        = (ulong) back ;
  gc                     = XCreateGC(display,
                                    root, GCForeground |
                                    GCBackground, &vals) ;
  XFlush(display) ;
}
```

The caller of this constructor supplies only the desired foreground and background colors for the new Context object. Note that the caller can provide CString arguments, and temporary Color object will be constructed for the call. This is quite convenient.

The constructor first checks to determine if the class has been constructed. It then assigns the arguments to the foreground and background fields of the GC values. Finally, it creates the X GC structure, assigns it to the gc member, and flushes the display. Flushing the display tells the X server to process all outstanding requests. This guarantees that X will know about the new context immediately.

Class destruction consists of destroying the GC structure created by X at construction:

```
Context::~Context(void)
{
  XFreeGC(display, gc) ;
}
```

The Color members fore and back are implicitly destroyed as part of the Context instance according to the standard behavior of C++.

CONTEXT METHODS

The remainder of the `Context` class consists of methods to set various rendering attributes and a number of access methods. We omit any discussion of access methods here because they are considered to be self-explanatory.

The first methods to discuss are the methods that change the colors of a `Context` object: `setForeground()` and `setBackground()`. Let's take a look at `setForeground()`:

```
void Context::setForeground(const Color &color)
{
  XSetForeground(display, gc, (ulong) (fore = color)) ;
}
```

This method simply calls the X function `XSetForeground()` with a new colormap index value representing the new color. The index value is obtained by casting the result of the assignment with the `ulong` cast operator provided by `Color`. Remember, `Color` assignment returns the right-hand side for exactly this reason (as any assignment operator for any class should!).

The `setBackground()` method is quite similar to `setForeground()`, except that it calls `XSetBackground()` instead of `XSetForeground()`.

The `toggleReverse()` method is a useful method to have. It switches the foreground and background colors, allowing for dramatic graphical effects.

```
void Context::toggleReverse(void)
{
  Color tcol = fore ;

  XSetForeground(GraphicalEnv::display, gc, (ulong)
      (fore = back)) ;
  XSetBackground(GraphicalEnv::display, gc, (ulong)
      (back = tcol)) ;
}
```

The `setFunction()` method allows the user to change the bitwise combination function used to draw a graphical element. It works by mapping the class enumerator to an X literal and then calling `XSetFunction()` with the new value.

```
static const int FunctionLookup[] =
{
  GXclear, GXset, GXand, GXnand, GXcopy,
  GXnoop, GXxor, GXor, GXnor, GXinvert
} ;

Boolean Context::setFunction(const DrawFunction func)
{
  if (func > DRAW_FUNC_INVERT) return FALSE ;

  // Set the function
  XSetFunction(GraphicalEnv::display, gc,
      FunctionLookup[func]) ;
  return TRUE ;
}
```

The setLineStyle() method is quite similar to setFunction().

```
// Maps our line style type to X type
static const int LineStyleLookup[] =
{
  LineSolid, LineOnOffDash, LineDoubleDash
} ;

Boolean Context::setLineStyle(const LineStyle ls)
{

  if (ls > LINE_STYLE_DOUBLE_DASH) return FALSE ;

  XGCValues  vals ;

  // Set the line style
  vals.line_style = LineStyleLookup[ls] ;
  XChangeGC(GraphicalEnv::display, gc, GCLineStyle, &vals) ;
  return TRUE ;
}
```

The `setLineWidth()` method is quite similar to the previous two methods. We also see the correct initialization for `LW1_FAST` and `LW1_PRECISE`.

```
const uint Context::LW1_FAST      = 0;
const uint Context::LW1_PRECISE   = 1;

void Context::setLineWidth(const uint lw)
{
  XGCValues   vals ;

  vals.line_width = lw ;
  XChangeGC(GraphicalEnv::display, gc, GCLineWidth, &vals) ;
}
```

Finally, the `setFillStyle()` method continues in the same vein, except that we use a `switch` statement instead of a lookup table because additional checks are performed against the optimum tile or stipple dimensions if a tile or stipple fill style, respectively, has been requested. See Section 5.5.3 for a discussion of the `PixelMap` class.

```
Boolean Context::setFillStyle(const FillStyle   fs,
                              PixelMap          *pmap,
                              int               x,
                              int               y)
{
  // If not solid fill, make sure we have a pixel map
  if (fs != FILL_SOLID and pmap == NULL) return FALSE ;

  XGCValues vals ;
  ulong     mask = GCFillStyle ;


  switch (fs)
  {
    case FILL_SOLID:
      vals.fill_style = FillSolid ;
      break ;
```

```
case FILL_TILE:
  {
    // Check against optimum dimensions
    if (pmap->getWidth()  != tileWidth or
        pmap->getHeight() != tileHeight) return FALSE ;

    // Formulate change mask
    mask |= GCTileStipXOrigin | GCTileStipYOrigin |
        GCTile ;

    // Set new GC values
    vals.fill_style          = FillTiled ;
    vals.tile                = (Pixmap) (*pmap) ;
    vals.ts_x_origin         = x ;
    vals.ts_y_origin         = y ;
  }
  break ;

case FILL_STIPPLE:
case FILL_STIPPLE_OPAQUE:
  {
    // Check against optimum dimensions
    if (pmap->getWidth()  != stipWidth or
        pmap->getHeight() != stipHeight) return FALSE ;

    // Formulate change mask
    mask |= GCTileStipXOrigin | GCTileStipYOrigin |
    GCStipple ;

    // Set new GC values
    vals.fill_style          = (fs == FILL_STIPPLE ?
                                FillStippled :
                                FillOpaqueStippled) ;
    vals.stipple             = (Pixmap) (*pmap) ;
    vals.ts_x_origin         = x ;
    vals.ts_y_origin         = y ;
  }
  break ;
```

```
default:
  return FALSE ;
}


XChangeGC(GraphicalEnv::display, gc, mask, &vals) ;
return TRUE ;
}
```

5.5.3 Pixel Maps

Pixel maps are as important as windows to a good GUI library. A pixel map can be used to store and display color images captured from a window or read from a file. Unfortunately, X does not provide an easy mechanism for storing color pixel maps in files. Rather, X only allows one plane at a time in pixel map files. A plane is a bitmap corresponding to a bit position within a pixel. For example, if our screen has a depth of 8 (i.e., each pixel is represented with 8 bits), we would need 8 planes to form a complete color pixel map. Files for such a pixel map would be extremely difficult to create manually. Furthermore, even if we were to create these files, they would be unreadable by humans.

We solve this problem by creating our own file format for pixel maps:

```
<width> <height>
0="<color1>"
1="<color2>"
      .


      .


      .



<image data>
```

A pixel map file consists of ASCII text, which is modifiable through any common text editor, such as VI or EMACS.[2] We use the first line to specify the

---

[2]EMACS is a free text editor published by the Free Software Foundation. If you wish to obtain it, contact the Foundation at 675 Massachusetts Ave., Cambridge, MA, 02139.

dimensions of the pixel map, in pixels. Following the dimensions, we specify which colors will be used in the pixel map and assign a single digit to each color. For example, we may choose 1 for "black," 2 for "red," and so on. The remainder of the file is an ASCII depiction of the pixel map image. The sample pixel map text file given in Figure 5.1 is for a red "X" on a black background. The pixel map corresponding to the text file is given in Figure 5.2.

As you have probably surmised, there are limitations to our file mechanism. The main disadvantage is that we are limited to 10 colors, because we can only use digits 0 through 9 in the file. However, we can easily extend our file mechanism to support characters other than digits for color specification. This should give us more than enough color. For example, we could allow

```
...
x="yellow"
...
```

In addition to providing a mechanism for reading pixel maps from a file, we also allow users to draw random shapes into our pixel maps. For this purpose, we will have to conjure up a bunch of fictitious classes. These classes represent various elements that can be rendered into a pixel map: FontString, Line, Polygon, Segment, and Vertex. These classes are used for illustration purposes only. The implementation of these classes is beyond the scope of this book.

In our library, pixel maps are represented by the PixelMap class, which is declared as follows:

```
// Forward declarations
class CString ;
class Color ;
class Context ;
class FontString ;
class Line ;
class Polygon ;
class Segment ;
class Vertex ;

// Includes
#include "GraphicalEnv.h"
```

```
24 24
0="black"
1="red"

000000000000000000000000
111100000000000000001111
111110000000000000011111
011111000000000000111110
001111100000000001111100
000111110000000011111000
000011111000000111110000
000001111100001111100000
000000111110011111000000
000000011111111110000000
000000001111111100000000
000000000111110000000000
000000000111110000000000
000000001111111100000000
000000011111111110000000
000000111110011111000000
000001111100001111100000
000011111000000111110000
000111110000000011111000
001111000000000011111000
011111000000000000111110
011110000000000000011111
111100000000000000001111
000000000000000000000000
```

Figure 5.1. Pixel map text file for red X.

Figure 5.2. Pixel map for a red X on a black background.

```
class PixelMap : public GraphicalEnv
{
    uint    width ;      // Width of pixel map
    uint    height ;     // Height of pixel map
    Pixmap  pixmap ;     // X representation of pixel map

    inline void zero(void)
    { width = height = 0 ; pixmap = (Pixmap) NULL ; }
        // Clears all members

public:

    inline PixelMap(void) : GraphicalEnv() { zero() ; }
        // Constructor

    inline PixelMap(uint w, uint h) : GraphicalEnv()
    {zero(); resize(w, h) ; }
        // Constructor for predefined dimensions

    PixelMap(const PixelMap &other) ;
        // Copy constructor

    ~PixelMap(void) ;
        // Destructor
```

```
Boolean read(const CString &fileName) ;
   // Obtains pixel map from file

Boolean resize(uint w, uint h) ;
   // Changes dimensions of pixel map
   // WARNING: Pixel map contents are destroyed

void clear(const CString &colName) ;
   // Clears pixel map to a known color

void draw(const Context &c, const Vertex      &v) ;
void draw(const Context &c, const Segment     &s) ;
void draw(const Context &c, const Line        &l) ;
void draw(const Context &c, const Polygon     &p) ;
void draw(const Context &c, const FontString &f) ;
   // Draws geometric shapes to pixel map

void fill(const Context &c, const Polygon &poly) ;
   // Fills polygon in pixel map

inline uint getWidth(void) const { return width ; }
   // Obtains the width of the pixel map in pixels

inline uint getHeight(void) const { return height ; }
   // Obtains the height of the pixel map in pixels

inline operator Pixmap(void) const { return pixmap ; }
   // Cast to X representation
} ;
```

For once, we do not have to worry about initializing class `static` members by way of a class constructor. In fact, we have just three data members. Two of them, `width` and `height`, store the dimensions of the pixel map. The third, `pixmap`, is the X representation of the pixel map.

It may seem redundant to store the dimensions, since X provides function calls to obtain the dimensions of a pixel map. However, the dimensions are used frequently, and therefore storing them makes sense if we desire better performance.

CONSTRUCTION AND DESTRUCTION

We provide three constructors for the `PixelMap` class. The first is the default constructor.

```
class PixelMap : public GraphicalEnv
{
  ...
  inline PixelMap(void) : GraphicalEnv() { zero() ; }
  ...
} ;
```

This consists of a call to the private method `zero()`, which clears all of the data members of the instance to 0.

```
class PixelMap : public GraphicalEnv
{
  ...
  inline void zero(void)
  { width = height = 0 ; pixmap = (Pixmap) NULL ; }
  ...
} ;
```

This effectively sets all of the data members to an invalid state. Once such a pixel map is instantiated, it can be made valid by either resizing it using the `resize()` method or reading it from a file (see below).

The second form of construction creates a `PixelMap` of preset dimensions. This constructor is basically a shortcut, which resizes the `PixelMap` at the point of construction. Otherwise, we would have to create a `PixelMap` using the default constructor, and then call the `resize()` method.

```
class PixelMap : public GraphicalEnv
{
  ...
  inline PixelMap(uint w, uint h) : GraphicalEnv()
  { zero() ; resize(w, h) ; }
  ...
} ;
```

Notice that the constructor calls the `zero()` method before resizing. This guarantees that all data members are set to a known value before `resize()` is called. The `resize()` method will not perform correctly if we do not do this.

```
Boolean PixelMap::resize(uint w, uint h)
{
  // Can't have 0 dimensions
  if (w == 0 or h == 0) return FALSE ;

  // See if we need to resize
  if (width == w and height == h) return TRUE ;

  // If an X pixel map already exists, free it
  if (pixmap) XFreePixmap(display, pixmap) ;

  // Initialize dimension members
  width     = w ;
  height    = h ;

  // Create the new pixel map
  pixmap = XCreatePixmap(display,
                         root,
                         width,
                         height,
                         depth) ;
  return TRUE ;
}
```

The `resize()` method checks the requested dimensions to see if the user requested a 0 dimension, which is, of course, illegal. Once we are sure that the dimensions are valid, we check to see if they actually change. If they don't, we are done. If the dimensions change, then we must delete the old pixel map and create a new one with the correct dimensions.

The third and final constructor is the copy constructor.

```
PixelMap::PixelMap(const PixelMap &other) : GraphicalEnv()
{
  // See if there is a pixel map to copy
```

```
if (not other.pixmap)
{
  zero();
  return ;
}

// Initialize dimensions
width  = other.width ;
height = other.height ;

// Create system representation
pixmap = XCreatePixmap(display,
                       root,
                       width,
                       height,
                       depth) ;

// Copy other pixel map to this
XCopyArea(display,
          other.pixmap,
          pixmap,
          DefaultGC(display, screen),
          0, 0,
          width, height,
          0, 0) ;
}
```

The copy constructor creates a new pixel map from the dimensions of the argument and then copies the contents of the argument to the pixmap member.

The PixelMap class does not provide a constructor for reading a pixel map from a file. This is because it is far more likely for file I/O to fail than it is for pixel map resizing to fail. Furthermore, the consequences of I/O failure can be far more devastating. Therefore, the class forces the user to call the read() method (see below), which explicitly returns the status of the operation.

Destruction of PixelMap objects is exceedingly simple. We just check if the pixmap member is valid, and, if so, destroy it.

```
PixelMap::~PixelMap(void)
{
  if (pixmap) XFreePixmap(display, pixmap) ;
}
```

OBTAINING IMAGES FROM FILES

The read() method is used to obtain a pixel map image from a file and draw it into the pixel map.

```
// Includes
#include <fstream.h>
#include "List.h"

// Defines
#define StringList List<CString>

// Prototypes
static Boolean readColors (ifstream        &inFile,
                           StringList       &colors) ;
static Boolean readImage  (ifstream        &inFile,
                           const StringList &colors,
                           PixelMap         &pm) ;

Boolean PixelMap::read(const CString &fileName)
{
  ifstream inFile(fileName) ;

  // Check status of input file
  if (not inFile) return FALSE ;

  uint w, h ;

  // Read in pixel map dimensions
  inFile.seekg(0L, ios::beg) ;
  inFile >> w >> h ;

  // Validate dimensions
```

```
    if (w == 0 or h == 0) return FALSE ;

    // Eat rest of line
    inFile.get() ;

    StringList    colors ;

    // Read the color specification from the file
    if (not readColors(inFile, colors)) return FALSE ;

    // Resize if necessary
    resize(w, h) ;

    // Read the image specification from the file
    if (not readImage(inFile, colors, *this)) return FALSE ;

    return TRUE ;
}
```

The read() method begins by opening and validating an input file stream inFile based on the file name argument of the method (see Ellis and Stroustrup, 1990, or Lippman, 1993, for a discussion of streams). Next, the method reads and validates the dimensions of the image specified in the file. If either the file or dimension validation fails, the read() method returns FALSE.

The next task is to read the color specification. The read() method uses the auxiliary function readColors() to read, parse, and validate the color specification within the file and to populate a list of strings representing the requested colors. The implementation of this function appears below.

```
static Boolean readColors(ifstream   &inFile,
                          StringList &colors)
{
  CString    color ;
  uint       start, finish ;

  // Read colors until there is a blank line
  while (TRUE)
```

```
{
  inFile >> color ;
  if (not color.isBlank())
  {
    // Get the name of the color.
    start  = color.find('\"') + 1;
    finish = color.rfind('\"') ;

    // Validate
    if (start > finish) return FALSE ;

    // Add to list
    colors += color.subString(start, finish - start) ;
  }
  else break ;
}
return colors.length() ;
}
```

The readColors() function is implemented as a loop that reads colors until a blank line is encountered. With each iteration of the loop, a substring of the current line is generated, which contains all characters inside the double quotes. The quotes are necessary in case a color is made up of multiple words, such as "light blue."

Notice that readColors() ignores the number assignment for the color name, as in

```
. . .
0="cyan"
. . .
```

The left-hand side of the assignment is ignored because the readColors() function assumes that the colors are given in order and that there are no gaps in the numbering scheme. In other words, the function treats the number assignments as a readability issue only. The readColors() function can easily be extended to solve both of the mentioned problems.

If the color specification is correct, then the read() method resizes the pixel map to fit the new dimensions and attempts to read the image from the file using the auxiliary function readImage().

There are a couple of ways to implement the readImage() function, depending upon performance and memory requirements for the library. The simplest implementation is as follows:

```
#define MY_ATOI(c) (int)((c) - 48)

static Boolean readImage(ifstream        &inFile,
                         const StringList &colors,
                         PixelMap         &pm)
{
  uint          width  = pm.getWidth(),
                height = pm.getHeight(),
                i ;
  StringList    textImage ;
  CString       string ;

  // Read in image specification
  for (i = 0 ; i < height ; i++)
  {
    // Get a line
    inFile >> string ;
    string.trim() ;

    // Check the length
    if (string.length() != width) return FALSE ;

    // Add the string
    textImage += string ;
  }

  Context       context(Color::defForeName(),
                        Color::defBackName()) ;
  uint          j ;
  int           colIndex,
                prevIndex      = -1 ;
```

```
Display      *display          = getDisplay() ;

// Loop through height
for (i = 0 ; i < height ; i++)
{
  CString &line = textImage[(long) i] ;

  // Loop through width
  for (j = 0 ; j < width ; j++)
  {
    // Get index
    colIndex = MY_ATOI(line[j]) ;
    if (colIndex >= colors.length()) colIndex = 0 ;

    // Change color
    if (colIndex != prevIndex)
    context.setForeground(colors[colIndex]) ;

    // Draw a point
    XDrawPoint(display, (Pixmap) pm, context, j, i) ;
    prevIndex = colIndex ;
  }
}

return TRUE ;
}
```

The for loop at the top of the function reads and validates the text image and populates textImage with all lines in the file that comprise the image specification. The second pair of loops traverses the image in a row major fashion, rendering each point in the requested color.

This implementation can be quite expensive in terms of network traffic, especially for large pixel maps. This is because we are making an individual draw request to the X server for each pixel within the pixel map. To solve this problem, we have to be smarter about collecting the points and rendering all points at the same time.

A good alternative to the above implementation is to use the XImage structure to store the graphical version of the pixel map image. This is a "client side" structure, which is not transmitted across the network until we need to render the image. Here is the alternative implementation of readImage() that illustrates the use of XImage:

```
#define MY_ATOI(c)  (int)((c) - 48)

static Boolean readImage(ifstream             &inFile,
                         const StringList      &colors,
                         PixelMap              &pm)
{
  uint          width  = pm.getWidth(),
                height = pm.getHeight(),
                i ;
  StringList    textImage ;
  CString       string ;

  // Read in image specification
  for (i = 0 ; i < height ; i++)
  {
      // Get a line
      inFile >> string ;
      string.trim() ;

      // Check the length
      if (string.length() != width) return FALSE ;

      // Add the string
      textImage += string ;
  }

  Display       *display   = getDisplay() ;
  int           depth      = getDepth(),
                screen     = getScreenNumber(),
                colIndex,
                prevIndex  = -1 ;
```

```cpp
ulong          cmapVal ;
uint           j ;

XImage *img = XCreateImage(display,
                          DefaultVisual(display,
                                       screen),
                          depth,
                          ZPixmap,
                          0, None,
                          width, height,
                          BitmapPad(display), 0) ;

// Allocate image information.
img->data = (char *) malloc(height *
    img->bytes_per_line) ;

// Loop through height
for (i = 0 ; i < height ; i++)
{
  CString &line = textImage[(long) i] ;

  // Loop through width
  for (j = 0 ; j < width ; j++)
  {
    // Get index
    colIndex = MY_ATOI(line[j]) ;
    if (colIndex >= colors.length()) colIndex = 0 ;

    // Change color
    if (colIndex != prevIndex)
    cmapVal = (ulong) Color(colors[colIndex]) ;

    // Draw a point
    XPutPixel(img, j, i, cmapVal) ;
    prevIndex = colIndex ;
  }
}
```

```
// Put image in the Pixel map.
XPutImage(display,
          (Pixmap) pm,
          DefaultGC(display, screen),
          img,
          0, 0,
          0, 0,
          width, height) ;

// Clean up memory.
free(img->data) ;
XFree((char *) img) ;

return TRUE ;
}
```

In this implementation, the first loop, which reads and validates the image specification, is exactly the same as in the previous implementation. However, after the loop, the implementation changes. First, we create an XImage structure called img and populate it using the XPutPixel() function, rather than the XDrawPoint() function. After population is complete, we put the image into the pixel map and clean up.

The disadvantage to this implementation is the fact that we are allocating and freeing img and img->data for each pixel map. This can lead to memory fragmentation within the application process. As always, it is up to the programmer to perform an analysis of these trade-offs and to choose the implementation that best suits his or her requirements.

RENDERING PIXEL MAPS

Before discussing the rendering methods provided by the PixelMap class, it is useful to spend a moment thinking about coordinate systems. X windows and pixel maps (*drawables*) place the origin at the top left corner of the drawable. However, most other coordinate systems place the origin at the bottom left or in the center, as in the latitude/longitude coordinate system used to track locations on earth. Therefore, translating coordinates from bottom-left-origin or center-origin systems to X coordinates requires us to "flip" values along the vertical axis (*y-axis*) in the former case, and perform a more complicated transformation in the latter case. If this situation occurs frequently, we may want to consider building support for these transformations directly into the `PixelMap` class and into any other classes that permit rendering. For example, we can force the user to specify all coordinates relative to a bottom-left origin and then flip values on the y-axis within each rendering method. In any case, we will ignore coordinate system variations, and assume that all coordinates are relative to the top-left corner of the window in question.

The `PixelMap` class supports three varieties of rendering: clearing, filling, and drawing. The `clear()` method fills the pixel map with a single color.

```
void PixelMap::clear(const CString &colName)
{
  GC           gc ;
  XGCValues    vals ;
  Color        col(colName) ;

  // Create a GC with the correct foreground color
  vals.foreground       = (ulong) col ;
  gc                    = XCreateGC(display, pixmap,
                                    GCForeground, &vals) ;

  // Fill pixel map with color
  XFillRectangle(display, pixmap, gc, 0, 0, width, height) ;

  // Clean up
  XFreeGC(display, gc) ;
}
```

The `fill()` method fills an instance of the fictitious `Polygon` class. We will assume that `Polygon` has a method called `pointCount()`, which returns the number of points in the instance. We will also assume that the points in the `Polygon` instance can be accessed by `operator [] ()`.

```
void PixelMap::fill(const Context &context,
                    const Polygon &poly)
{
  // A polygon with less than 3 points can't be filled
```

```
if (poly.pointCount() < 3) return ;

int i ;
XPoint pts[poly.pointCount() + 1] ;

// Populate array of X points
for (i = 0 ; i < poly.pointCount() ; i++)
{
  pts[i].x = (short) poly[i].x ;
  pts[i].y = (short) poly[i].y ;
}

// Repeat the first point
pts[i].x = (short) poly[0].x ;
pts[i].y = (short) poly[0].y ;

// Fill the polygon
XFillPolygon(display,
             pixmap,
             (GC) context,
             pts,
             poly.pointCount() + 1,
             Complex,
             CoordModeOrigin) ;
}
```

Each of the draw() methods is similar in terms of implementation. Let's take a look at the version for Polygon:

```
void PixelMap::draw(const Context &context,
                    const Polygon &poly)
{
  // There is no need to draw a polygon with less than
  // 3 points
  if (poly.pointCount() < 3) return ;

  int    i ;
  XPoint pts[p.pointCount() + 1] ;
```

```
// Populate array of X points
for (i = 0 ; i < poly.pointCount() ; i++)
{
  pts[i].x = (short) poly[i].x ;
  pts[i].y = (short) poly[i].y ;
}

// Repeat the first point
pts[i].x = (short) poly[0].x ;
pts[i].y = (short) poly[0].y ;

// Draw the polygon
XDrawLines(display,
           pixmap,
           (GC) context,
           pts,
           poly.pointCount() + 1,
           CoordModeOrigin) ;
}
```

The other draw() methods are quite similar, so we will not discuss them here.

5.5.4 Events

The XEvent structure in X windows is quite complicated. It is a union containing a number of structures, each designed to hold information for a certain kind of event, such as a key press or the border crossing of a window. Our class will be called LEvent for "library event" in order to avoid naming conflicts with X.

We must make some important decisions in the design of the LEvent class. Ideally, we can take advantage of the C++ inheritance mechanism to derive a number of different classes from a base LEvent class, such as a LKeyEvent or LButtonPressEvent class. Each of the derived classes can support a particular kind of event. Alternatively, we can create a "wrapper" class, which can be implemented directly on top of the X representation of events. Either way, there are advantages and disadvantages.

The advantages of creating an LEvent class hierarchy include greater efficiency and conceptual clarity. The efficiency would result from the natural sharing of code that occurs when using the inheritance mechanism. It would also prevent numerous `switch` statements needed to distinguish between event types. Because we would maintain separate classes for each event kind, this would also lead to greater conceptual clarity. However, we need to distinguish between different kinds of events during event processing. Creating a class hierarchy would make it difficult to determine the kind of event in the absence of a built-in `typeof()` function supported by the compiler. This is because event instances would be passed back and forth as objects of the parent class `LEvent`, and the actual class would be difficult to ascertain. To get around this, we could create an enumeration representing each supported event kind. This enumeration would be placed within the parent class. The problem in doing this manifests itself when we need to add a new kind of event. In this case we would need to modify the parent class in order to add a literal representing the new event kind to the enumeration. This means we would have to recompile all classes derived from `LEvent`, in effect making unrelated classes dependent upon the new class. This is bad programming practice.

If we implemented the `LEvent` class as a wrapper for the X representation of events, we would not have the problem of distinguishing among different kinds of events during event processing. Furthermore, we could use the `XEvent` structure itself to hold all of the necessary information. The main disadvantage to this technique is the fact that X shows through a bit more than it would in the case of a class hierarchy. For the sake of this discussion, we can live with this disadvantage. Therefore, this is the approach we will take.

Another decision we have to make concerns which kinds of events we should support. It would be extremely tedious to support every single kind of event, since we will probably be concerned only with a few specific kinds of events. In the `LEvent` class we will only provide support for a few kinds of events. However, the `LEvent` class can be extended easily to support other kinds of events.

Our `LEvent` class is declared as follows:

```
class LEvent : public GraphicalEnv
{
  public:

    // Supported events
    enum Kind
```

```
  {
    UnknownEvent,              // Unsupported event
    KeyPressEvent,             // Key press
    ButtonPressEvent,          // Mouse button (1..5) press
    ButtonReleaseEvent,        // Mouse button (1..5) release
    MotionEvent,               // Mouse motion
    EnterEvent,                // Pointer entered
    LeaveEvent                 // Pointer left
  } ;

  // Non ASCII Keys (server dependent)
  enum SpecialKey
  {
    LHomeKey = -100, LLeftKey,     LUpKey,
    LRightKey,       LDownKey,     LPriorKey,
    LNextKey,        LEndKey,      LInsertKey,
    LHelpKey,        LBreakKey,    LF1Key,
    LF2Key,          LF3Key,       LF4Key,
    LF5Key,          LF6Key,       LF7Key,
    LF8Key,          LF9Key,       LF10Key,
    LF11Key,         LF12Key,      LF13Key,
    LF14Key,         LF15Key,      LF16Key,
    LF17Key,         LF18Key,      LF19Key,
    LF20Key,         LF21Key,      LF22Key,
    LF23Key,         LF24Key,      LF25Key,
    LF26Key,         LF27Key,      LF28Key,
    LF29Key,         LF30Key,      LF31Key,
    LF32Key,         LF33Key,      LF34Key,
    LF35Key,         LUnknownKey
  } ;

  const XEvent *event ;

  uint  state(void) const ;
        // State field of X event is not always
        // in same position within union

public:
```

```
inline LEvent(void) : GraphicalEnv() { event = NULL ; }
   // Constructor

inline LEvent(const XEvent &xevent) : GraphicalEnv()
{ event = &xevent ; }
   // Conversion constructor

inline LEvent(const LEvent &other) : GraphicalEnv()
{ event = other.event ; }
   // Copy constructor

inline ~LEvent(void) {} // NULL
   // Destructor

inline void set(const XEvent &xevent)
{ event = &xevent ; }
   // Changes X event, so object can be reused

Kind kind(void) const ;
   // Obtains kind of event

inline uint button(void) const
{ return event->xbutton.button ; }
   // Obtains button for event
   // WARNING: This is only valid for events which
   // contain button information

int key(void) const ;
   // Obtains ASCII key for event. If key is non-
   // ASCII, result is SpecialKey.
   // WARNING: This is only valid for events which
   // contain key information

inline Boolean button1Pressed(void) const
{ return state() & Button1Mask ; }
inline Boolean button2Pressed(void) const
{ return state() & Button2Mask ; }
inline Boolean button3Pressed(void) const
```

```
{ return state() & Button3Mask ; }
inline Boolean button4Pressed(void) const
{ return state() & Button4Mask ; }
inline Boolean button5Pressed(void) const
{ return state() & Button5Mask ; }
inline Boolean controlPressed(void) const
{ return state() & ControlMask ; }
inline Boolean lockPressed(void) const
{ return state() & LockMask ; }
inline Boolean shiftPressed(void) const
{ return state() & ShiftMask ; }
    // Indicates whether modifier key or button was
    // pressed during event

inline int x(void) const { return event->xbutton.x ; }
inline int y(void) const { return event->xbutton.y ; }
   // Obtains location of event, relative to event
   // window

inline int screenx(void) const
{ return event->xbutton.x_root ; }
inline int screeny(void) const
{ return event->xbutton.y_root ; }
    // Obtains location of event, relative to screen
} ;
```

The LEvent class supports the following kinds of events:

- UnknownEvent: The event type is either unsupported, or some other exception (such as a NULL value for the event member) has occurred.
- KeyPressEvent: A keyboard key has been pressed.
- ButtonPressEvent: A mouse button has been pressed. Buttons 1 through 5 are supported.
- ButtonReleaseEvent: A mouse button has been released. Buttons 1 through 5 are supported.
- MotionEvent: The pointer has been moved.

- EnterEvent: The pointer has entered a particular window of interest.
- LeaveEvent: The pointer has left a particular window of interest.

The only data member in the LEvent class is event, which is a XEvent *. We have declared this member a pointer for three reasons:

1. Events are obtained at the top of the event loop, as discussed in Section 2.7. Each iteration of the loop should process <u>one and only one</u> event. Therefore, the pointer will remain valid for the entire iteration, as the X event should never go out of scope.
2. By the very nature of the event-driven paradigm, events are used quite frequently. If we do not use a pointer for the X event, we will be forced to use a memory copy whenever assigning the event data member. This can be time consuming.
3. We can easily reuse the object by changing the pointer.

You may have noticed that LEvent methods use the xbutton field of the event member, even when it cannot be sure that it is processing a button-related event. This is because the position of certain fields of the xbutton structure is the same as the position of these fields within other structures, such as xmotion. For example, the x_root field is in the same position in both xbutton and xmotion.

Unfortunately, this is not the case with the various state fields for different structures within XEvent. Therefore, the LEvent class defines a private method called state(), which returns the X state depending on the kind of event it is processing.

```
uint LEvent::state(void) const
{
  // Check the type
  switch (event->xany.type)
  {
    case KeyPress:
      return event->xkey.state ;
      break ;
```

```
    case ButtonPress:
    case ButtonRelease:
      return event->xbutton.state ;
      break ;

    case MotionNotify:
      return event->xmotion.state ;
      break ;

    default:
      return 0 ;
  }
}
```

Notice that the `state()` method does not determine if the `event` member is valid before using it. This is true of many LEvent class methods. The LEvent class leaves it to the user to determine if the kind of event is appropriate before calling any of these methods.

Most of the other methods in the LEvent class are self-explanatory. Therefore, a further discussion of these will be omitted. However, it is worth looking at a couple of more complicated methods in detail.

One of the methods which is certainly worth looking at is the `kind()` method. This method translates an X event type into the library type `LEvent::Kind`.

```
LEvent::Kind LEvent::kind(void) const
{
  // See if event has been initialized
  if (event == NULL) return UnknownEvent ;

  // Check the type
  switch (event->xany.type)
  {
    case KeyPress:
      return KeyPressEvent ;
      break ;
```

```
   case ButtonPress:
     return ButtonPressEvent ;
     break ;

   case ButtonRelease:
     return ButtonReleaseEvent ;
     break ;

   case MotionNotify:
     return MotionEvent ;
     break ;

   case EnterNotify:
     return EnterEvent ;
     break ;

   case LeaveNotify:
     return LeaveEvent ;
     break ;

   default:
     return UnknownEvent ;
  }
}
```

Key handling is a bit more complicated than it may seem at first glance. When the end user generates a key-related event, X gives us a server-dependent code representing the key. However, the programmer is interested only in the ASCII representation of the key. Therefore, the LEvent class must provide a translation mechanism from X key code to ASCII character. Actually, X can do this for us.

X provides a function called XLookupString(), which translates a key code to ASCII text. X also returns a variable of type KeySym representing the key, which is independent of the X server. If a key, such as an arrow key, does not have an ASCII representation (i.e., the length of the key text is greater than 1), we must look at the KeySym and translate it into a LEvent::SpecialKey.

Notice that the `key()` method returns an integer instead of a character. This is because we define special keys as negative numbers, and we can never be sure that the `char` type will be signed.

The `key()` method is implemented on top of `XLookupString()`.

```
// Includes
extern "C"
{
# include <string.h>
# include <X11/keysym.h>
}

int LEvent::key(void) const
{
  static const int BufSize = 20 ;

  char    buffer[BufSize + 1] ;        // Text for key
  KeySym keysym ;                      // X server independent
                                       // key symbol


  // Get key text and symbol
  int count = XLookupString((XKeyEvent *) event,
                            buffer,
                            BufSize,
                            &keysym,
                            NULL) ;
  buffer[count] = EOS ;

  // Check if we have a special key
  if (strlen(buffer) > 1)
  {
    switch (keysym)
    {
      case XK_Home:
        return LHomeKey ;
```

```
      case XK_Left:
        return LLeftKey ;

      case XK_Up:
        return LUpKey ;

              .


              .


              .

      default:
      return LUnknownKey ;
    }
  }

  // Return the ASCII code
  return (int) buffer[0] ;
}
```

The key() method first looks up the text and KeySym associated with the key code for the event. Next, the method determines if the text length is greater than 1. If so, the key is a "special" key, which is non-ASCII. In this case, the key() method must use keysym to translate the key to a LEvent::SpecialKey literal. The translation is accomplished by using a rather large switch statement. Of course, depending on how many special keys we wish to support, we can use an array or even a Set<int> for this translation.

CHAPTER *6*

The Graphical Object

The GraphicalObject class is one of the most important classes in our library. It serves as a base class for any class representing a Motif widget. We use this class to complete the initialization of Xt (as discussed in Section 5.3.2), and to store all of the common data and methods for all of the derived classes.

In formulating the GraphicalObject class, we must make some extremely important decisions about which Motif widgets, widget resources, and other mechanisms we will support in our library. Remember, the primary goal of developing a Motif-based GUI library is to make life easier for library users. This means that we must not burden the library user with all kinds of program elements that are rarely, if ever, used. At the same time, we must be careful to provide enough for the user to write the necessary applications.

In the remainder of this book, we will look at widgets, resources, and mechanisms that can be extrapolated to GUI classes that do not explicitly appear within this book. Treat the classes introduced hereafter as representative only. Obviously, different applications will make use of different classes and different methods within each class.

6.1 **Class Declaration**

The `GraphicalObject` class is declared as follows:

```
extern "C"
{
#  include <Xm/Xm.h>
}

#include "GraphicalEnv.h"
#include "LEvent.h"
#include "Boolean.h"
#include "Set.h"

// Defines
#define HandlerSet        Set<GraphicalObject::HandlerRec *>
#define RepSet            Set<GraphicalObject::RepRec *>
#define HandlerSetIndex   SetIndex<GraphicalObject::HandlerRec *>
#define RepSetIndex       SetIndex<GraphicalObject::RepRec *>

// Forward declarations
class PixelMap ;

class GraphicalObject : public GraphicalEnv
{
  friend class HandlerSet ;
  friend class RepSet ;

public:

  enum CallbackType
  {
    CB_ACTIVE,    CB_APPLY,    CB_CANCEL,
    CB_HELP,      CB_OK,       CB_VALUE_CHANGED
  } ;

  // Function types
```

```
   typedef void (* EventHandler)      (GraphicalObject &,
                                        LEvent &,
                                        void *) ;
   typedef void (* CallbackHandler) (GraphicalObject &,
                                        CallbackType,
                                        void *) ;

protected:

   // Holds event/function or callback/function pairs
   // along with user data associated with the function
   struct HandlerRec
   {
     // Name of event or callback
     union
     {
       LEvent::Kind   evKind ;
       CallbackType   cbKind ;
     } ;

     // Function to be executed
     union
     {
       EventHandler eh ;
       CallbackHandler ch ;
     } ;

     void            *udata ;   // User data

     inline const HandlerRec &operator =(const
         HandlerRec &hr)
     {
       udata       =      hr.udata ;
       evKind      =      hr.evKind ;
       eh          =      hr.eh ;
       return *this ;
     }
```

```cpp
    // Assigns one record to another

  inline HandlerRec(void) { eh = NULL ; }
    // Constructor

  inline HandlerRec(CallbackType        kind,
                    CallbackHandler     handler,
                    void                *ud)
  { cbKind = kind ; ch = handler ; udata = ud ; }
    // Constructor for callbacks

  inline HandlerRec(LEvent::Kind   kind,
                    EventHandler   handler,
                    void           *ud)
  { evKind = kind ; eh = handler ; udata _ ud ; }
    // Constructor for event handlers

  inline HandlerRec(const HandlerRec &hr)
  { *this = hr ; }
    // Constructor

  inline ~HandlerRec(void) {} // NULL
    // Destructor

  inline Boolean operator ==(const HandlerRec &hr) const
  {return evKind == hr.evKind ; }
    // Compares two records

  inline KeyType getKey(void) const
  { return (KeyType) evKind ; }
    // For set storage
} ;

protected:

  // Maps Motif representation to our representation
  struct RepRec
```

```
{
  Widget              mrep ;      // X representation
  GraphicalObject   *lrep ;      // Our graphical object

  inline const RepRec &operator =(const RepRec &rtr)
  {
     mrep = rtr.mrep ;
     lrep = rtr.lrep ;
     return *this ;
  }
    // Assigns one record to another

  inline RepRec(void) { lrep = NULL ; }
    // Constructor

  inline RepRec(const RepRec &rtr) { *this = rtr ; }
    // Copy constructor

  inline ~RepRec(void) {} // NULL
    // Destructor

  inline Boolean operator ==(const RepRec &rtr) const
  { return lrep == rtr.lrep ; }
    // Compares two records

  inline KeyType getKey(void) const
  { return (KeyType) mrep ; }
    // For set storage
} ;

// Class members
static Widget topLevel ;    // Top level graphical item
static RepSet rtset ;       // Representation tracking


// Instance members
RepRec rtr ;                // Maps to system rep
```

```
    HandlerSet evHandlers ;       // Event handlers
    HandlerSet cbHandlers ;       // Callback handlers

private:

  friend void internalEH(Widget w,
                         XtPointer calld,
                         XEvent *xevent) ;
    // Internal event handler

  friend void internalCB(Widget w,
                         XtPointer clientd,
                         XtPointer calld) ;
    // Internal callback handler

  static void classConstruct(void) ;
    // Initializes class statics

protected:

  GraphicalObject(void) ;
    // Constructor

public:

  virtual ~GraphicalObject(void) ;
    // Destructor

  Boolean registerEventHandler (LEvent::Kind   kind,
                                EventHandler   handler,
                                void           *ud = NULL) ;
  Boolean unregisterEventHandler (LEvent::Kind k) ;
    // (Un)registers event handler for graphical item

  Boolean registerCallback  (CallbackType    type,
                             CallbackHandler cb,
                             void            *ud = NULL) ;
```

```
Boolean unregisterCallback (CallbackType k) ;
   // (Un)registers callback handler for graphical item

inline virtual void manage(void) const
{ XtManageChild(rtr.mrep) ; }

inline virtual void unmanage(void) const
{ XtUnmanageChild(rtr.mrep) ; }
   // Places/removes graphical item under supervision
   // of parent

inline virtual void realize(void) const
{ XtRealizeWidget(rtr.mrep) ; }
inline virtual void unrealize(void) const
{ XtUnrealizeWidget(rtr.mrep) ; }
inline virtual Boolean isRealized(void) const
{ return XtIsRealized(rtr.mrep) ; }
static inline void realizeAll(void)
{ XtRealizeWidget(topLevel) ; }
   // Controls realization of graphical items

inline void sensitize(void) const
{ XtSetSensitive(rtr.mrep, True) ; }
inline void desensitize(void) const
{ XtSetSensitive(rtr.mrep, False) ; }
inline Boolean isSensitive(void) const
{ return XtIsSensitive(rtr.mrep) ; }
   // Controls event sensitivity of object

static inline void raise(void)
{ XRaiseWindow(display, XtWindow(topLevel)) ; }
static inline void lower(void)
{ XLowerWindow(display, XtWindow(topLevel)) ; }
static inline void iconify(void)
{ XtVaSetValues(topLevel, XmNiconic, True, NULL) ; }
   // Raises/lowers/iconifies entire widget hierarchy
```

```
uint getHeight(void) const ;
uint getWidth(void)  const ;
void setDimensions(uint w, uint h) ;
    // Controls dimensions of graphical item (in pixels)

int x(void) const ;
int y(void) const ;
void setPosition(int x, int y) ;
    // Controls position of graphical item,
    // relative to parent (in pixels)

inline operator Widget(void) const
{ return rtr.mrep ; }
    // Retrieves system representation for graphical item

static inline Widget getTopLevel(void)
{ return topLevel ; }
    // Obtains top level widget

private:
  friend class HandlerSet;
  friend class RepSet;
} ;
```

Before discussing the GraphicalObject class itself, let's take a moment to discuss class portability.

In the class declaration, we are certainly violating many of the portability design rules discussed in Section 3.2. Among other things, we are including a system file Xm/Xm.h and allowing X, Xt, and Motif to show through in the various inlined class methods. This is done for the sake of brevity. If we wish to declare the class so that it is truly portable, we would have to devise a class such as the SystemPart class, as discussed in Section 5.4.

The GraphicalObject class itself contains many nested types and classes. Many of these are used in callback and event processing, so a discussion of these is postponed until Section 6.3. The same is true of many of the data members, static and otherwise.

The nested type RepRec is central to GraphicalObject. This class maps a Motif widget, represented by the mrep member, to the corresponding GraphicalObject instances represented by the lrep member. The static data member rtset stores RepRec records, one for each GraphicalObject instance. In fact, the rtr (for "representation tracking record") member of each instance is inserted into rtset upon construction and removed on destruction. Storing the rtr member in a set allows us to find a GraphicalObject instance if we know the corresponding Motif widget. The need for this will become apparent when we discuss callback and event processing.

Notice that RepSet and HandlerSet are declared friends of the GraphicalObject class. This friendship is needed because the nested classes involved are private or protected; otherwise the Set<T> template would have no access to them.

The topLevel data member is the root of the widget tree for library applications, as discussed briefly in Section 2.4. This widget is used for any Xt or Motif function that recursively operates on the entire application widget tree, as in the implementation of the realizeAll(), raise(), lower(), and iconify() methods. These methods do not validate topLevel. Therefore it is conceivable that the user can crash the system by calling one of these static methods before any GraphicalObject is instantiated. This problem can be solved by declaring a method such as testConstruct() for GraphicalEnv (see Section 5.3.2).

All of the inlined methods in the GraphicalObject class are implemented as direct calls to X, Xt or Motif functions. Any further discussion of these is left to X, Xt; and Motif documentation (e.g., Heller, 1992; Nye and O'Reilly, 1992; Flanagan, 1993; Nye, 1993a,b).

6.2 Construction and Destruction

The GraphicalObject instance constructor is declared protected so that no GraphicalObject can be constructed, except by a descendant class. While not a true abstract base class (see Ellis and Stroustrup, 1990; Lippman, 1993), this class is intended to be used as such. As we shall see, it makes no sense to directly instantiate GraphicalObject, because any Motif widget stored in rtr.mrep will be created in a descendant class.

The instance constructor is implemented as follows:

```
GraphicalObject::GraphicalObject(void) : GraphicalEnv()
{
  static Boolean classInit = FALSE ;

  // Class construction
  if (classInit == FALSE)
  {
    classConstruct() ;
    classInit = TRUE ;
  }

  // Assign our representation to tracking record, and
  // insert into set
  rtr.lrep = this ;
  rtset.insert(&rtr) ;

  // NOTE: It is up to each of the derived classes to
  //       initialize the rtr.mrep member !!!!
}
```

The constructor first performs class construction, if necessary, and then assigns `this` object into the representation tracking record. The constructor then inserts the record into the `rtset` for purposes of future lookup. The assignment of a widget to `rtr.mrep` is the responsibility of the descendant class, as we cannot know what widget to create at this point.

Class construction for `GraphicalObject` completes the Xt initialization as discussed in Section 5.3.2. This is done to avoid making Motif visible at the `GraphicalEnv` level.

```
// Includes
#include "Color.h"

// Class static initialization
RepSet GraphicalObject::rtset ;
Widget GraphicalObject::topLevel = (Widget) NULL ;
```

```
void GraphicalObject::classConstruct(void)

{
  topLevel = XtVaAppCreateShell(appName,
                                appClass,
                                applicationShellWidgetClass,
                                display,
                                XmNvisual, Color::getVisual(),
                                XmNcolormap,
                                Color::getColorMap(),
                                NULL) ;
}
```

The `topLevel` widget is a Motif `ApplicationShell`, which is responsible for negotiating application geometry with the window manager, among other things. See Section 2.2 for a brief discussion of shell widgets.

In performing instance destruction we must eliminate the `rtr` member from the representation tracking set `rtset` and destroy any widget that has been created by a descendant class.

```
GraphicalObject::~GraphicalObject(void)
{
  // Remove the widget from the set
  if (rtset.eliminate(&rtr) == FALSE)
  {
    // Tell end user something is wrong...
  }

  // Destroy the widget
  XtDestroyWidget(rtr.mrep) ;

  // Make widget destruction take place immediately
  XSync(display, FALSE) ;
  XmUpdateDisplay(topLevel) ;
}
```

The calls to `XSync()` and `XmUpdateDisplay()` tell the X server to read and process all events in queue.

Once again, we let the operating system take care of class destruction by way of termination of the application process.

6.3 Managing Callback and Event Processing

The mechanisms we use to implement both callback and event processing in our library are quite similar. The general idea behind both of these mechanisms is described in the following steps:

1. The user registers a handler function for a particular callback or event with a particular `GraphicalObject` instance. The user may also register some *user data* to be passed back when the handler is invoked. User data is the term we will use for client data passed to one of <u>our</u> callbacks.
2. The user function is stored within the `GraphicalObject`, and an internal callback or event handler is registered with Motif.
3. When the callback or event occurs in the given `GraphicalObject`, Xt invokes the internal callback or event handler.
4. The internal handler finds the user handler function associated with the callback or event type for the given `GraphicalObject` and invokes the user function. If the user registered any user data for the callback or event, it is passed to the user function.

Now that we understand the general idea behind these mechanisms, let's continue by looking at callback processing.

We implement the callback processing mechanism by way of the internal `friend` function to the `GraphicalObject` class, called `internalCB()`. The user registers a callback handler function using the `GraphicalObject` method `registerCallback()`. The registered user function must match the following `GraphicalObject` prototype:

```
class GraphicalObject : public GraphicalEnv
{
    . . .
```

```
typedef void (* CallbackHandler)(GraphicalObject &,
                                  CallbackType,
                                  void *) ;
  ...
} ;
```

We store the user function, along with any user data passed with it, in a
HandlerRec object. The HandlerRec structure is a storage device used to
store a handler function, any user data for the function, and the kind of callback or event handling for which the function is intended.

```
class GraphicalObject : public GraphicalEnv
{
  ...
  struct HandlerRec
  {
    // Name of event or callback
    union
    {
      LEvent::Kind evKind ;
      CallbackType cbKind ;
    } ;

    // Function to be executed
    union
    {
      EventHandler    eh ;
      CallbackHandler ch ;
    } ;

    void *udata ;    // User data

    // Methods...
  } ;
  ...
} ;
```

Notice that `HandlerRec` supports <u>both</u> callback and event processing by way of two `union`s. Each `union` holds a field for event processing information and for callback processing information. The correct field within each `union` is selected based upon the context in which the `HandlerRec` is being used. The `udata` member is valid for either kind of processing.

Once the function and user data are registered with a `GraphicalObject`, we store the corresponding `HandlerRec` instance in the `HandlerSet` member `cbHandlers`. This set is keyed for lookup by `CallbackType`. At the same time, we register `internalCB()` with Xt for the particular kind of callback in the particular widget represented by the `GraphicalObject`.

```
// Maps our callbacks to Motif callbacks
static char *callbackTable[] =
{
  XmNactivateCallback,    XmNapplyCallback,
  XmNcancelCallback,      XmNhelpCallback,
  XmNokCallback,          XmNvalueChangedCallback

} ;


Boolean GraphicalObject::registerCallback(CallbackType kind,
                                          CallbackHandler ch,
                                          void *udata)
{
  // See if a callback of this kind is already registered
  if (cbHandlers.inRange(cbHandlers.find((KeyType) kind)))
  {
    // Tell end user that there is already such a
    // callback...
    return FALSE ;
  }

  // Allocate and populate handler record
  HandlerRec *hrp = new HandlerRec(kind, ch, udata) ;

  // Insert record into set
  cbHandlers.insert(hrp) ;
```

```
// Add callback
XtAddCallback(rtr.mrep,
              callbackTable[kind],
              internalCB,
              (XtPointer) hrp) ;

    return TRUE ;
}
```

Notice that the `registerCallback()` method checks whether a callback for a given callback type already exists. This points out the major limitation of this mechanism: only one callback can be registered for a `GraphicalObject` and a given type of callback. This may be highly undesirable. For example, we may have a number of extremely minor callbacks that can be used in various combinations, depending on the nature of the `GraphicalObject` in question. In such a situation, we would need the ability to register multiple handlers for a single callback and `GraphicalObject`. This problem can be solved by replacing the `ch` member in `HandlerRec` with a list. Every single function on the list would be invoked if the callback were triggered.

However, life is further complicated by the fact that C++ does not allow objects as direct members of `unions` (see Ellis and Stroustrup, 1990). This is because the compiler is not able to determine which members of a `union` to construct when the `union` is created. If we changed members of the second `union` within `HandlerRec` to be of `List<T>` type we would run into this limitation. However, we could easily work around it by making the members `List<T>` * type and calling the `new` operator for the correct list, based on the context of the `HandlerRec` construction. A similar problem (and solution) also exists for the event handling mechanism.

When registering `internalCB()` with Xt, `registerCallback()` passes the address of the `HandlerRec` corresponding to the user callback handler as the client data for the callback. This way, when `internalCB()` is invoked by Xt, the `HandlerRec` will be passed back via the client data parameter. Thus, `internalCB()` will have all the information it needs about the callback function registered with the `GraphicalObject` by the user, including a pointer to the function and the associated user data. The `internalCB()` function then invokes the user callback handler.

```
void internalCB(Widget      w,
                XtPointer   clientd,
                XtPointer   calld)
{
  // Find the GraphicalObject for the Motif widget
  RepSetIndex rti = GraphicalObject::rtset.find((KeyType) w) ;

  // Verify that the GraphicalObject was found
  if (GraphicalObject::rtset.inRange(rti) == FALSE)
  {
    // Tell end user something is wrong...
    return ;
  }

  GraphicalObject::HandlerRec *hrp =
      (GraphicalObject::HandlerRec *) clientd ;

  // Invoke the user function
  hrp->ch(*GraphicalObject::rtset[rti] lrep,
        hrp->cbKind,
        hrp->udata) ;
}
```

Unregistering a callback handler is accomplished through use of the unreg-isterCallback() method.

```
Boolean GraphicalObject::unregisterCallback
  (CallbackType kind)
{
  HandlerSetIndex   hsi = cbHandlers.find((KeyType) kind) ;

  // See if a callback handler was registered
  if (not cbHandlers.inRange(hsi))
  {
    // Tell the user something is wrong...
    return FALSE ;
  }
```

```
HandlerRec *hrp = cbHandlers[hsi] ;

// Unregister internal callback
XtRemoveCallback(rtr.mrep,
                 callbackTable[kind],
                 internalCB
                 hrp->udata) ;

// Eliminate handler record from set
cbHandlers.eliminate(hrp) ;
delete hrp ;

return TRUE ;
}
```

The event processing mechanism is extremely similar to the callback processing mechanism. User event handlers must match the following GraphicalObject prototype:

```
class GraphicalObject : public GraphicalEnv
{
  ...
  typedef void (* EventHandler) (GraphicalObject &,
                                 LEvent &,
                                 void *) ;
  ...
} ;
```

The user registers an event handler with a GraphicalObject by using the registerEventHandler() method. Once again, we create a HandlerRec corresponding to the user handler and data (if any), and insert it into a set. However, we maintain a separate set for event handlers, evHandlers.

```
// Maps our event kinds to X event masks
static EventMask eventMaskTable[] =
{
  NoEventMask,
```

```
  KeyPressMask,
  ButtonPressMask,
  ButtonReleaseMask,
  PointerMotionMask | ButtonMotionMask,
  EnterWindowMask,
  LeaveWindowMask
} ;


Boolean GraphicalObject::registerEventHandler
    (LEvent::Kind  kind,
     EventHandler  eh,
     void          *udata)
{
  // See if an event handler already exists
  if (evHandlers.inRange(evHandlers.find((KeyType) kind)))
  {
    // Tell end user something is wrong...
    return FALSE ;
  }

  // Allocate and populate handler record
  HandlerRec *hrp = new HandlerRec(kind, eh, udata) ;

  // Insert record into set
  evHandlers.insert(hrp) ;

  // Register internal event handler with Xt
  XtAddEventHandler(rtr.mrep,
                    eventMaskTable[kind],
                    False,
                    (XtEventHandler) internalEH,
                    (XtPointer) hrp) ;
  return TRUE ;
}
```

When the user registers an event handler with a GraphicalObject, reg-
isterEventHandler() registers an internal event handler with Xt. This

internal handler is called `internalEH()`. As in `registerCallback()`, `registerEventHandler()` registers the `HandlerRec` corresponding to the user event handler and data (if any) as the client data for Xt. When populating the `HandlerRec`, `registerEventHandler()` uses the members of the `unions` meant for event handling, `evKind` and `eh`, instead of those meant for callback handling.

```
void internalEH(Widget w, XtPointer clientd, XEvent *event)
{
  RepSetIndex rti =
     GraphicalObject::rtset.find((KeyType) w) ;

  // Verify that the GraphicalObject was found
  if (not GraphicalObject::rtset.inRange(rti))
  {
    // Tell end user something is wrong...
    return ;
  }

  LEvent levent(*event) ;
  GraphicalObject::HandlerRec *hrp =
    (GraphicalObject::HandlerRec *) clientd ;

  // See if event is valid
  if (levent.kind() != hrp->evKind)
  {
    // Tell end user something is wrong...
    return ;
  }

  // Call user event handler
  hrp->eh(*GraphicalObject::rtset[rti]->lrep,
          levent,
          hrp->udata) ;
}
```

Remember, this function is a `friend` of the `GraphicalObject` class, so it is okay to mention the internals of GraphicalObject. Upon invocation, internalEH() finds the GraphicalObject corresponding to the w argument. It then constructs an LEvent instance from the event argument and invokes the user event handler with these items and any data the user might have registered.

User event handlers are unregistered with the GraphicalObject method unregisterEventHandler().

```
Boolean GraphicalObject::unregisterEventHandler
    (LEvent::Kind kind)
{
  HandlerSetIndex  hsi = evHandlers.find((KeyType) kind) ;

  // See if an event handler was registered
  if (not evHandlers.inRange(hsi))
  {
    // Tell end user something is wrong...
    return FALSE ;
  }

  HandlerRec *hrp = evHandlers[hsi] ;

  // Remove system handler
  XtRemoveEventHandler(rtr.mrep,
                       eventMaskTable[kind],
                       True,
                       (XtEventHandler) internalEH,
                       (XtPointer) hrp) ;

  // Remove handler record from set
  evHandlers.eliminate(hrp) ;
  delete hrp ;

  return TRUE ;
}
```

6.4 **Positions and Dimensions**

The `GraphicalObject` class provides methods for obtaining positional information relative to an instance's parent. These methods are implemented on top of the `XtGetValues()` and `XtSetValues()` functions, discussed in Section 2.6.

The `x()` and `y()` methods are used to obtain the horizontal (*x-axis*) position and y-axis position, respectively, of a `GraphicalObject` within its parent, in pixels.

```
int GraphicalObject::x(void) const
{
  Position   x ;

  XtVaGetValues(rtr.mrep, XmNx, &x, NULL) ;
  return x ;
}

int GraphicalObject::y(void) const
{
  Position   y ;

  XtVaGetValues(rtr.mrep, XmNy, &y, NULL) ;
  return y ;
}
```

We can change the position of a `GraphicalObject` within its parent by using the method `setPosition()` and supplying x-axis and y-axis values in pixels.

```
void GraphicalObject::setPosition(int x, int y)
{
  XtVaSetValues(rtr.mrep,
                XmNx, (Position) x,
                XmNy, (Position) y,
                NULL) ;
}
```

There is an analogous set of methods for obtaining and setting the dimensions of a GraphicalObject. The getWidth() and getHeight() methods are used to obtain the width and height, respectively, (in pixels) of a GraphicalObject.

```
uint GraphicalObject::getWidth(void) const
{
  Dimension    w ;

  XtVaGetValues(rtr.mrep, XmNwidth, &w, NULL) ;
  return (uint) w ;
}

uint GraphicalObject::getHeight(void) const
{
  Dimension    h ;

  XtVaGetValues(rtr.mrep, XmNHeight, &h, NULL) ;
  return h ;
}
```

We can set the dimensions (in pixels) of a GraphicalObject by using the setDimensions() method. However, the parent of the GraphicalObject must allow this change, or it will fail.

```
void GraphicalObject::setDimensions(uint w, uint h)
{
  if (w == 0 or h == 0) return ;

  XtVaSetValues(rtr.mrep,
                XmNwidth,   (Dimension) w,
                XmNheight,  (Dimension) h,
                NULL) ;
}
```

All of these methods are straightforward. However, in a typical application, both the position and dimension values for a GraphicalObject are used quite frequently (especially the dimension values). Therefore, it might be prudent to store these values redundantly within the `GraphicalObject` instance. This will allow us to obtain the dimensions of a `GraphicalObject` without calling a function, thereby enhancing the performance of our applications.

To accomplish this, we must add some new data members called `gobjWidth` and `gobjHeight` to the `GraphicalObject` declaration.

```
class GraphicalObject : public GraphicalEnv
{
  ...
  uint gobjWidth ;
  uint gobjHeight ;
  ...
} ;
```

However, there is a serious problem with storing the dimensions in a `GraphicalObject` instance. Any `GraphicalObject` instance may be subject to resizing by the end user. If the end user resizes the `GraphicalObject`, the values contained in the new data members will no longer be valid.

We can solve this problem by registering a callback handler (called `monitorCB()`) for resizing with Xt. This function should be a `friend` so it can access the `gobjWidth` and `gobjHeight` members of any `GraphicalObject`. We can allow the user to specify whether to monitor dimensions for a given `GraphicalObject` by calling a method called `monitorDimensions()`. This way, the user monitors only those `GraphicalObject` instances in which he or she is interested.

First, we should modify the `GraphicalObject` class declaration to support the monitoring mechanism.

```
class GraphicalObject : public GraphicalEnv
{
  private:

    friend void monitorCB(Widget      w,
                          XtPointer   clientd,
                          XtPointer   calld) ;
```

```
...
Boolean dimsMonitored ; // Are we monitoring?
...

public:

  void monitorDimensions(void) ;
      // Start monitoring dimensions of graphical object
  ...
} ;
```

These modifications consist of declarations for the `friend` callback function `monitorCB()` and the class method `monitorDimensions()`. We also add the flag `dimsMonitored` to indicate whether a particular instance falls under the monitoring regimen.

Next we must define the `monitorCB()` function, which will act as the resize handler.

```
void monitorCB(Widget     widget,
               XtPointer  clientd,
               XtPointer  calld)
{
  GraphicalObject *gobj = clientd ;

  // Widget is placed on screen for first time
  // NOTE: Handle Xt bug with resizes
  if (calld->reason == XmCR_EXPOSE or
      calld->reason == XmCR_RESIZE and
      calld->event  == NULL)
  {
    Dimensions  w = 0, h = 0 ;

    // Obtain values from Xt
    XtVaGetValues(widget,
                  XmNwidth,   &w,
                  XmNheight,  &h,
                  NULL) ;
```

```
  // Assign new values into object
  gobj->gobjWidth   = (uint) w ;
  gobj->gobjHeight  = (uint) h ;
}


// Xt resize bug not present
else if (cbs->reason == XmCR_RESIZE)
{
  gobj->gobjWidth     =
      (uint) cbs->event->xresizerequest.width ;
  gobj->gobjHeight    =
      (uint) cbs->event->xresizerequest.height ;
}
}
```

This function acts as a handler for both resizing and *exposure* callbacks. An exposure occurs when a widget is first mapped to the screen, or when another window which had been covering it is removed. You should note that there is a flaw in Xt with regard to resize callbacks (see Heller, 1992, p. 324). These callbacks are implemented in Xt such that the event for the callback is NULL. We work around this flaw by testing for NULL events in the if statement. If the event field is NULL, we use XtVaGetValues() to obtain the dimensions of a widget.

We now must define the monitorDimensions() method, which the user can call to set the monitoring mechanism in motion.

```
void GraphicalObject::monitorDimensions(void)
{
  // Initialize gobjWidth and gobjHeight when widget is
  // mapped to screen
  XtAddCallback(rtr.mrep,
                XmNexposeCallback,
                monitorCB,
                this) ;


  // Change gobjWidth and gobjHeight when widget is resized
  XtAddCallback(rtr.mrep,
```

```
                XmNresizeCallback,
                monitorCB, this) ;

  // Dimensions are now monitored
  dimsMonitored = TRUE ;
}
```

We must also initialize the values of the gobjWidth, gobjHeight, and dimsMonitored members in the constructor.

```
GraphicalObject::GraphicalObject(void)  :  GraphicalEnv()
{
  ...
  dimsMonitored = FALSE ;
  gobjWidth = gobjHeight = 0 ;
  ...
}
```

Finally, we must change the implementation of the getWidth() and get-Height() methods to support the new mechanism.

```
uint GraphicalObject::getWidth(void) const
{
  if (dimsMonitored) return gobjWidth ;

  Dimension   w ;

  XtVaGetValues(rtr.mrep, XmNwidth, &w, NULL) ;
  return (uint) w ;
}

uint GraphicalObject::getHeight(void) const
{
  if (dimsMonitored) return gobjHeight ;

  Dimension   h ;
```

```
    XtVaGetValues(rtr.mrep, XmNheight, &h, NULL) ;
    return h ;
}
```

The modifications to these methods are quite simple. If we are monitoring the dimensions of the `GraphicalObject`, we just return the data members, which are now guaranteed to be holding the correct dimension values. Otherwise, we get them from Xt. If necessary, we can implement a similar mechanism for monitoring the position of `GraphicalObject` instances. However, position changes are less likely than are dimension changes for widgets.

7

Essential
Graphical
Objects

U p to this point, we have been discussing classes that lay the foundation for our GUI library but that cannot be used to place anything meaningful on the screen. We are now ready to discuss the graphical elements for our GUI library that will actually be displayed on the screen.

This chapter is devoted to classes that are essential for a typical GUI library. All of the classes in this chapter are descendants of `GraphicalObject`, which is discussed in Chapter 6.

7.1 Forms

Motif `Form` widgets are containers for other widgets, which allow flexible and dynamic placement and sizing of widgets as a group. We give an example of the use of Motif `Forms` in the discussion of `MainWindows` in Section 7.2. However, `Forms` have many uses other than for `MainWindows`. In fact, `Forms` are so useful we will encapsulate them into a class for our GUI library.

```cpp
// Includes
#include "GraphicalObject.h"

// Forward declarations
class CString ;

class Form : public GraphicalObject
{
public:

  // Indicates kind of attachment
  enum Edge
  {
    TOP, BOTTOM, LEFT, RIGHT
  } ;

  private:

  Widget findAttachWidget(const GraphicalObject &gobj) const ;
    // Finds immediate child of form given any
    // ancestor of form

  void makeAttachment(Edge                    edge,
                      unsigned char           constraint,
                      int                     offset,
                      const GraphicalObject &gobj1,
                      const GraphicalObject *gobj2 = NULL) ;
    // Sets appropriate constraint resources of
    // specified graphical object for given
    // edge and attachment type

  public:

    // Spacing constants
    enum { DefaultDivisions   = 100 } ;
    enum { DefaultHorizSpace  = 0 } ;
    enum { DefaultVertSpace   = 0 } ;
```

```
    enum { DefaultOffset     = 0 } ;

Form(const   CString          &name,
     const GraphicalObject *parent = NULL,
     uint                     divisions = DefaultDivisions,
     uint                     hspace = DefaultHorizSpace,
     uint                     vspace = DefaultVertSpace) ;
     // Constructor

inline ~Form(void) {} // NULL
     // Destructor

void attachObjects(const GraphicalObject &gobj1,
                   const GraphicalObject &gobj2,
                   Edge                   edge,
                   int                    offset =
                                          DefaultOffset) ;
     // Attaches an edge of first graphical object
     // to second graphical object with specified
     // offset

void alignObjects(const GraphicalObject  &gobj1,
                  const GraphicalObject  &gobj2,
                  Edge                    edge,
                  int                     offset =
                                          DefaultOffset) ;
     // Aligns indicated edge of first graphical
     // object with same edge of a second graphical
     // object and then offsets by a specified amount

void attachForm(const GraphicalObject    &gobj,
                Edge                       edge,
                int                        offset =
                                           DefaultOffset) ;
     // Attaches specified edge of graphical
     // object to same edge of form with specified
     // offset
```

```
void attachPosition(const GraphicalObject    &gobj,
                          Edge                  edge,
                          int                   position)  ;
    // Attaches specified edge of a specified
    // graphical object
    // to a relative position in form
} ;
```

The Form class has no data members of its own: it uses the data members of its parent class, GraphicalObject. When we create a Form we must specify its name, its parent GraphicalObject, and some values which control the spacing of widgets within the corresponding Motif Form. The meaning of the spacing parameters is defined below:

- **divisions:** When positioning widgets within a Motif Form, we divide the Form into a number of tiny "slices" represented by this value along both the x- and y-axes. In effect, this value is used as a denominator in a fraction in which the positioning value is used as a numerator. This fraction actually determines the position as a percentage of a given Motif Form. For example, if the divisions value is 100, and the position value for a widget from the top of the Form is 10, then the widget placed 10/100 = 10% from the top of the Form.
- **vertical spacing:** This is the number of pixels between widgets that are attached on the top or bottom. This value is only a default and is used only when the spacing is not specified during the attachment.
- **horizontal spacing:** This is the number of pixels between widgets that are attached on the left or right. This value is only a default and is used only when the spacing is not specified during the attachment.

The Form constructor is implemented as follows:

```
// Includes
extern "C"
{
# include <Xm/Form.h>
}
#include "Form.h"
#include "CString.h"
```

```
Form::Form(const CString          &name,
           const GraphicalObject  *parent,
           uint                   divisions,
           uint                   hspace,
           uint                   vspace) : GraphicalObject()
{
  // Figure out the parent
  Widget wparent = parent ? (Widget) *parent : topLevel ;

  // Create the widget
  rtr.mrep = XtVaCreateWidget(name,
                             xmFormWidgetClass,
                             wparent,
                             XmNfractionBase,       divisions,
                             XmNhorizontalSpacing, hspace,
                             XmNverticalSpacing,   vspace,
                             NULL) ;
}
```

The first task that the constructor performs is to figure out the widget parent for the Motif Form widget. If the user fails to specify a valid GraphicalObject for the Form parent, we assume that the Form should be a child of topLevel. The second and final task is to create the widget. In creating the widget, we specify the spacing as indicated by the arguments passed though the spacing parameters.

The GraphicalObject destructor handles destruction of the widget. We provide an empty destructor so that the compiler does not provide one for us.

The remaining methods provide support for the various kinds of attachment supplied by Motif Forms. The methods are all implemented as calls to the private method makeAttachment(). This method encapsulates the code necessary to perform any kind of attachment.

```
void Form::makeAttachment(Form::Edge        edge,
                          unsigned char     constraint,
                          int               offset,
                          const GraphicalObject &gobj1,
                          const GraphicalObject *gobj2)
```

```
{
  Widget      child,
              child2 ;


  // Get widget corresponding to first graphical object
  if (not (child = findAttachWidget(gobj1)))
  {
    // Tell end user something is wrong...
    return ;
  }

  // Get widget corresponding to second graphical object
  if (gobj2 and not (child2 = findAttachWidget(*gobj2)))
  {
    // Tell end user something is wrong...
    return ;
  }

  char     *mOffset,
           *mAttachment,
           *mWidget,
           *mPos ;

  // Get Motif resource names corresponding to our edge type
  switch (edge)
  {
    case Form::TOP:
     mAttachment = XmNtopAttachment ;
     mOffset     = XmNtopOffset ;
     mWidget     = XmNtopWidget ;
     mPos        = XmNtopPosition ;
     break ;

    case Form::LEFT:
     mAttachment = XmNleftAttachment ;
     mOffset     = XmNleftOffset ;
```

```
      mWidget       = XmNleftWidget ;
      mPos          = XmNleftPosition ;
      break ;

  case Form::BOTTOM:
   mAttachment     = XmNbottomAttachment ;
   mOffset         = XmNbottomOffset ;
   mWidget         = XmNbottomWidget ;
   mPos            = XmNbottomPosition ;
   break ;

  case Form::RIGHT:
   mAttachment     = XmNrightAttachment ;
   mOffset         = XmNrightOffset ;
   mWidget         = XmNrightWidget ;
   mPos            = XmNrightPosition ;
   break ;
  }

  Arg argv[3] ;
  Cardinal argc = 0 ;

  // One argument is Motif attachment type
  XtSetArg(argv[argc], mAttachment, constraint) ; argc++ ;

  // Are we attaching to another widget?
  if (gobj2) XtSetArg(argv[argc], mWidget, child2), argc++ ;

  // Are we attaching to a position?...
  if (constraint == XmATTACH_POSITION)
      XtSetArg(argv[argc], mPos, offset), argc++ ;

  // ...otherwise set the offset for attachment
  else XtSetArg(argv[argc], mOffset, offset), argc++ ;

  // Set the attachment
  XtSetValues(child, argv, argc) ;
}
```

This method performs the following steps to specify an attachment:

1. It finds the widgets corresponding to the `GraphicalObject` arguments for attachment within the `Form`. These are not necessarily the same as the widgets returned by the `Widget` cast operator provided by the `GraphicalObject` class. (See below for a further discussion of this.)
2. It translates the edge specified by the `Form` class type `Edge` into the corresponding Motif resource name.
3. It sets the target resource for the attachment, such as the second widget (`child2`) or a position (`offset`) within the form.
4. If the target resource for the attachment is not a position, it sets the spacing resource (`offset`) for the attachment.

Quite often, a Motif widget actually consists of a number of distinct widgets, instead of being monolithic. We call such widgets *composite* widgets. For example, the various Motif dialog widgets are composite, because each one consists of a `DialogShell` widget parented to some other kind of widget. When creating a dialog, Motif returns a handle to the child of the `DialogShell`, making dialog widgets seem like they are monolithic.

The `private` method `findAttachWidget()` is used to find the correct Motif widget for attachment. This returns the root of the widget subhierarchy for composite widgets or the widget itself for any other kind of widget.

```
Widget Form::findAttachWidget(const GraphicalObject &gobj) const
{
  Widget  child   = (Widget) gobj,
          parent  = XtParent(child) ;

  // Loop until root of sub-hierarchy
  while (parent != topLevel)
  {
    if (parent == rtr.mrep) return child ;
    child   = parent ;
    parent  = XtParent(child) ;
  }
```

```
    // If we get here, the attachment widget
    // was not found
    return (Widget) NULL ;
}
```

Note that we assume that widgets that are placed in the Form are descended from the Form. Motif requires this to be the case in order for the Form to reconfigure its contained widgets.

The first of the attachment methods is called attachObjects(). This attaches a GraphicalObject to another GraphicalObject within the Form. The offset parameter is used to set the distance, in pixels, of GraphicalObjects. For example, assume we call attachObjects() with a value of BOTTOM for the edge parameter and a value of 20 for the offset parameter. Then gobj1 will be attached to the bottom edge of gobj2 with a spacing of 20 pixels. See Figure 7.1 for an illustration of this.

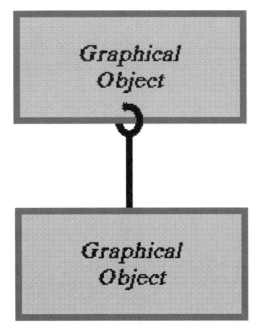

Figure 7.1. Object-to-object attachment.

```
void Form::attachObjects(const GraphicalObject  &gobj1,
                         const GraphicalObject  &gobj2,
                         Form::Edge             edge,
                         int                    offset)
{
  makeAttachment(edge,
                 XmATTACH_WIDGET,
                 offset,
                 gobj1,
                 &gobj2) ;
}
```

The next attachment method, alignObjects(), aligns two Graph-icalObjects within a Form along a given edge. The offset parameter sets the distance, in pixels, between the GraphicalObjects being aligned. For example, if two GraphicalObjects are aligned along their left edges, these edges will be exactly the same distance from the left edge of the Form. See Figure 7.2 for an illustration of this.

```
void Form::alignObjects(const GraphicalObject  &object1,
                        const GraphicalObject  &object2,
                        Form::Edge             edge,
                        int                    offset)
{
  makeAttachment(edge,
                 XmATTACH_OPPOSITE_WIDGET,
                 offset,
                 object1,
                 &object2) ;
}
```

Next we have the attachForm() method, which attaches the edge of a GraphicalObject to the same edge of a Form. The offset parameter is used to set the distance, in pixels, between the GraphicalObject and the edge of the Form. For example, if we specify a value of TOP for the edge para-meter, the top edge of the GraphicalObject will be attached to the top edge of the Form. See Figure 7.3 for an illustration of this.

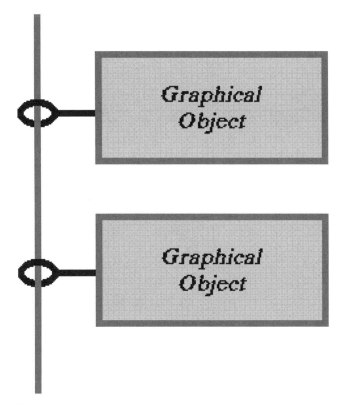

Figure 7.2. Object-to-object alignment.

```
void Form::attachForm(const GraphicalObject     &gobj,
                      Form::Edge                 edge,
                      int                        offset)

{
  makeAttachment(edge,
               XmATTACH_FORM,
               offset,
               gobj) ;
}
```

We can attach an edge of a `GraphicalObject` to a specified position within a `Form` by calling the method `attachPosition()`. The value of posi-

tion parameter is interpreted in the context of the divisions value specified at construction of the Form, as discussed above. For example, assume we specified 100 for the value of divisions at Form construction, and specify 20 for the value of position, and Form::LEFT for the value of edge. Then gobj will be placed in the form at a position 20% into the form from the left. See Figure 7.4 for an illustration of this.

```
void Form::attachPosition(const GraphicalObject  &gobj,
                          Form::Edge              edge,
                          int                     position)
```

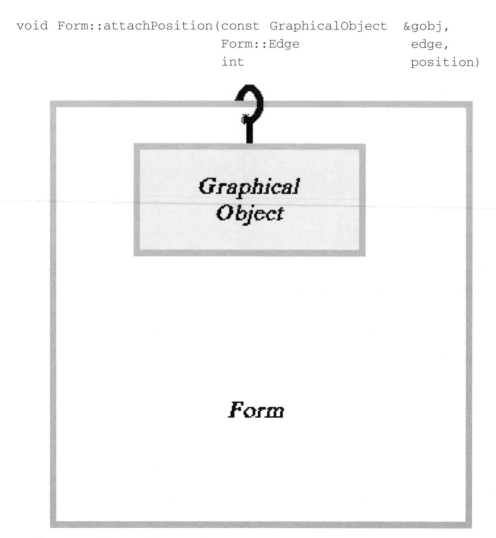

Figure 7.3. Object-to-form attachment.

```
{
  makeAttachment(edge, XmATTACH_POSITION, position, gobj) ;
}
```

We will see many examples of the use of forms in Chapter 8.

7.2   Main Windows

In Section 3.3.1 we discussed the place of external consistency within the GUI library. One of the most important factors in maintaining external consistency is the placement of the graphical elements within an interface. For example, if

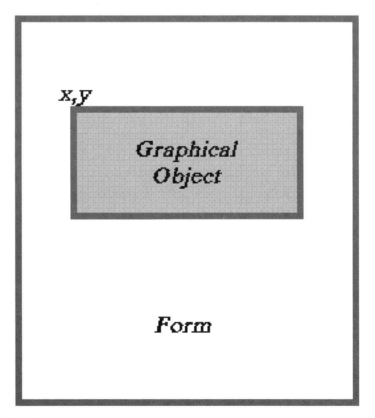

Figure 7.4. Attachment by position.

we provide a control panel, as most GUI applications do, it should always appear in the same place, regardless of the actual application in which the panel appears. This means that if we place the control panel on the left for one application interface, the control panel should <u>always</u> appear on the left for any application interface that provides a control panel.

The `MainWindow` class is used to maintain this consistency. A `MainWindow` may consist of three separate regions.

1. **Work space:** this is the area in which the main task of the application takes place. For example, in a text editor application, this would be the window in which we could edit text. In a drawing application, this would be the window in which we could draw pictures.

2. **Control panel:** this is an area that contains buttons an end user can press to select major modes or functions for the application. For example, in a drawing application these buttons may allow the end user to switch between drawing (e.g., polygons, lines, text), and erasing drawn elements.

3. **Menu bar:** this is an area that displays the titles of pull-down menus from which the end user can perform various operations. For example, in a text editor application there might be a "File" menu from which the end user can open, close, create, or destroy files.

We will require all applications that are implemented on top of our library to have a work space. However, the control panel and menu bar will be optional.

Figure 7.5 depicts a main window for a mapping application. In this case, the work space is the map.

Note that Motif provides a `MainWindow` widget, which we are not using here. This widget provides support for five separate regions within its confines:

1. Menu bar
2. Command window
3. Work space
4. Horizontal scrollbar
5. Vertical scrollbar

However, Motif does not provide any special support for control panels. I believe that control panels are essential to a great number of applications, more important in fact than command windows or scroll bars. Therefore, we imple-

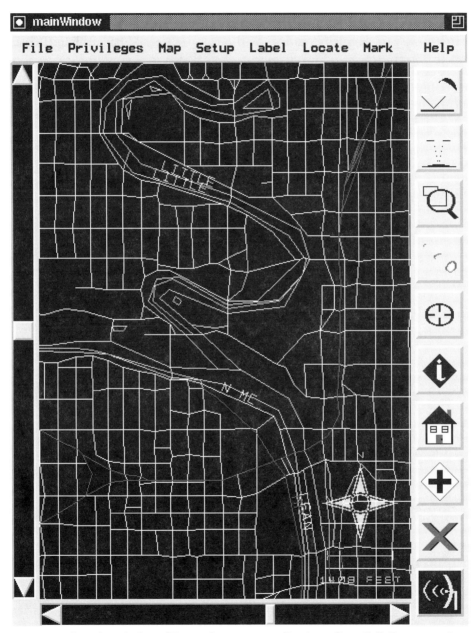

Figure 7.5. A main window. [From the *mapx* application. One Call Concepts, Inc., Hanover, MD, USA Copyright © 1992, 1993, 1994, 1995. All rights reserved. Reproduced with permission.]

ment our own version of main windows. If the reader does not feel comfortable with this, the implementation of the class can easily be modified to support the Motif `MainWindow` widget.

```cpp
// Includes
#include "Form.h"

// Forward declarations
class MenuBar ;
class ControlPanel ;
class CString ;

class MainWindow : public Form
{
    // Data members
    const GraphicalObject      *workSpace ;
    const MenuBar              *menuBar ;
    const ControlPanel         *controlPanel ;

  public:

    MainWindow(const CString &name) ;
        // Constructor

    inline ~MainWindow(void) {} // NULL
        // Destructor

    void set(const GraphicalObject   &ws,
            const MenuBar            *mb = NULL,
            const ControlPanel       *cp = NULL) ;
        // Sets the regions of main window

    inline const GraphicalObject *getWorkSpace (void) const
    { return workSpace ; }
    inline const MenuBar *getMenuBar (void) const
    { return menuBar ; }
    inline const ControlPanel *getControlPanel (void) const
```

```
      { return controlPanel ; }
        // Obtains pointer to any of the regions
} ;
```

As we can see, the interface to `MainWindow` is simple. We provide a constructor, a destructor, and three access methods, one for each component.

Our `MainWindow` class is derived from the `Form` class. A `Form` serves as a container widget for other widgets and allows a flexible arrangement of these widgets by allowing us to attach them in various ways (see Section 7.1 or Heller, 1992). The constructor just initializes its data members.

```
#include "MainWindow.h"
#include "CString.h"

MainWindow::MainWindow(const CString &name) : Form(name)
{
  // Invalidate regions
  workSpace        = NULL ;
  controlPanel     = NULL ;
  menuBar          = NULL ;
}
```

This is the only `GraphicalObject`-descended class in our library that does not provide a "parent" parameter for its constructor. This is because we wish to force the widget to be created as a child of `topLevel`, with no intervening widgets.

There is nothing special about destroying a `MainWindow`. We just call `XtDestroyWidget()` for `rtr.mrep`, which is already done in the destructor for the parent class `GraphicalObject`. Therefore, the definition of the `MainWindow` destructor is empty.

Once we have created a main window, we must define the regions for it. The regions are not defined at the point of construction for a very important reason: We want the user to be able to use the `MainWindow` as a parent `GraphicalObject` for the regions. The `MainWindow` class cannot be used as a parent class if the regions are used as arguments to the `MainWindow` constructor, because we must have already created them. Therefore, the regions must be created and set in the `MainWindow` according to the following steps:

1. Create a `MainWindow`.
2. Create regions with the `MainWindow` as the parent.
3. Set the regions for the `MainWindow`.

The user can set the regions for a `MainWindow` with the method `set()`. This method takes as arguments a `GraphicalObject &` for the work space, a `MenuBar *` for the menu bar, and a `ControlPanel *` for the control panel. See Section 7.5 for a discussion of the `MenuBar` class. See Section 7.6 for a discussion of the `ControlPanel` class.

```
void MainWindow::set(const GraphicalObject    &ws,
                     const MenuBar             *mb,
                     const ControlPanel        *pn)

{
    // Assign the data members
    workSpace      = &ws ;
    menuBar        = mb ;
    controlPanel   = pn ;

    // Attach top, right and left edge menu bar, if it exists
    if (menuBar)
    {
      attachForm(*menuBar, Form::RIGHT) ;
      attachForm(*menuBar, Form::TOP) ;
      attachForm(*menuBar, Form::LEFT) ;
    }



    // Attach work space
    if (workSpace)
    {
      // Attach bottom and right edge of work
      // space to form
      attachForm(*workSpace, Form::BOTTOM) ;
      attachForm(*workSpace, Form::RIGHT) ;
```

```
      // Attach top of workspace to menu bar, if it exists...
      if (menuBar) attachObjects(*workSpace, *menuBar, Form::TOP) ;

      // ...otherwise attach it to the form
      else attachForm(*workSpace, TOP) ;

      // Attach left edge of workspace to control panel, if
      // it exists...
      if (controlPanel)
          attachObjects(*workSpace, *controlPanel, Form::LEFT) ;

      // ...otherwise attach it to the form
      else attachForm(*workSpace, Form::LEFT) ;
   }

   // Attach control panel
   if (controlPanel)
   {
     // Attach control panel to bottom and left of form
     attachForm(*controlPanel, Form::BOTTOM) ;
     attachForm(*controlPanel, Form::LEFT) ;

     // Attach top of control panel to menu bar, if it
     // exists...
     if (menuBar)
         attachObjects(*controlPanel, *menuBar, Form::TOP) ;

     // ...otherwise attach it to the form
     else attachForm(*controlPanel, Form::TOP) ;
   }
}
```

As we can see, the implementation of the set() method consists of setting the various attachments of the regions (if they exist) to each other and to the form.

The following code fragment shows us how to define a `MainWindow` for a generic application.

```
// Includes
#include "ControlPanel.h"
#include "MenuBar.h"

// Functions defined elsewhere
extern ControlPanel    *buildPanel(GraphicalObject *parent) ;
extern MenuBar          *buildMenus(GraphicalObject *parent) ;

// Objects defined elsewhere
extern GraphicalObject *workSpace ;

main(int argc, char **argv)
{
  // Initialize environment
  GraphicalEnv::setEnvironment("sample", argc, argv) ;

  MainWindow      mainWindow("mainWindow") ;
  ControlPanel   *panel      = buildPanel(&mainWindow) ;
  MenuBar        *menuBar    = buildMenus(&mainWindow) ;

  // Set the main window
  mainWindow.set(*workSpace, menuBar, panel) ;

  // Put everything on screen
  mainWindow.realizeAll() ;
  mainWindow.manage() ;

  // Start application
  GraphicalEnv::startApplication() ;
}
```

We will see more examples involving the `MainWindow` class in the remainder of this book.

7.3 Buttons

Our GUI library will provide three different types of buttons:

1. **Text buttons:** these are buttons placed in a pulldown menu. The face of a text button displays text.
2. **Cascade buttons:** these are buttons placed in menu bars or pulldown menus. When a cascade button is depressed, it activates a "cascading" pulldown menu. The face of a cascade button displays text.
3. **Picture buttons:** these are buttons placed in a control panel. The face of a picture button displays a pixel map.

We support each of these button varieties with a distinct class. It may seem like these classes are likely candidates for inheritance, since each button variety is similar to the others. This is especially true of text and cascade buttons. Conceptually, these classes <u>are</u> related to one another. Unfortunately, Motif implements them as distinct classes with no relationships whatsoever. However, we may still want to design a class hierarchy for buttons, because we do not want to let the implementation dictate the structure of our library.

This may seem a little awkward at first, but consider that if we ever port our GUI library to some other graphical platform, these classes are likely to be more closely related. In this case, we would not have to adapt the library by introducing the inheritance relationships especially for the port.

7.3.1 Button Base Class

We begin by formulating a base class called `Button`, which will act as a parent class for all of our other button classes. This class is a stub: it does nothing at all.

```
#include "GraphicalObject.h"

class Button : public GraphicalObject
{
  public:

    inline Button(void) : GraphicalObject() {} // NULL
      // Constructor
```

```
inline ~Button(void) {} // NULL
    // Destructor
} ;
```

7.3.2 Text Buttons

Motif text buttons are represented by the library class `TextButton`, which is derived from class `Button`. Text buttons are intended for pulldown menus, as discussed in Section 7.5. In practice, we register an activation callback for each text button. The activation callback will be invoked when an end user presses the button. Each callback will perform the application-level operation associated with the button when invoked. See Figure 7.6 for an illustration of text buttons.

```
// Includes
#include "Button.h"

// Forward declarations
class CString ;
class PulldownMenu ;

class TextButton : public Button
{
  public:
```

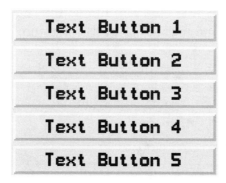

Figure 7.6. Text buttons.

```
    TextButton(const CString          &label,
            const GraphicalObject *parent) ;
      // Constructor

    inline ~TextButton(void) {} // NULL
      // Destructor

    void setColor(const CString &colName) ;
      // Sets color for button text

    void setLabel(const CString &label) ;
      // Sets displayed button text
} ;
```

The `TextButton` class provides only four `public` methods: a constructor, a destructor, and the ability to change the color and text of the button label.

The constructor takes the label string and parent of the `TextButton` instance as arguments. The label string will act as both the name of the button within Xt and the text that appears on the face of the button.

```
extern "C"
{
# include <Xm/PushB.h>
}
#include "TextButton.h"
#include "PulldownMenu.h"
#include "CString.h"

TextButton::TextButton(const CString          &label,
                    const GraphicalObject  *parent) :
                    Button()
{
    // Figure out the parent
    Widget wparent = parent ? (Widget) *parent : topLevel ;

    // Create button
    // NOTE: name acts as name of widget and button label
```

```
      rtr.mrep = XmCreatePushButton(wparent,
                               (const char *) label,
                               NULL, 0) ;
}
```

The destructor for TextButton is empty. Once again, we let the destructor for GraphicalObject take care of destroying the Motif widget.

We may wish to provide methods to set various attributes of a TextButton instance. An example of such an attribute is the color of the text displayed on the face of the button. We can change the text color with the setColor() method.

```
#include "Color.h"

void TextButton::setColor(const CString &colName)
{
  Color    col(colName) ;

  XtVaSetValues(rtr.mrep, XmNforeground, (ulong) col, NULL) ;
}
```

We can change the text displayed upon the face of the button by using the setLabel() method.

```
void TextButton::setLabel(const CString &label)
{
  XmString   mtext =
     XmStringCreateSimple((const char *) label) ;

  XtVaSetValues(rtr.mrep, XmNlabelString, mtext, NULL);
  XmStringFree(mtext);
}
```

These last two methods are just examples of how to set button attributes. The reader may wish to allow the user to change other text button attributes by providing methods to perform these changes.

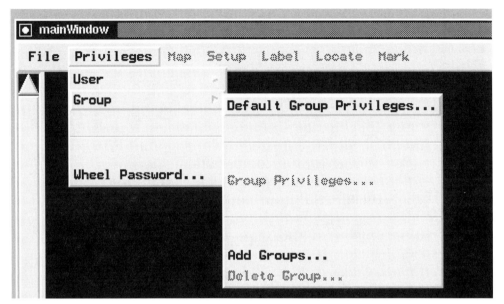

Figure 7.7. Cascade buttons in a pulldown menu. [From the *mapx* application. One Call Concepts, Inc., Hanover, MD, USA Copyright © 1992, 1993, 1994, 1995. All rights reserved. Reproduced with permission.]

7.3.3 Cascade Buttons

Motif cascade buttons are represented in our library by the `CascadeButton` class, which is derived from the `Button` class. Cascade buttons are intended for menu bars or pulldown menus, as discussed in Section 7.5. A cascade button is used to activate a pulldown menu if it resides in a menu bar, or a submenu if it resides in a pulldown menu. The only difference in appearance between cascade buttons and text buttons is an arrow indicator at the extreme right side of the face of a cascade button. However, this arrow only appears when the `CascadeButton` is placed in a `PulldownMenu`.

Figure 7.7 contains an illustration of two cascade buttons inside a pulldown menu. The second button has been activated, revealing a submenu.

```
#include "Button.h"

// Forward declarations
class CString ;
```

```
class MenuBar ;
class PulldownMenu ;

class CascadeButton : public Button
{
  public:

    CascadeButton(const CString        &label,
                  const PulldownMenu    &menu,
                  const MenuBar         &parent) ;
      // Constructor for menu bar buttons

    CascadeButton(const CString        &label,
                  const PulldownMenu    &menu,
                  const PulldownMenu    &parent) ;
      // Constructor for pulldown menu buttons

    inline ~CascadeButton() {} // NULL
      // Destructor
} ;
```

The only `public` methods the `CascadeButton` class provides are constructor and destructor methods. All other manipulation of `CascadeButtons`
takes place through the `GraphicalObject` ancestor class. Both constructors
are implemented as a call to a `static` function called `createButton()`,
which encapsulates code for creating the Motif `CascadeButton` widgets.

```
extern "C"
{
# include <Xm/CascadeB.h>
}

static Widget createButton(const char   *name,
                           Widget        parent,
                           Widget        menu)
{
    Arg   arg ;
```

```
   XtSetArg(arg, XmNsubMenuId, menu) ;

   // Create the widget
   // NOTE: The name here acts as the name of the
   // widget AND the button label
   return XmCreateCascadeButton(parent, name, &arg, 1) ;
}
```

The CascadeButton constructor for buttons parented to a menu bar calls createButton() with the proper arguments.

```
#include "CString.h"
#include "MenuBar.h"
#include "PulldownMenu.h"
#include "CascadeButton.h"

CascadeButton::CascadeButton(const CString      &label,
                             const PulldownMenu &menu,
                             const MenuBar      &parent) :
                             Button()
{
    rtr.mrep = createButton(label, (Widget) parent,
                            (Widget) menu) ;
}
```

The CascadeButton constructor for buttons parented to a pulldown menu is quite similar.

```
#include "CString.h"
#include "PulldownMenu.h"

CascadeButton::CascadeButton(const CString      &label,
                             const PulldownMenu &menu,
                             const PulldownMenu &parent) :
                             Button()
{
    rtr.mrep = createButton (label,
                             (Widget) parent,
                             (Widget) menu) ;
}
```

The constructors (as implemented through `createButton()`) are quite similar to that of `TextButton`. Like the `TextButton` constructor, the `CascadeButton` constructor takes a string as an argument, which acts as both the name of the button and the text displayed on the face of the button. The only difference between the constructors is that we tell the `CascadeButton` instance which menu to display when it is depressed. We do this by associating the widget corresponding to the `menu` argument with the widget's `XmNsubMenuId`.

7.3.4 Picture Buttons

Motif picture buttons are represented by the library class `PictureButton`, which is derived from the class `Button`. A picture button is used in the context of a control panel, which is discussed in Section 7.6. A picture button displays not just one, but two pixel maps. The first pixel map is displayed on the face of the button when the button is *sensitive,* that is, available for end user input. Otherwise, it displays the second pixel map. When depressed, a panel button should activate a major mode or perform a major operation within the application. See Figure 7.8 for an illustration of picture buttons.

Figure 7.8. Picture buttons. [From the *mapx* application. One Call Concepts, Inc., Hanover, MD, USA Copyright © 1992, 1993, 1994, 1995. All rights reserved. Reproduced with permission.]

```
// Includes
#include "Button.h"

// Forward declarations
class CString ;
class ControlPanel ;
class PixelMap ;

class PictureButton : public Button
{
    PixelMap *sensPm ;          // Pixel map to be used when
                                // button is sensitive
                                // (enabled for input)
    PixelMap *insensPm ;        // Pixel map to be used when
                                // button is insensitive

    friend void drawButtonCB(Widget          pbutres,
                             XtPointer        clientd,
                             XtPointer        calld) ;
      // Xt callback which draws picture button after
      // exposure

  public:

    PictureButton(const CString         &name,
                  const ControlPanel    &parent,
                  PixelMap              *pm,
                  PixelMap              *ipm = NULL) ;
      // Constructor

    inline ~PictureButton(void) {} // NULL
        // Destructor
} ;
```

The PictureButton class contains pointers to two PixelMap instances, one
each for the sensitive and insensitive versions. These are passed as arguments to

the constructor, along with the name and parent of the button. We force the class of the parent to be `ControlPanel`. This is required by Motif in order for the panel to configure the buttons it contains.

```
// Includes
extern "C"
{
# include <Xm/DrawnB.h>
}
#include "ControlPanel.h"
#include "CString.h"
#include "PixelMap.h"
#include "PictureButton.h"

PictureButton::PictureButton(const CString      &name,
                             const ControlPanel &parent,
                             PixelMap           *pm,
                             PixelMap           *ipm) :
                             Button()
{
    // Validate
    if (pm == NULL)
        // Tell end user something is wrong...

    Arg           args[4] ;

    // Set some attributes
    XtSetArg(args[0], XmNshadowThickness, 3) ;
    XtSetArg(args[1], XmNmultiClick, XmMULTICLICK_DISCARD) ;
    XtSetArg(args[2], XmNpushButtonEnabled, True) ;
    XtSetArg(args[3], XmNshadowType, XmSHADOW_ETCHED_OUT) ;

    // Create the Motif button
    rtr.mrep = XmCreateDrawnButton((Widget) parent,
                                   (const char *) name,
                                   args, 4) ;
```

```
    // Set the pixel maps
    sensPm   = pm ;
    insensPm = ipm ;

    // Add resize callback
    XtAddCallback(rtr.mrep,
                  XmNresizeCallback,
                  drawButtonCB,
                  this) ;

    // Add exposure callback
    XtAddCallback(rtr.mrep,
                  XmNexposeCallback,
                  drawButtonCB,
                  this) ;
}
```

In addition to creating the Motif widget represented by the class, we register the `friend` function `drawButtonCB()` as a callback when the button is exposed or resized.

We must ourselves handle the rendering of the pixel map displayed on the face of the button. This is because if we allow Motif to do it (which is possible), our button will "flicker" because of the way Motif handles refreshing in `DrawnButton` widgets (See Heller, 1992, p. 382). The `drawButtonCB()` callback implements the `PictureButton`-rendering mechanism. The client data for this function is a pointer to the `Picture-Button` to be rendered. Any time the button is exposed or resized, Xt will invoke the callback handler.

```
void drawButtonCB (Widget w,
                   XtPointer clientd,
                   XtPointer calld)
{
    // If resources for widget do not exist, do nothing
    if (XtIsRealized(w) == False) return ;

    PictureButton *button = (PictureButton *) clientd ;
```

```cpp
// If sensitive pixel map was not specified, do nothing
if (button->sensPm == NULL)
{
  // Tell end user something is wrong...
  return ;
}

Dimension      highlight, shadow,    // Width of highlight
                                     // and shadow
               bdrw,                 // Width of the
                                     // actual "border"
               winw, winh ;          // Window dimensions
Bool           sens ;

// Get information about dimensions of button face
XtVaGetValues(w,
               XmNwidth,                 &winw,
               XmNheight,                &winh,
               XmNborderWidth,           &bdrw,
               XmNhighlightThickness,    &highlight,
               XmNshadowThickness,       &shadow,
               XmNsensitive,             &sens,
               NULL) ;

// Use correct pixel map
PixelMap *pm = sens or button->insensPm == NULL ?
               button->sensPm : button->insensPm ;

int pmw, pmh ;          // Pixel map dimensions

pmw = pm->getWidth() ;
pmh = pm->getHeight() ;

int  border,        // Number of pixels in button border
     dimNoBorders ; // Width/height of button face,
                    // without borders
```

```
// Calculate the total border width
border = bdrw + highlight + shadow ;

// Find width of button face without borders
dimNoBorders = winw - (2 * border) ;

int     srcx, srcy,     // Origin of pixel map for copy
        destx, desty ;  // Where to place pixel
                        // map in button face


// Center the drawing horizontally
if (dimNoBorders > pmw)
{
  srcx  = 0 ;
  destx = (dimNoBorders - pmw) / 2 + border ;
}
else
{
  srcx  = (pmw - dimNoBorders) / 2 ;
  destx = border ;
  pmw   = dimNoBorders ;
}

// Find height of button face, without borders
dimNoBorders = winh - (2 * border) ;

// Center the drawing vertically
if (dimNoBorders > pmh)
{
  srcy  = 0;
  desty = (dimNoBorders - pmh) / 2 + border ;
}
else
{
  srcy  = (pmh - dimNoBorders) / 2 ;
  desty = border ;
```

```
    pmh    = dimNoBorders ;
  }

  // We need a graphics context for drawing
  GC gc = XtGetGC(w, 0L, NULL) ;

  // Draw it
  XCopyArea(getDisplay(),
            (Pixmap) *pm,
            XtWindow(w),
            gc,
            srcx, srcy,
            pmw, pmh,
            destx, desty) ;

  // Clean up
  XtReleaseGC(w, gc) ;
}
```

We implement the drawButtonCB() function to validate the button by check-ing to see whether it has been realized and whether it has any valid pixel map to draw. We then calculate the placement of the pixel map within the button face.

When we render a pixel map to the button face, we must be concerned about the relationship of the button width and height to the pixel map width and height. For each dimension, we handle this according to one of three pos-sibilities:

1. **Button face is smaller than pixel map:** we "shave" the sides (left and right for width, top, and bottom for height) of the pixel map to "squeeze" it into the button face.
2. **Button face is equal to pixel map:** we copy the pixel map directly to the button face for the dimension in question.
3. **Button face is greater than pixel map:** we center the pixel map along the dimension in question.

Notice that drawButtonCB() handles cases 2 and 3 as a single case in the body of the else statement.

Finally, we draw the pixel map to the button face by obtaining a temporary graphics context from Xt and calling `XCopyArea()` to render the pixel map to the computed position within the button face.

7.4 Separators

A separator is a horizontal line that gives the end user a visual cue as to how various graphical elements are grouped. Separators are represented in our library by the `Separator` class.

```
// Includes
#include "GraphicalObject.h"

// Forward declarations
class CString ;

class Separator : public GraphicalObject
{
  public:

    Separator(const CString          &name,
              const GraphicalObject  *parent) ;
    // Constructor

    inline ~Separator(void) {} // NULL
    // Destructor
} ;
```

The `Separator` class provides only a constructor and a destructor. The constructor calls the Motif convenience function `XmCreateSeparator()`.

```
extern "C"
{
#  include <Xm/Separator.h>
}
#include "CString.h"
```

```
Separator::Separator(const CString          &name,
                     const GraphicalObject   *parent):
                     GraphicalObject()
{
    // Figure out the parent
    Widget wparent = parent ? (Widget) *parent : topLevel ;

    // Create separator
    rtr.mrep = XmCreateSeparator(wparent,
                                  (const char *) name,
                                  NULL, 0) ;
}
```

All other manipulation of Separator objects is accomplished via Graph-icalObject methods. We will see some examples of how to use Separator objects in Sections 7.5 and 8.1.

7.5 Pulldown Menus

Pulldown menus are used in an interface to give the end user quick access to various operations and utilities and to organize these into logical groups. Pulldown menus are pulled down from a menu bar across the top of the application window, rather like pulling down a window shade. Each button within a menu contains text indicating the operation or utility invoked when the button is depressed or contains the name of another cascading pulldown menu, which appears when the button is depressed. The buttons that invoke operations or utilities are instances of class TextButton and are discussed in Section 7.3.2. The buttons that cause cascading menus to appear are instances of class CascadeButton and are discussed in Section 7.3.3.

7.5.1 The Menu Bar

Before we discuss pulldown menus, we must define a class to support Motif menu bars. A menu bar is a long thin area, at the top of the application window, which contains the name of various menus. An illustration of the menu

File Privileges Map Setup Label Locate Mark   Help

Figure 7.9. A menu bar. [From the *mapx* application. One Call Concepts, Inc., Hanover, MD, USA, Copyright © 1992, 1993, 1994, 1995. All rights reserved. Reproduced with permission.]

bar for our mapping application appears in Figure 7.9. We represent Motif MenuBar widgets in our library with the class MenuBar.

```
// Includes
#include "GraphicalObject.h"

// Forward declarations
class CString ;
class CascadeButton ;
class MainWindow ;

class MenuBar : public GraphicalObject
{
  public:

    MenuBar(const CString &name, const MainWindow &parent) ;
      // Constructor

    inline ~MenuBar(void) {} // NULL
      // Destructor

    void setHelpButton(const CascadeButton &hb) ;
      // Sets help button, which is at the extreme
      // right hand side of the menu bar
} ;
```

The MenuBar constructor consists of a call to the Motif convenience function XmCreateMenuBar().

```
extern "C"
{
```

```
# include <Xm/RowColumn.h>
}
#include "CString.h"
#include "MainWindow.h"
#include "MenuBar.h"

MenuBar::MenuBar(const CString      &name,
                const MainWindow    &parent) :
                  GraphicalObject()
{
    rtr.mrep = XmCreateMenuBar((Widget) parent,
                               (const char *)
                               name, NULL, 0) ;
}
```

By convention, most GUIs, including Motif and Microsoft Windows, reserve the button at the extreme right-hand side of the menu bar for help utilities. We will follow this convention in our GUI library.

```
void MenuBar::setHelpButton(const CascadeButton &helpb)
{
    XtVaSetValues(rtr.mrep,
                  XmNmenuHelpWidget, (Widget) helpb,
                  NULL) ;
}
```

7.5.2 Pulldown Menu Class

We represent pulldown menus in our library by the PulldownMenu class. Pulldown menus may contain a mixture of three elements: text buttons, cascade buttons, and separators. Separators are displayed lines that allow us to functionally or logically group the other two elements within a menu, as discussed in Section 7.4. An illustration of the File pulldown menu for our mapping application appears in Figure 7.10.

```
// Includes
#include "GraphicalObject.h"
```

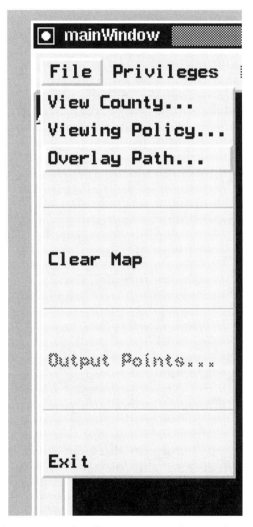

Figure 7.10. A pulldown menu for file operations. [From the *mapx* application. One Call Concepts, Inc., Hanover, MD, USA, Copyright © 1992, 1993, 1994, 1995. All rights reserved. Reproduced with permission.]

```
#include "List.h"

// Forward declarations
class CString ;
```

```
class MenuBar ;
class Separator ;

// Defines
#define SepList        List<Separator *>
#define SepListIndex   ListIndex<Separator *>

class PulldownMenu : public GraphicalObject
{
    SepList sepList ;

  public:

    PulldownMenu(const CString &name, const MenuBar &parent) ;
      // Constructor

    ~PulldownMenu(void) ;
      // Destructor

    void addSeparator(void) ;
      // Adds "separator" line in order of
      // constituent button creation
} ;
```

The data member `sepList` stores all of the separators that the user has added to the menu. A user must add a separator while creating the menu buttons. In addition, the user must create the buttons in the order in which they are to appear in the menu. In order for a user to add a separator between two buttons, he or she must create the first button, add a separator using the `addSeparator()` method, and create the second button. This process is illustrated by the code fragment below:

```
...
MainWindow      mainWindow      ("mainWindow") ;
MenuBar         menuBar         ("menuBar", mainWindow) ;
PulldownMenu    menu            ("menu", menuBar)
TextButton      tb1             ("button 1", menu) ;
```

```
menu.addSeparator() ;

TextButton       tb2                  ("button 2", menu) ;
...
```

In this fragment we declare a `PulldownMenu` called `menu`. We then declare a `TextButton` called `tb1`, which will be the first button to appear in the menu. The `addSeparator()` method is then called for `menu`, causing a separator line to appear between `tb1` and the next button placed in `menu`, namely, `tb2`.

The constructor for `PulldownMenu` creates a Motif `RowColumn` widget with the convenience function `XmCreatePulldownMenu()`.

```
// Includes
extern "C"
{
#  include <Xm/RowColumn.h>
}
#include "CString.h"
#include "GraphicalObject.h"
#include "MenuBar.h"
#include "PulldownMenu.h"

PulldownMenu::PulldownMenu(const CString &name,
                          const MenuBar &parent) :
                          GraphicalObject()
{
    // Create the widget
    rtr.mrep = XmCreatePulldownMenu((Widget) parent,
                                    (const char *) name,
                                    NULL, 0) ;
}
```

The method `addSeparator()` creates a `Separator` instance and places it after the last button added to the menu. The name of the `Separator` is generated from a prefix of "sep_" and the digit representing the current separator count.

```
void PulldownMenu::addSeparator(void)
{
    // Generate a name for the separator
    CString name = CString ("sep_") +
                    ntos((long) sepList.length()) ;

    // Create the separator
    Separator *sep = new Separator(name, this) ;

    // Insert into list
    sepList += sep ;

    // Display the separator when menu is displayed
    sep->manage() ;
}
```

The `PulldownMenu` destructor destroys all of the `Separators` in the menu. The `GraphicalObject` destructor destroys the Motif widget representing the menu.

```
PulldownMenu::~PulldownMenu(void)
{
    SepListIndex  i ;

    // Destroy the separators
    ListLoop(sepList, i) delete sepList[i]) ;
}
```

7.5.3   Using Pulldown Menus

The following code fragment illustrates how to create and use a couple of `PulldownMenus`. One of these is a "File" menu containing buttons for file operations for an application. The other `PulldownMenu` is a "Help" menu.

```
// Includes
#include "MainWindow.h"
#include "PulldownMenu.h"
```

```
#include "TextButton.h"
#include "CascadeButton.h"
#include "MenuBar.h"

// Functions defined elsewhere
GraphicalObject::CallbackHandler getFileCB ;
GraphicalObject::CallbackHandler changeDirCB ;
GraphicalObject::CallbackHandler contentsCB ;

// Objects defined elsewhere
extern GraphicalObject *workSpace ;

main(int argc, char **argv)
{
    // Initialize environment
    GraphicalEnv::setEnvironment("pmDemo", argc, argv) ;

    // Build menus
    MainWindow      mainWindow  ("mainWindow") ;
    MenuBar         menuBar     ("menuBar",       mainWindow) ;
    PulldownMenu    fileMenu    ("fileMenu",      menuBar),
                    helpMenu    ("helpMenu",      menuBar) ;
    CascadeButton   fileButton  ("File",          fileMenu,
                                                  menuBar),
                    helpButton  ("Help",          helpMenu,
                                                  menuBar) ;
    TextButton      tb1         ("New File",    &fileMenu),
                    tb2         ("Change Path", &fileMenu),
                    tb3         ("Contents",      helpMenu) ;


    // Register callbacks
    tb1.registerCallback
       (GraphicalObject::CB_ACTIVE, getFileCB) ;
    tb2.registerCallback
       (GraphicalObject::CB_ACTIVE, changeDirCB) ;
    tb3.registerCallback
       (GraphicalObject::CB_ACTIVE, contentsCB) ;
```

```
        // Set help button in menu bar
        menuBar.setHelpButton(helpButton) ;

        // Set the main window
        mainWindow.set(*workSpace, &menuBar) ;

        // Put everything on screen
        mainWindow.realizeAll() ;
        mainWindow.manage() ; // ...and everything else

        // Start application
        GraphicalEnv::startApplication() ;
}
```

See Figure 7.11 for an illustration of the interface resulting from this fragment.

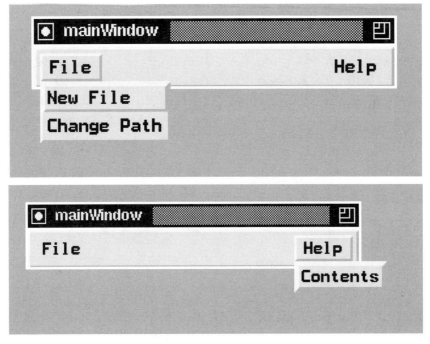

Figure 7.11. File and help menus.

7.6   Control Panels

Control panels are used to group and configure the picture buttons (see Section 7.3.4) for an application. By convention, each picture button allows the end user to switch among major application modes or functions. The grouping of these buttons takes place vertically, in columns. Control panels are represented by the library class `ControlPanel`. Figure 7.12 contains the `ControlPanel` for our mapping application.

```
// Includes
#include "GraphicalObject.h"

// Forward declarations
class CString ;
class MainWindow ;

class ControlPanel : public GraphicalObject
{
  public:

    ControlPanel(const CString      &name,
                 const MainWindow   &parent,
                 uint               columns = 1);
      // Constructor

    inline ~ControlPanel(void) {} // NULL
      // Destructor
} ;
```

The `ControlPanel` class provides only a constructor and an empty destructor. The constructor creates a Motif `RowColumn` widget with the specified name, parent, and number of columns, using the (possibly misnamed) Motif function `XmCreateWorkArea()`.

```
extern "C"
{
# include <Xm/RowColumn.h>
```

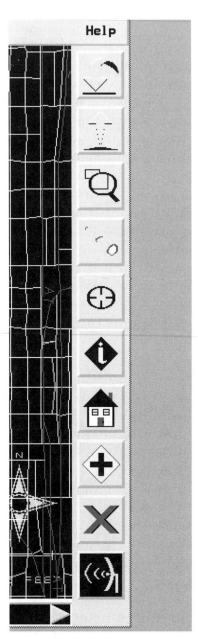

Figure 7.12. A control panel. [From the *mapx* application. One Call Concepts, Inc., Hanover, MD, USA, Copyright © 1992, 1993, 1994, 1995. All rights reserved. Reproduced with permission.]

```
}
#include "CString.h"
#include "MainWindow.h"
#include "ControlPanel.h"

ControlPanel::ControlPanel(const CString        &name,
                          const MainWindow      &parent,
                          uint                  columns) :
                          GraphicalObject()
{
    Arg    args[3] ;

    // Set some attributes
    XtSetArg(args[0], XmNpacking,        XmPACK_COLUMN) ;
    XtSetArg(args[1], XmNorientation,    XmVERTICAL) ;
    XtSetArg(args[2], XmNnumColumns,     (short) columns) ;

    // Create the widget
    rtr.mrep = XmCreateWorkArea((Widget) parent,
                                (const char *) name,
                                args, 3) ;
}
```

The following fragment illustrates the use of ControlPanels for a "real" application.

```
// Includes
#include "MainWindow.h"
#include "PixelMap.h"
#include "ControlPanel.h"
#include "PictureButton.h"

// Functions defined elsewhere
GraphicalObject::CallbackHandler zoomInCB ;
GraphicalObject::CallbackHandler zoomOutCB ;

// Objects defined elsewhere
```

```
extern GraphicalObject *workSpace ;

main(int argc, char **argv)
{
    // Initialize environment
    GraphicalEnv::setEnvironment("cpDemo", argc, argv) ;

    // Pixel maps for picture buttons
    PixelMap *pm1  = new PixelMap,
             *ipm1 = new PixelMap,
             *pm2  = new PixelMap,
             *ipm2 = new PixelMap ;

    // Read in the images
    if (not pm1->read  ("zoom_in.pm"))   exit(1) ;
    if (not ipm1->read ("zoom_in.ipm"))  exit(1) ;
    if (not pm2->read  ("zoom_out.pm"))  exit(1) ;
    if (not ipm2->read ("zoom_out.ipm")) exit(1) ;

    MainWindow     mainWindow ("mainWindow") ;
    ControlPanel   panel      ("panel",   mainWindow) ;
    PictureButton  pb1        ("zoomIn",  panel, pm1, ipm1) ;
    PictureButton  pb2        ("zoomOut", panel, pm2, ipm2) ;

    // Register callbacks
    pb1.registerCallback
    (GraphicalObject::CB_ACTIVE, zoomInCB) ;
    pb2.registerCallback
    (GraphicalObject::CB_ACTIVE, zoomOutCB) ;

    // Set the main window
    mainWindow.set(*workSpace, NULL, &panel) ;

    // Put everything on screen
    mainWindow.realizeAll() ;
    mainWindow.manage() ; // ...and everything else
```

```
    // Start application
    GraphicalEnv::startApplication() ;
}
```

The preceding code fragment illustrates a complete `main()` function, which creates a `ControlPanel` object containing buttons for "zooming in" and for "zooming out" to or from some kind of workspace. The particular application defines the zooming operations and the workspace.

7.7 **Labels**

Labels are used to display unmodifiable text within other widgets. This text may be aligned such that it is flush with the left or right margins of the widget, or it may be centered within the widget. The `Label` class represents labels in our library.

Figure 7.13 contains an illustration of three `Labels` for our mapping application, one each for latitude, longitude, and distance within a map.

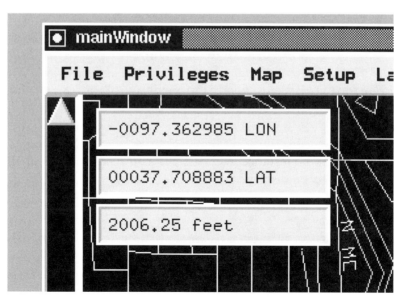

Figure 7.13. Labels for position and distance. [From the *mapx* application. One Call Concepts, Inc., Hanover, MD, USA, Copyright © 1992, 1993, 1994, 1995. All rights reserved. Reproduced with permission.]

```
// Includes
#include "GraphicalObject.h"
#include "CString.h"

class Label : public GraphicalObject
{
  public:

    enum AlignmentType
    {
      LEFT, CENTER, RIGHT
    } ;

    Label(const CString                &name,
          const GraphicalObject        *parent = NULL) ;
      // Constructor

    inline ~Label(void) {} // NULL

    void changeText(const CString &text = CString::Empty) ;
      // Changes text displayed in label

    void align(AlignmentType alignment = LEFT) ;
      // Aligns text within label
};
```

When creating a `Label` instance, we pass the name and parent of the label, plus any initial text to be displayed within the label.

```
extern "C"
{
# include <Xm/Label.h>
}
#include "Label.h"
#include "CString.h"

Label::Label(const CString                &name,
```

```
                const GraphicalObject  *parent) :
                GraphicalObject()
{
   // Get the parent object for the label
   Widget wparent = parent ? (Widget) *parent : topLevel ;

   // Create label widget
   rtr.mrep = XmCreateLabel(wparent,
                            (const char *) name,
                            NULL, 0) ;
}
```

The first task we perform in the `Label` constructor is to validate the `GraphicalObject` `*` specified as a parent. If the value of this is `NULL`, we set the parent to be `topLevel`. Next we create the Motif `Label` widget. We set the text for the `Label` instance using the method `changeText()`.

```
void Label::changeText(const CString &text)
{
   XmString  mtext =
          XmStringCreateSimple((const char *) text) ;

   XtVaSetValues(rtr.mrep, XmNlabelString, mtext, NULL);
   XmStringFree(mtext);
}
```

Notice that if we call this method with a blank string, we effectively erase the displayed text within the label.

We also allow users to change the alignment of the text within a `Label` instance.

```
static unsigned char AlignLookup[] =
{
   XmALIGNMENT_BEGINNING,
   XmALIGNMENT_CENTER,
   XmALIGNMENT_END
} ;
```

```
void Label::align(Label::AlignmentType alignment)
{
    // Set the alignment
    XtVaSetValues(rtr.mrep,
                  XmNalignment, AlignLookup[alignment],
                  NULL) ;
}
```

In Section 8.2, we will see some examples of how to use `Labels`.

7.8 Text Fields

Text fields allow the end user to enter a single line of text into an application. The purpose of this text varies. It could be a file name or have some other application-defined meaning. Text fields are represented in our library by class `TextField`. Figure 7.14 contains a graphical depiction of a generic `TextField`.

```
// Includes
#include "GraphicalObject.h"
#include "CString.h"

class TextField : public GraphicalObject
{
  public:

    // Defaults number of characters to display
    static const uint DefaultWidth ;

    // Number of characters in field is unlimited
    static const uint Unlimited ;

    TextField(const CString          &name,
              const GraphicalObject *parent,
              uint                   width   = DefaultWidth,
              uint                   maxLen  = Unlimited) ;
        // Constructor
```

Figure 7.14. A text field.

```
inline ~TextField(void) {} // NULL
   // Destructor

operator CString(void) ;
   // Obtains text currently displayed in text field

const CString &operator =(const CString &text) ;
   // Replaces current text with specified text

CString operator +=(const CString &text) ;
   // Appends text to current text

void showText(uint pos) const ;
   // Shows text at specified character position
   // Position numbering starts at 0

inline void clearText(void) { *this = CString::Empty ; }
   // Clears contents of text field

void     lock   (void) ;
void     unlock (void) ;
Boolean  locked (void) const ;
   // Manipulates the editing status of text field
} ;
```

We pass to the `TextField` constructor the name and parent for the instance, as usual. We also pass the width of the `TextField` instance, in characters, and the maximum length allowed for entered text.

```
// Includes
extern "C"
{
```

```cpp
# include <Xm/TextF.h>
}
#include "TextField.h"

// Class static initialization
const uint TextField::DefaultWidth = 0 ;
const uint TextField::Unlimited    = 0 ;

TextField::TextField(const CString        &name,
                     const GraphicalObject *parent,
                     uint                  cwidth,
                     uint                  maxLen) :
                     GraphicalObject()
{
    // Get the parent object for the text field
    Widget wparent = parent ? (Widget) *parent : topLevel ;

    Arg       argv[10] ;
    Cardinal argc = 0 ;

    // If width has been specified...
    if (cwidth)
        XtSetArg(argv[argc], XmNcolumns, cwidth), argc++ ;

    // If maximum for entered text length has been
    // specified...
    if (maxLen)
        XtSetArg(argv[argc], XmNmaxLength, (int) maxLen) ,
        argc++ ;

    // Turn off blinking for cursor
    XtSetArg(argv[argc++], XmNblinkRate, 0) ; argc++ ;

    // Create widget
    rtr.mrep = XmCreateTextField(wparent,
                                 (const char *)
                                 name, argv, argc) ;
}
```

If the user specifies DefaultWidth for the value of cwidth, we do not set the number of columns, and thereby use the Motif default. By the same token, if the user specifies Unlimited for the value of maxLen, we do not place a limit on the amount of entered text. Also, we turn the blinking off for the text insertion cursor within the field. The blink rate is a matter of personal preference and would be an excellent candidate for another TextField method, such as set-BlinkRate().

We provide three operators for TextField to enhance interoperability with the CString class. The first of these is a cast to CString. This allows us to use a TextField at any point where a CString is expected.

```
TextField::operator CString(void) const
{
    char *mtext = XmTextFieldGetString(rtr.mrep) ;
    CString text ;

    if (mtext)
    {
      text = mtext ;
      XtFree(mtext);
    }

    return text ;
}
```

Our second operator, operator =(), allows us to assign a CString directly to a TextField. This can be quite convenient in so far as we can, for example, assign the result of a function that returns a CString or CString & directly into a TextField.

```
const CString &TextField::operator =(const CString &text)
{
    XmTextFieldSetString(rtr.mrep, (const char *) text);
    return text ;
}
```

We return the argument to allow chained assignment for TextFields.

Our third and final operator, operator +=(), allows us to append a CString to the current contents of the TextField. This offers us much of the same convenience as the assignment operator.

```
CString TextField::operator +=(const CString &text)
{

    // Find the last valid text position
    XmTextPosition endPos =
        XmTextFieldGetLastPosition(rtr.mrep) ;

    // Append the text
    XmTextFieldInsert(rtr.mrep, endPos, (const char *) text) ;

    return (CString) *this ;
}
```

Once again, we return the argument to allow chained assignment for TextFields.

A peculiar problem arises when we append text to a TextField. If the new text goes beyond the right side of the TextField, the portion that is beyond the field is not seen. If the new text is completely outside of the field, the end user may not get any feedback showing that the text was appended. For this reason we provide a method called showText(), which places the text beginning at the specified character position (0-based) as the first character in the field. No characters to the left of the position are shown.

```
void TextField::showText(uint pos)
{
    XmTextFieldShowPosition(rtr.mrep, (XmTextPosition) pos);
}
```

We can now modify operator +=() to show the appended text automatically, if we so desire.

The final three methods we will discuss have to do with locking and unlocking a TextField for editing. There may arise a situation in which we temporarily wish to keep the end user from entering any text into a TextField.

We accomplish this through the `lock()` method.

```
void TextField::lock(void)
{
    XtVaSetValues(rtr.mrep,
                XmNeditable,                    False,
                XmNcursorPositionVisible,       False,
                NULL) ;
}
```

In addition to making the `TextField` uneditable, we also turn off the cursor in order to signal the end user that this has occurred.

Once we have locked a `TextField`, we can make the field editable again by invoking the `unlock()` method. The implementation of `unlock()` is precisely the same as for `lock()`, except we set the resources to `True`. The `isLocked()` predicate tells the user whether the `TextField` is currently locked. The `isLocked()` predicate is implemented as a call to `XtVaGetValues()` for the `XmNeditable` resource of the Motif widget.

On a final note, text fields can be powerful tools for data entry and validation, especially for database applications. In the next chapter, we will discuss some techniques for extending the `TextField` class to perform validation of entered text.

7.9 Simple Dialogs

The dialog is one of the most powerful and essential elements in any GUI library. Dialogs can be used for many different purposes, such as informing an end user of a problem or getting a file name from an end user. Dialogs come in many flavors, an infinite number in fact, as they can be completely customized for any purpose. When we mention *simple* dialogs, the "simple" does not mean that the dialogs themselves are simple. It means that Motif supports them directly so that it is "simple" to define classes around them. Any dialog variety that Motif does not directly support we will call *custom* dialogs.

In our library, we will implement dialogs as a class hierarchy with two main branches for input and output dialog classes. This will draw the distinction between dialogs used to obtain input from the end user and those used to tell the end user something.

We will provide support for all of the following simple input dialogs:

- **prompt dialogs:** prompts the end user for a text string.
- **file dialogs:** prompts the end user for a file name.

In addition, we will provide support for all of the following simple output dialogs:

- **error dialogs:** tells the end user that an error has occurred.
- **information dialogs:** gives the end user an informational message.
- **warning dialogs:** warns the end user about an application-specific problem.

Figure 7.15 contains a depiction of the entire dialog class hierarchy.

7.9.1 Dialog Base Class

The `Dialog` class is an *abstract base class* (see Ellis and Stroustrup, 1990; Lippman, 1993), and therefore objects may not be directly declared to be of type `Dialog`.

```
// Includes
#include "GraphicalObject.h"

// Forward declarations
class CString ;

class Dialog : public GraphicalObject
{
  public:

    // Defines
    enum PoseType
    {
      WAIT,          // Wait for end user to respond
      NO_WAIT        // Allow normal processing to continue
    } ;
```

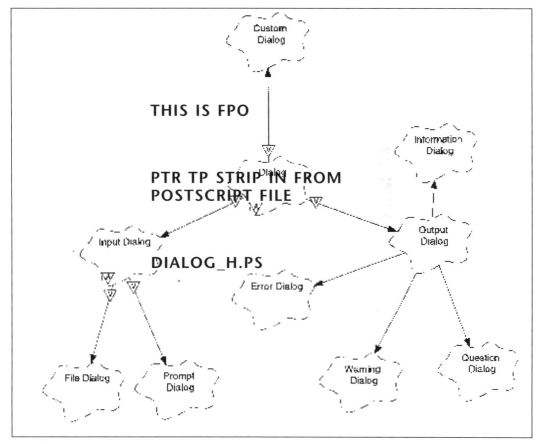

Figure 7.15. Dialog class hierarchy.

```
// How to calculate position
enum PosCalc
{
  FROM_PARENT,    // Position are relative to parent
  FROM_SCREEN     // Positions are absolute
} ;

// Dialog position types
enum PosType
```

```
{
  EXPLICIT,           // Position dialog explicitly
  TOP_LEFT,           // Position dialog at top left
  TOP_RIGHT,          // Position dialog at top right
  CENTER,             // Position dialog at center
  BOTTOM_LEFT,        // Position dialog at bottom left
  BOTTOM_RIGHT        // Position dialog at bottom right
} ;

// Dialog button types
enum StandardButton
{
  OK,                 // Button with default label "Ok"
  APPLY,              // Button with default label "Apply"
  CANCEL,             // Button with default label "Cancel"
  HELP,               // Button with default label "Help"
  UNKNOWN             // Exception condition
} ;

// Standard button labels
static const char *APPLY_LABEL ;
static const char *CANCEL_LABEL ;
static const char *FILTER_LABEL ;
static const char *HELP_LABEL ;
static const char *NO_LABEL ;
static const char *OK_LABEL ;
static const char *YES_LABEL ;

protected:

  // Dialog create function prototype
  typedef Widget (* CreateHook)(Widget,
                                const char *,
                                ArgList,
                                Cardinal) ;
```

```
PosCalc        posCalc ;        // Position relative to ???
PosType        posType ;        // Indicates placement for
                                // first pose
int            dx ;             // Explicit horizontal
                                // position
int            dy ;             // Explicit vertical position
StandardButton lastButton ;     // Most recent button
                                // activated
Boolean        dismissed ;      // Has dialog been dismissed?
Boolean        cancelled ;      // Has dialog been cancelled?
Boolean        applied ;        // Has dialog been applied?
Boolean        dismissOnApply ; // Dismiss with apply button?

friend void positionCB(Widget     w,
                       XtPointer   clientd,
                       XtPointer   calld) ;
  // Calculates dialog placement before it
  // is mapped to the screen

friend void stateCB(Widget     mbutton,
                    XtPointer   clientd,
                    XtPointer   calld) ;
  // Updates state of dialog, depending on
  // button end user pressed

virtual Widget findButton(StandardButton b) const = 0 ;
  // Locates button widget according to our button type

void setSensitivity(StandardButton b, Boolean on) ;
  // Sets sensitivity of specified button in dialog

void setVisibility(StandardButton b, Boolean on) ;
  // Sets visibility of specified button in dialog

Dialog(CreateHook            cfn,
     const CString           &name,
```

```
          const GraphicalObject    *parent = NULL) ;
          // Constructor

public:

  inline virtual ~Dialog(void) {} // NULL
     // Destructor

  virtual void pose(PoseType wait = Dialog::WAIT) ;
     // Displays dialog and optionally waits
     // for it to be dismissed before returning

  void setPosition(PosCalc calc   = FROM_PARENT,
                   PosType pos     = CENTER,
                   int x           = 0,
                   int y           = 0) ;
     // Sets position of dialog before first pose

  inline void sensitize    (StandardButton b)
  { setSensitivity(b, TRUE) ; }
  inline void desensitize (StandardButton b)
  { setSensitivity(b, FALSE) ; }
     // Button sensitization methods

  inline void showButton (StandardButton b)
  { setVisibility(b, TRUE) ; }
  inline void hideButton (StandardButton b)
  { setVisibility(b, FALSE) ; }
     // Button visibility methods

  virtual void setButtonLabel(StandardButton b,
                              const CString &label) ;
     // Sets label of specified button

  inline StandardButton getLastButton(void) const
  { return lastButton; }
```

```
        // Obtains last button activated in the dialog

    inline void setApplyDismiss(Boolean on)
    { dismissOnApply = on ; }
        // Sets behavior of dialog to automatically
        // dismiss (or not) when applied

    inline Boolean wasDismissed (void) const
    { return dismissed ; }
    inline Boolean wasCancelled (void) const
    { return cancelled ; }
    inline Boolean wasApplied (void) const
    { return applied ; }
        // Determines what happened to dialog
} ;
```

CLASS TYPES

The `Dialog` class provides a number of `public` and `protected` types used for various purposes. Let's take a look at each one of these types in some depth.

PoseType

We present a dialog to the end user by *posing* it, that is, placing it on screen so that the end user may interact with it. We can pose a dialog in two ways:

1. `WAIT`: we block further processing and wait for the end user to respond to the dialog.
2. `NO_WAIT`: we allow the event loop to continue and let the end user interact with the dialog at his or her leisure.

We specify the `WAIT` literal when it is important to get some kind of response from the end user before allowing any further processing. For example, it may be critical to make the end user aware of an application error before processing can continue. We specify the `NO_WAIT` literal when the timing of the end user response is not critical to application flow. This usually happens when we pose a custom dialog for application-specific data entry.

Note that when a dialog is nonblocking (i.e., has been posed using NO_WAIT), the user must explicitly take it off screen by using the Graphical Object method unmanage(). Otherwise, it is taken off screen automatically when the end user dismisses it.

PosCalc

Positioning a dialog is very important with regard to making the interface easy to use and maintaining internal and external consistency within and among applications. For example, when we pose a dialog and block on an end user response, we should place the dialog prominently within the interface, so it gets the end user's attention. Depending on context, this may be in the middle of the interface. On the other hand, we may want to position nonblocking dialogs to the side of the interface, so the end user can continue performing other tasks. This type allows us to specify whether positioning directives from the user are interpreted as being relative to the parent of the dialog or as being absolute (screen-relative).

Note that user positioning directives are valid only the first time a dialog is posed. After the first time, the end user is in control of the position of the dialog.

PosType

The literals of this type are used in association with literals of type PosCalc to specify the position of a dialog. If we use the literal EXPLICIT, then we will also provide coordinates when positioning.

StandardButton

The literals of this type refer to standard buttons presented by a simple dialog. The standard buttons include:

an approval button usually displaying the text "Ok";

an application button usually displaying the text "Apply";

a cancellation button usually displaying the text "Cancel";

a help button usually displaying the text "Help".

CreateHook

This is the prototype for all of the Motif dialog creation functions, XmCreate*Dialog(). This is used as a parameter type for the Dialog constructor and tells the base class which dialog to create.

Note that placing this type in the class interface makes the `Dialog` class inherently nonportable. See the discussion on `Dialog` portability below.

DATA MEMBERS

The `Dialog` class maintains a significant number of data members to maintain information about the state of the dialog.

- `posCalc`: This indicates how to interpret position information.
- `posType`: This indicates the position at which the dialog should appear the first time it is posed.
- `dx`, `dy`: These are coordinates for dialog placement when `posType` is `EXPLICIT`.
- `lastButton`: This indicates the last standard dialog button pressed by the end user.
- `dismissed`, `cancelled`, `applied`: These indicate how the end user disposed of the dialog.
- `dismissOnApply`: This indicates whether we should dismiss the dialog when the end user presses the standard "apply" button.

All of the `static` constants `*_LABEL` allow the user to standardize the names of standard dialog buttons. These are initialized as follows:

```
const char *Dialog::FILTER_LABEL    = "Filter" ;
const char *Dialog::APPLY_LABEL     = "Apply" ;
const char *Dialog::CANCEL_LABEL    = "Cancel" ;
const char *Dialog::HELP_LABEL      = "Help" ;
const char *Dialog::NO_LABEL        = "No" ;
const char *Dialog::OK_LABEL        = "OK" ;
const char *Dialog::YES_LABEL       = "Yes" ;
```

CONSTRUCTION AND DESTRUCTION

The constructor for the `Dialog` class takes a function pointer argument of class type `CreateHook` specifying the Motif dialog creation function to use when creating the Motif widget. This isolates dialog widget creation to this class. As usual, it also takes the name and the parent of the widget.

Note that the name of a Dialog is a bit more important than the name of other GraphicalObjects because a Dialog will usually be *decorated* (i.e., have a titlebar) by the window manager. This means that the name of the Dialog will appear in the titlebar, so be sure to choose meaningful names for Dialogs.

```cpp
// Includes
extern "C"
{
# include <Xm/MessageB.h>
}
#include "Dialog.h"
#include "CString.h"

Dialog::Dialog(CreateHook            cfn,
               const CString         &name,
               const GraphicalObject *parent) :
               GraphicalObject()
{
    // Get the parent object for the dialog
    Widget wparent = parent ? (Widget) *parent : topLevel ;

    // Initialize data members
    posCalc     = FROM_PARENT ;
    posType     = CENTER;
    dx          = dy = 0 ;
    dismissed   = cancelled = applied = dismissOnApply
                = FALSE ;
    lastButton  = UNKNOWN;

    XmString mtitle =
        XmStringCreateSimple((const char *) name) ;

    Arg   args[4] ;

    // Set some resources for the dialog
    XtSetArg(args[0], XmNautoUnmanage,   False) ;
```

```
    XtSetArg(args[1], XmNdefaultPosition, False) ;
    XtSetArg(args[2], XmNdialogTitle,     mtitle) ;
    XtSetArg(args[3], XmNdefaultButtonType,
                      XmDIALOG_CANCEL_BUTTON) ;

    // Create the dialog
    rtr.mrep = cfn(wparent,
                   (const char *) name,
                   args, 4) ;

    // Clean up
    XmStringFree(mtitle) ;

    // Add positioning callback
    XtAddCallback(XtParent(rtr.mrep),
                  XmNpopupCallback,
                  positionCB,
                  this) ;
}
```

After initializing the `Dialog` instance data members, we set some default behaviors for the `Dialog` with Motif. We set `XmNautoUnmanage` and `XmNdefaultPosition` to `False` because we will handle posing and positioning explicitly.

Next we call the Motif dialog creation function passed to us to create the Motif dialog widget. The Motif widget is a composite widget. In Section 2.2 we discussed Xt shell widgets and their role in communicating application geometry to the window manager. The Motif dialog widgets actually consist of a dialog (which is composite unto itself) and a Motif `DialogShell` widget, which is the parent of the Motif dialog. The Motif dialog creation function returns a handle to the child of this shell. This means that the `wparent` is actually the parent of the `DialogShell` widget, not the dialog itself. Therefore, we must be careful when using the dialog parent widget.

Our final task is to register an internal callback handler with the Motif dialog widget called `positionDialog()`, which will correctly position the dialog before it is posed. Notice that we register this callback handler with the parent shell of the Motif dialog widget.

The destructor is once again empty, as the `GraphicalObject` destructor destroys the Motif widget representing the dialog.

POSING DIALOGS

A `Dialog` can be placed on screen by using the `pose()` method. When posing a dialog we can tell Xt whether or not we wish to block on an end user response, as discussed above. A posed `Dialog` is removed from the screen upon end user dismissal automatically if we are blocking on end user response. Otherwise the user may take it off screen by using the `unmanage()` method provided by the `GraphicalObject` parent class.

```
static unsigned char ModeLookup[] =
{
    XmDIALOG_FULL_APPLICATION_MODAL,
    XmDIALOG_MODELESS
} ;


void Dialog::pose(PoseType wait)
{
    // Set the modality of the dialog
    // blocking specification
    XtVaSetValues (rtr.mrep,
                   XmNdialogStyle,
                   ModeLookup[wait], NULL) ;

    // Reset dialog state
    dismissed   = cancelled = applied = FALSE ;
    lastButton  = UNKNOWN ;

    // Put dialog on screen
    manage() ;

    // Wait for dismissal?
    if (wait == WAIT)
    {
      while (not dismissed) GraphicalEnv::processEvent() ;
      unmanage() ;
```

```
            XmUpdateDisplay(topLevel) ;
        }
}
```

The first thing we must do when posing a `Dialog` is to set the *modality*. Modality indicates which user events should be allowed for the rest of the application. If we block on end user response, we must lock the end user out of doing anything but responding to the dialog.

Our next tasks are to reset the state of the `Dialog` and to place it on screen. The state of a `Dialog` indicates how the end user interacted with it. The state is changed via a callback handler, depending on which standard button the end user pressed. This is discussed below.

Finally, we must perform blocking, if so requested. We accomplish this by remaining in an event subloop until the end user dismisses the `Dialog`.

MANAGING DIALOG STATE

Any time the end user presses a standard dialog button, we must update the state of the corresponding `Dialog` instance in order for us to manage posing and blocking. We register the internal callback handler `stateCB()` as an activation callback for each standard dialog button. This callback handler will automatically update the state of the `Dialog` instance.

```
void stateCB (Widget mbutton,
              XtPointer clientd,
              XtPointer calld)
{
  XmAnyCallbackStruct         *cbs   =
      (XmAnyCallbackStruct *)  calld ;
  Dialog                       *dialog= (Dialog *) clientd ;
  Dialog::StandardButton       button ;

  // Translate the system reason code into a button type
  switch (cbs->reason)
  {
    case XmCR_OK:
      button             = Dialog::OK ;
      dialog->dismissed  = TRUE ;
      break ;
```

```
    case XmCR_APPLY:
     button                  = Dialog::APPLY ;
     dialog->applied         = TRUE ;
     if (dialog->dismissOnApply) dialog->dismissed = TRUE ;
     break ;

    case XmCR_CANCEL:
     button                  = Dialog::CANCEL ;
     dialog->dismissed       = TRUE ;
     dialog->cancelled       = TRUE ;
     break ;

    case XmCR_HELP:
     button = Dialog::HELP ;
     break ;

    default:
     {
       // Tell end user something is wrong...
       button = Dialog::UNKNOWN ;
     }
     break ;
   }

   // Store the last button pressed
   dialog->lastButton = button ;
}
```

POSITIONING DIALOGS

We allow the user to set the position of a `Dialog` by calling the method `set-Position()`. This method sets the positioning data members of the `Dialog` instance. These members are later used in the popup callback `positionCB()` to correctly position the `Dialog`.

```
void Dialog::setPosition(Dialog::PosCalc    calc,
                         Dialog::PosType    pos,
                         int                x,
                         int                y)
```

```
{
    posCalc    = calc ;
    posType    = pos ;
    dx         = x ;
    dy         = y ;
}
```

Positioning dialogs on screen can be tricky. First of all we must remember that there is an intervening `DialogShell` widget between the Motif widget corresponding to the `Dialog` and its `GraphicalObject` parent. Secondly, we must calculate the position relative to either the `GraphicalObject` parent or the screen.

The `friend` function `positionCB()` is registered as the popup callback for each `Dialog` instance. This callback is invoked by Xt just prior to the moment when Xt places the `Dialog` on screen. This callback handler is responsible for telling Xt where to place the `Dialog`.

```
void positionCB(Widget w, XtPointer clientd, XtPointer
    calld)
{
    Dialog    *dialog = (Dialog *) clientd ;
    Dimension  shellw, shellh ; // Dialog shell dimensions

    // Get width and height of dialog shell
    XtVaGetValues(XtParent(dialog->rtr.mrep),
                XmNwidth,  &shellw,
                XmNheight, &shellh,
                NULL) ;

    Position  parentx, parenty ; // Graphical object parent
                                 // coordinates
    Dimension parentw, parenth ; // Graphical object parent
                                 // or screen dimensions

    // Obtain dimensions and position of
    // graphical object parent
    if (dialog->posCalc == Dialog::FROM_PARENT)
```

```
{
  // Get dimensions and position
  // of our parent graphical object
  XtVaGetValues(XtParent(XtParent(dialog->rtr.mrep)),
                XmNwidth,          &parentw,
                XmNheight,         &parenth,
                XmNx,              &parentx,
                XmNy,              &parenty, NULL);

  // Get grand parent of dialog shell
  Widget grandParent =
    XtParent(XtParent(XtParent(dialog->rtr.mrep))) ;

  // Translate grandparent-relative coordinates
  // to screen coordinates
  if (grandParent != (Widget) 0)
  {
    XtTranslateCoords(grandParent,
                      parentx,   parenty,
                      &parentx, &parenty) ;
  }
}

// The parent dimensions and position are
// already screen-relative
else
{
  parentw = screenWidth() ;
  parenth = screenHeight() ;
  parentx = parenty = 0 ;
}

Position newx, newy ; // New screen-relative position
                      // for the dialog shell

// Adjust screen-relative dialog shell position based on
// desired placement
```

```
switch (dialog->posType)
{
  case Dialog::EXPLICIT:
    newx = parentx + (Position) dialog->dx,
    newy = parenty + (Position) dialog->dy ;
    break;

  case Dialog::TOP_LEFT:
    newx = parentx ;
    newy = parenty ;
    break ;

  case Dialog::TOP_RIGHT:
    newx = parentx + (parentw - shellw) ;
    break ;

  case Dialog::BOTTOM_LEFT:
    newy = parenty + (parenth - shellh) ;
    break ;

  case Dialog::BOTTOM_RIGHT:
    newx = parentx + (parentw - shellw) ;
    newy = parenty + (parenth - shellh) ;
    break ;

  case Dialog::CENTER:
    newx = parentx + (parentw - shellw) / 2 ;
    newy = parenty + (parenth - shellh) / 2 ;
    break ;
}

// Set the position of the shell
XtVaSetValues(XtParent(dialog->rtr.mrep),
              XmNx, newx,
              XmNy, newy,
              NULL) ;
```

```
// We want this called only the first time
XtRemoveCallback(XtParent(dialog->rtr.mrep),
                 XmNpopupCallback,
                 positionCB,
                 dialog) ;
}
```

The parent of the Motif `DialogShell` widget is either one of our `Graph-icalObjects` or is `topLevel`. Our first task is to obtain the position of the parent of the shell, relative to the screen. This is <u>very</u> tricky.

First of all, the `XmNx` and `XmNy` resources for Motif `DialogShell` widgets seem to have some strange behavior. When you <u>get</u> them they are relative to the parent widget, but when you <u>set</u> them they are screen-relative. This is why we must translate everything to screen coordinates.

Second, we must be very careful when translating parent relative shell widget coordinates to screen-relative coordinates. When performing this translation we must use the "grandparent" of the shell widget, because the position of the parent of the shell is relative to this grandparent. This grandparent may be the screen itself, if the parent of the shell is `topLevel`.

Once we have the screen-relative coordinates of the parent, we can calculate the new, screen-relative position of the shell and set it. This is calculated according to the user-specified position, stored in the `dialog` argument's data member `posType`.

Finally, we must unregister this callback for `dialog` in order to hand positioning control over to the end user for `dialog`.

MANAGING DIALOG BUTTONS

The remaining `Dialog` methods perform various operations on standard dialog buttons. The first of these is `findButton()`, which is a *pure virtual* method (see Ellis and Stroustrup, 1990; Lippman, 1993). This means that it is up to each derived class to provide an implementation of this method. The purpose of `findButton()` is to return the Motif widget corresponding to each standard button for a `Dialog`. This is not as straightforward as it may seem. For simple dialogs, Motif creates the standard buttons for us. For custom dialogs (see Section 8.1), we create our own dialog buttons.

The `setSensitivity()` method is defined for convenience only. It allows us to sensitize or desensitize each standard dialog button for end user input.

```
void Dialog::setSensitivity(Dialog::StandardButton button,
                            Boolean                on)
{
    // Find the Motif button widget
    Widget mbutton = findButton(button) ;

    // Set sensitivity
    if (mbutton) XtSetSensitive(mbutton, (Bool) on) ;
}
```

This method is called with the appropriate `Boolean` value from the `inlined` `public` methods `sensitize()` and `desensitize()`.

We also provide the `protected` method `setVisibility()` methods, which is a convenience method for changing standard dialog button visibility.

```
void Dialog::setVisibility (Dialog::StandardButton button,
                            Boolean                on)
{
    // Find the Motif widget for the button
    Widget mbutton = findButton(button) ;

    // Set the visibility
    if (mbutton)
    {
      on ? XtManageChild(mbutton) : XtUnmanageChild(mbutton) ;
    }
}
```

This method is called with the appropriate `Boolean` value from the inlined `public` methods `showButton()` and `hideButton()`.

Finally we define the `public` and `virtual` method `setButtonLabel()`, which allows us to change the labels of the standard dialog buttons.

```
static char *LabelStringLookup[] =
{
    XmNokLabelString,
    XmNapplyLabelString,
```

```
    XmNcancelLabelString,
    XmNhelpLabelString
} ;

void Dialog::setButtonLabel(Dialog::StandardButton   button,
                            const CString             &text)
{
    // Create Motif compound string
    XmString label =
        XmStringCreateSimple((const char *) text) ;

    // Set the label
    XtVaSetValues(rtr.mrep,
                  LabelStringLookup[button], label,
                  NULL) ;

    // Clean up
    XmStringFree(label) ;
}
```

We make this method `virtual` to allow derived classes to override it. This way, if an object of a derived class is treated as a `Dialog`, the correct version of `setButtonLabel()` can still be called.

NOTES ON PORTABILITY

The fact that the `Dialog` class provides the `CreateHook` prototype for Motif dialog creation makes the class inherently nonportable. This is compounded by the declaration of the two Xt callback handlers, `positionCB()` and `stateCB()`.

It is not as easy for us to make the `Dialog` class portable as it is for, say, `GraphicalEnv`. This is because the `Dialog` constructor uses the `Create-Hook` prototype. In order for us to avoid this problem, we would have to either pass the creation function as a `void *` and cast to the prototype in the .C file, or we would have to distribute the responsibility for dialog creation among the various classes derived from `Dialog`. Furthermore, we would have to eliminate the callback handler declarations from the class declaration, essentially destroying the `friend` relationship. We would then have to provide some additional methods for `Dialog` so that the callback handlers could accomplish their tasks.

7.9.2 *Input Dialogs*

Input dialogs are dialogs that allow us to obtain some application-specific information, such as a file name, from the end user. These classes are all derived from the `InputDialog` class, which itself is derived from class `Dialog`.

The `InputDialog` class is an abstract base class (see Ellis and Stroustrup, 1990; Lippman, 1993).

```
// Includes
#include "Dialog.h"
#include "CString.h"

class InputDialog : public Dialog
{
  protected:

    InputDialog(CreateHook                  cfn,
                const CString               &name,
                const GraphicalObject       *parent) ;
      // Constructor

  public:

    inline ~InputDialog(void) {} // NULL
      // Destructor

    void setPrompt(const CString &prompt) ;
      // Sets prompt

    virtual operator CString(void) const = 0 ;
      // Obtain text from dialog

    virtual const CString &operator =(const CString &) = 0 ;
      // Assigns text to dialog
} ;
```

The constructor for `InputDialog` passes the Motif dialog creation function and the name and parent of the dialog to the `Dialog` constructor. It also sets the button state management callback for each standard button.

```
#include "InputDialog.h"

InputDialog::InputDialog(Dialog::CreateHook      cfn
                         const CString           &name
                         const GraphicalObject   *parent
                         Dialog(cfn, name, parent)
{
  //Add state manangement callbacks
  XtAddCallback(rtr.mrep, XmNokCallback,     stateCB, this) ;
  XtAddCallback(rtr.mrep, XmNapplyCallback,  stateCB, this) ;
  XtAddCallback(rtr.mrep, XmNhelpCallback,   stateCB, this) ;
  XtAddCallback(rtr.mrep, XmNcancelCallback, stateCB, this) ;
}
```

Each input dialog displays a prompt and contains a Motif TextField for text input by the end user. The setPrompt() method allows the user to set the prompt string.

```
void InputDialog::setPrompt(const CString &prompt)
{
    // Create a Motif compound string
    XmString mprompt =
        XmStringCreateSimple((const char *) prompt) ;

    // Set the prompt
    XtVaSetValues(rtr.mrep,
                  XmNselectionLabelString, mprompt,
                  NULL) ;

    // Clean up
    XmStringFree(mprompt);
}
```

The CString cast operator allows us to retrieve the text from the Motif TextField. Unfortunately, the widget resource for the dialog text is different

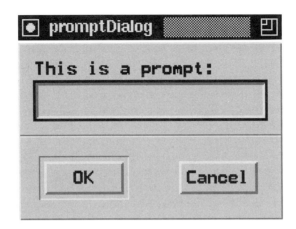

Figure 7.16. A prompt dialog.

for each input dialog. Therefore, this method is pure virtual.

The `CString` assignment operator allows us to set the text in the Motif `TextField` widget for the `InputDialog`. We must declare this as a pure virtual method because the method of setting text is different for each derived class.

PROMPT DIALOGS

Prompt dialogs allow the user to prompt the end user for a text string. Our library represents prompt dialogs with the `PromptDialog` class. An illustration of a `PromptDialog` appears in Figure 7.16.

```
#include "InputDialog.h"

class PromptDialog : public InputDialog
{
    Widget findButton(StandardButton b) const ;
        // Locates Motif widget for our button type

  public:

    PromptDialog(const CString        &name,
            const GraphicalObject  *parent  = NULL,
```

```
                    const CString              &prompt  =
                                               CString::Empty,
                    const CString              &text    =
                                               CString::Empty) ;
        // Constructor

     inline ~PromptDialog(void) {} // NULL
        // Destructor

     operator CString(void) const ;
        // Obtains text for dialog

     const CString &operator =(const CString &text) ;
        // Sets text for dialog
} ;
```

In addition to the name and parent of the `PromptDialog`, we pass the prompt and initial text to the constructor.

```
PromptDialog::PromptDialog(const CString          &name,
                           const GraphicalObject  *parent,
                           const CString          &prompt,
                           const CString          &text) :
                           InputDialog(XmCreatePromptDialog,
                                       name, parent)
{
    hideButton(HELP);
    setPrompt(prompt) ;
    PromptDialog::operator =(text) ;
}
```

Motif implements prompt dialogs on top of a `SelectionBox` widget. Therefore, we implement the `findButton()` method as a call to `XmSelectionBoxGetChild()`.

```
unsigned char ButtonLookup[] =
{
```

```
    XmDIALOG_OK_BUTTON,
    XmDIALOG_APPLY_BUTTON,
    XmDIALOG_CANCEL_BUTTON,
    XmDIALOG_HELP_BUTTON
} ;


Widget PromptDialog::findButton
    (Dialog::StandardButton button) const
{
    return XmSelectionBoxGetChild(rtr.mrep,
                              ButtonLookup[button]) ;
}
```

In order for the `PromptDialog` to be a usable class, we must provide implementations for both the `CString` cast operator and assignment operator.

The `CString` cast operator for a `PromptDialog` returns the value of the `XmNtextString` resource for the corresponding widget.

```
PromptDialog::operator CString(void) const
{
    XmString    mtext ;

    // Get the Motif compound string
    XtVaGetValues(rtr.mrep, XmNtextString, &mtext, NULL) ;

    char        *ctext ;

    // Translate to character pointer
    XmStringGetLtoR(mtext,
                XmSTRING_DEFAULT_CHARSET, &ctext) ;

    CString    text ;

    // Translate to our string
    text = ctext ;
```

```
// Clean up
XtFree(ctext) ;
XmStringFree(mtext) ;

return text ;
}
```

Finally, the `CString` assignment operator sets the value of the `XmN-textString` resource for the Motif `SelectionBox` widget.

```
const CString &PromptDialog::operator =(const CString &text)
{
    // Create a Motif compound string
    XmString mtext =
        XmStringCreateSimple((const char *) text) ;

    // Set the text
    XtVaSetValues(rtr.mrep,
                  XmNtextString, mtext,
                  NULL) ;

    // Clean up
    XmStringFree(mtext) ;

    return text ;
}
```

The argument is returned to allow for chained assignment.

FILE DIALOGS

Motif file dialogs provide us with a very nice mechanism to obtain file names from the user. Motif allows the end user to switch directories and filter the file names by pattern, all from within the dialog. Our library represents file dialogs with the `FileDialog` class. An illustration of a `FileDialog` appears in Figure 7.17.

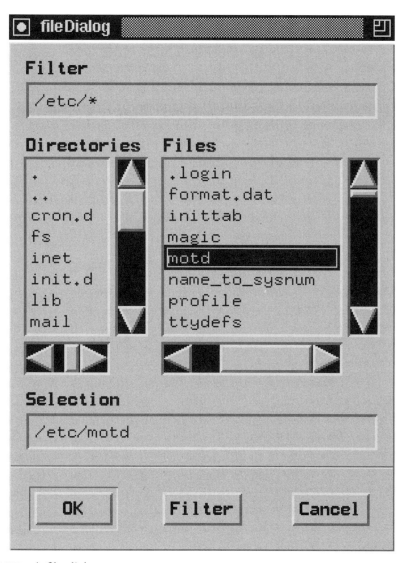

Figure 7.17. A file dialog.

```
// Includes
#include "InputDialog.h"

class FileDialog : public InputDialog
{
```

```
    Widget findButton(StandardButton b) const ;
        // Locates Motif button widget corresponding to
        // our type

  public:

    // Dialog button types
    enum ModeType
    {
      MODE_ANY,     // Existence check only
      MODE_READ,    // Existence and read permission check
      MODE_UPDATE   // Existence and read/write permission
                    // check
    } ;

    FileDialog(const CString          &name,
               const GraphicalObject  *parent  = NULL,
               ModeType                mode     = MODE_ANY,
               const CString          &fname    =
                                       CString::Empty) ;
        // Constructor

    inline ~FileDialog(void) {} // NULL
        // Destructor

    void setFilter(const CString &text) ;
        // Stores text as file name filter,
        // as if typed by end user

    operator CString(void) const ;
        // Obtains selected file name

    const CString &operator =(const CString &text) ;
        // Stores text as selected file,
        // as if typed by end user
} ;
```

The `FileDialog` class provides a type called `ModeType`, which allows the user to specify whether he or she is interested in read-only or read/write files, or if it doesn't matter.

The user can specify the mode and initial file name upon construction, along with the name and parent.

```
extern "C"
{
# include <stdlib.h>
# include <unistd.h>
# include <sys/types.h>
# include <sys/stat.h>
# include <dirent.h>
# include <Xm/FileSB.h>
}
#include "FileDialog.h"

FileDialog::FileDialog(const CString        &name,
                       const GraphicalObject *parent,
                       FileDialog::ModeType  mode,
                       const CString         &fname) :
                       InputDialog
                       (XmCreateFileSelectionDialog, name,
                        parent)
{
    // Set default button behavior for file dialogs
    hideButton(HELP) ;
    setButtonLabel(APPLY, FILTER_LABEL) ;

    // Add appropriate Motif search procedure
    switch (mode)
    {
      case MODE_ANY:
        break ;

      case MODE_READ:
        XtVaSetValues(rtr.mrep,
```

```
                    XmNfileSearchProc, fileSearchRead,
                    NULL) ;
        break ;

    case MODE_UPDATE:
      XtVaSetValues(rtr.mrep,
                    XmNfileSearchProc, fileSearchWrite,
                    NULL) ;
        break ;
  }

  // Set the file name
  if (not fname.isBlank()) FileDialog::operator =(fname) ;
}
```

We use `mode` to set the proper value for the `XmNfileSearchProc` widget resource. This is a function that filters the files from which the end user can select. As this resource can be set to a user defined function, we will use it to filter files with certain permissions, as indicated by `mode`. Note that if we do not set this resource, as is the case for a `mode` value of `MODE_ANY`, Motif provides a default function.

We use the filtering functions `fileSearchRead()` and `fileSearch-Write()` to filter the files by permission. The implementation of these is similar, so only `fileSearchRead()` is presented here.

```
//For filtering file name
extern Boolean match(const CString  &fn,
                    const XmString &filter);

inline static Boolean isReadable(const CString &fileName)
{
    return (Boolean)
    (access((const char *) fileName, R_OK) != -1) ;
}

inline static Boolean isDirectory(const CString &dirName)
{
    struct stat ftest ;
```

```
    if (stat((const char *) dirName, &ftest) == -1)
    return FALSE ;
    return
    ((ftest.st_mode & S_IFMT) == S_IFDIR ? TRUE : FALSE) ;
}

static DIR *getDirectory(XmString &mdirName,
                         CString &dirName)
{
    char    *dir ;

    // Get directory mask
    if (not XmStringGetLtoR(mdirName
                            XmSTRING_DEFAULT_CHARSET,
                            &dir)) return NULL ;

    // Standardize directory name
    dirName = dir ;
    if (dirName[dirName.length() - 1] != '/')
        dirName += '/' ;

    // Clean up
    XtFree(dir) ;

    return opendir(dirName) ;
}

static void fileSearchRead(XmFileSelectionBoxWidget fs,
                           XmFileSelectionBoxCallbackStruct *cbs)
{
    CString dirName ;
    DIR    *dir   = getDirectory(cbs->dir, dirName) ;

    // Check for bad directory
    if (not dir) return ;

    struct dirent *ent ;
```

```
XmString  names[FD_MAX_FILES] ;
int       fileCount = 0 ;

// Loop through files in directory
while (ent = readdir(dir))
{
  CString  fileName (dirName + ent->d_name) ;

  // Check for readability
  if (not isDirectory(fileName)     and
      isReadable(fileName)          and
      not isWriteable(fileName)     and
      match(fileName, cbs->pattern))
  {
    name[fileCount++] = XmStringCreateSimple(ent->d_name) ;
  }
}

Arg         argv[5] ;
Cardinal    argc = 0 ;

// Set file names in dialog
XtSetArg(argv[argc], XmNlistUpdated,       True) ;
    argc++ ;
XtSetArg(argv[argc], XmNfileListItemCount, fileCount) ;
    argc++ ;
XtSetArg(argv[argc], XmNfileListItems,     names) ;
    argc++ ;
if (fileCount) XtSetArg(argv[argc], XmNdirSpec, names[0]),
    argc++ ;

// Do it
XtSetValues((Widget) fs, argv, argc) ;
}
```

These functions make heavy use of Unix operating system facilities. The correct implementations for various flavors of Unix might differ.

In addition to the mechanism for filtering files by permission, we also provide the user of `FileDialog` with a mechanism for filtering file names that do not match a wildcard pattern. The `setFilter()` method accomplishes this.

```
void FileDialog::setFilter(const CString &text)
{
    // Build Motif compound string
    XmString mtext =
        XmStringCreateSimple((const char *) text) ;

    // Filter the file names
    XmFileSelectionDoSearch(rtr.mrep, mtext) ;

    // Clean up
    XmStringFree(mtext) ;
}
```

Of course, we can use just about any criterion for filtering files. All we need to do is change the file search function resource for the Motif `FileDialog` widget, as discussed above.

The remaining undiscussed methods are implementations of pure virtual methods declared in ancestor classes. If we do not provide any implementation for these, the user will not be able to declare objects of type `FileDialog`.

First of all, we must provide an implementation for the `findButton()` method.

```
// See PromptDialog.C
extern unsigned char ButtonLookup[] ;

Widget FileDialog::findButton
    (Dialog::StandardButton button) const
{
    return XmFileSelectionBoxGetChild(rtr.mrep,
                                ButtonLookup[button]) ;
}
```

Next we must implement the CString cast operator.

```
FileDialog::operator CString(void) const
{
    XmString mtext ;

    // Get the file name from the dialog
    XtVaGetValues(rtr.mrep, XmNdirSpec, &mtext, NULL) ;

    char *fname ;

    // Translate to our string
    if (not XmStringGetLtoR(mtext,
                          XmSTRING_DEFAULT_CHARSET,
                          &fname))
        return CString::Empty ;

    CString fileName = fname ;

    // Clean up
    XtFree(fname) ;

    return fileName ;
}
```

Finally, we must implement the CString assignment operator.

```
const CString &FileDialog::operator =(const CString &text)
{
    // Build the Motif compound string
    XmString mtext =
        XmStringCreateSimple((const char *) text) ;

    // Set the file name
    XtVaSetValues(rtr.mrep, XmNdirSpec, mtext, NULL) ;

    // Clean up
```

```
    XmStringFree(mtext) ;

    return text ;
}
```

7.9.3 Output Dialogs

Output dialogs are dialogs that allow us to convey some application-specific information, such as error messages, to the end user. These classes are all derived from the OutputDialog class, which itself is derived from class Dialog.

Unlike the InputDialog class, the OutputDialog class is <u>not</u> an abstract base class. This is because the classes derived from OutputDialog are so similar that we can encapsulate much of the functionality in this class. However, the constructor is protected, so that instances of this class cannot be easily defined.

```
// Includes
#include "Dialog.h"
#include "CString.h"

class OutputDialog : public Dialog
{
  protected:

    Widget findButton(StandardButton b) const ;
      // Locates system resource for our button type

    OutputDialog(Dialog::CreateHook      cfn,
                 const CString           &name,
                 const GraphicalObject   *parent) ;
      // Constructor

  public:

    inline ~OutputDialog(void) {} // NULL
      // Destructor
```

```
    virtual const CString &operator =(const CString &text) ;
      // Sets output message string
} ;
```

Just as for `InputDialog`s, the constructor for this class passes on the name, parent, and Motif dialog creation function directly to the `Dialog` base class.

```
#include "OutputDialog.h"

OutputDialog::OutputDialog(CreateHook              cfn,
                           const CString           &name,
                           const GraphicalObject   *parent) :
                           Dialog(cfn, name, parent)
{
   // Add state management callbacks
   XtAddCallback(rtr.mrep, XmNokCallback,      stateCB, this) ;
   XtAddCallback(rtr.mrep, XmNhelpCallback,    stateCB, this) ;
   XtAddCallback(rtr.mrep, XmNcancelCallback,  stateCB, this) ;
   hideButton(Help) ;
}
```

Fortunately, all classes derived from `OutputDialog` are implemented on top of Motif `MessageBox` widgets, so we can define the `findButton()` method at this point.

```
// See PromptDialog.C
extern unsigned char ButtonLookup[] ;

Widget OutputDialog::findButton
    (Dialog::StandardButton button) const

{
    return XmMessageBoxGetChild(rtr.mrep,
                        ButtonLookup[button]) ;
}
```

Finally, we require all `OutputDialog` classes to provide a `CString` assignment operator. However, we do not make this method a pure virtual, because of the commonalities shared by the `OutputDialog` classes. We declare the method as virtual so that a derived class may choose to override the default, as defined here.

```
const CString &OutputDialog::operator =
    (const CString &message)
{
    // Build a Motif compound string
    XmString mmessage =
        XmStringCreateSimple((const char *) message) ;

    // Set the message resource
    XtVaSetValues(rtr.mrep, XmNmessageString, mmessage, NULL) ;

    // Clean up
    XmStringFree(mmessage) ;

    return message ;
}
```

As usual, we return the argument to allow for chained assignment.

Because of the similarities in implementation among error, information, and warning dialogs, we present only a discussion of error dialogs.

Error dialogs are used to display application-specific errors for the end user to acknowledge. They are represented in our library by the `ErrorDialog` class.

```
// Includes
#include "OutputDialog.h"

class ErrorDialog : public OutputDialog

{
  public:

    ErrorDialog(const CString          &name,
            const GraphicalObject  *parent   = NULL,
            const CString          &message  =
                                    CString::Empty) ;
```

```
   // Constructor

 inline ~ErrorDialog(void) {} // NULL
   // Destructor
} ;
```

We pass the message to be displayed at the point of construction. Of course, we can always change the message by using the CString assignment operator provided by the OutputDialog class.

```
ErrorDialog::ErrorDialog(const  CString        &name,
                    const  GraphicalObject  *parent,
                    const  CString          &message) :
                    OutputDialog
                    (XmCreateErrorDialog, name, parent)
{
    OutputDialog::operator =(message) ;
    hideButton(Dialog::CANCEL) ;
}
```

The declarations and definitions of classes for information dialogs (class InfoDialog) and warning dialogs (class WarningDialog) are extremely similar to those for ErrorDialog. The only real difference lies in the Motif dialog creation function we pass to the OutputDialog constructor. For InfoDialogs this function is XmCreateInformationDialog(). For WarningDialogs this function is XmCreateWarningDialog().

7.9.4 Using Dialogs

Let's take a look at some "real-world" uses for our library dialogs.

The following code fragment shows how we can use a PromptDialog to obtain the name of a color from the end user. The PromptDialog for this fragment is depicted in Figure 7.18.

```
...
#include "PromptDialog.h"
#include "CString.h"
```

Figure 7.18. A prompt dialog for color.

```
// Defined elsewhere
extern GraphicalObject *parent ;

CString getUserColor(void)
{
    PromptDialog  dialog("colorDialog",
                         parent,
                         "Enter name of color:") ;

    // Wait for user response
    dialog.pose() ;

    // Return file name
    return dialog.wasCancelled() ?
         CString::Empty : (CString) dialog ;
}
...
```

The next code fragment shows how we can use a `FileDialog` to obtain a read-only file matching the pattern `*.txt`. The `FileDialog` for this fragment is depicted in Figure 7.19.

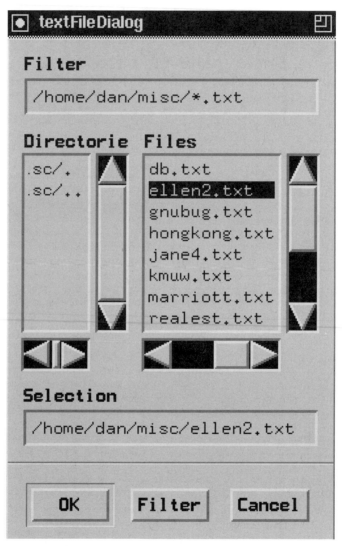

Figure 7.19. A file dialog for .txt files.

```
...
#include "FileDialog.h"
#include "CString.h"

// Defined elsewhere
extern GraphicalObject *parent ;
```

Figure 7.20. Using an error dialog.

```
CString getReadOnlyTextFile(void)
{
    FileDialog  dialog("textFileDialog",
                        parent,
                        FileDialog::MODE_READ) ;

    // We only want files ending in ".txt"
    dialog.setFilter("*.txt") ;

    // Wait for user response
    dialog.pose() ;

    // Return file name
    return dialog.wasCancelled() ?
        CString::Empty : (CString) dialog ;
}
...
```

The final code fragment shows how we can tell the end user that an error has occurred by using an ErrorDialog. The ErrorDialog for this fragment is depicted in Figure 7.20.

```
...
#include "ErrorDialog.h"
#include "CString.h"
```

```
// Defined elsewhere
extern GraphicalObject *parent ;

void tellUser(const CString &message)
{
    ErrorDialog dialog("textFileDialog",
                       parent, message) ;

    // Wait for user acknowledgement
    dialog.pose() ;
}
...
```

The use of InfoDialogs and WarningDialogs is exactly the same as for ErrorDialogs.

7.10   Radio and Check Boxes

Radio boxes allow the end user to select an arbitrary subset from some discrete range of values. These values are represented by graphical elements called *toggles*, which are a special kind of button.

To illustrate the use of radio boxes, consider a geographic mapping application. In this application, we may wish turn on or off the display of certain map features, such as highways or railroads. To do this we can formulate a toggle for the display state of each feature and group them together into a radio box. This radio box is depicted in Figure 7.21.

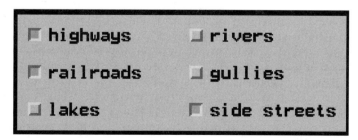

Figure 7.21. A radio box for map features.

The radio box illustrated in Figure 7.21 allows the end user to select as many toggles as he or she pleases. Such radio boxes, in which the end user may select more than one toggle, are termed *check boxes*.

7.10.1 Class Declaration

Radio boxes are represented by the RadioBox class in our library. They are implemented on top of Motif RadioBox widgets. These widgets consist of a number of small Motif ToggleButton widgets. Each button has an associated text label, explaining what the toggle is for. Going back to our mapping example, two of the toggle labels might read "highways" or "railroads".

```cpp
// Includes
#include "GraphicalObject.h"
#include "CString.h"
#include "List.h"

// Defines
#define WidgetList          List<Widget>
#define WidgetListIndex     ListIndex<Widget>

class RadioBox : public GraphicalObject
{
  public:

    // Possible behaviors
    enum Behavior
    {
      ONE_OR_NONE,  // Zero or one toggles may be set
      ALWAYS_ONE,   // Exactly one toggle must ALWAYS be set
      MANY          // Zero or more toggles may be set
                    // (check box)
    } ;

    // No toggles set
    static const uint NONE_SELECTED ;
```

```
    // Callback for toggling
    typedef void (* ToggleCallback)(RadioBox     &radioBox,
                                    uint          pos,
                                    void         *udata) ;

private:

    Behavior        behavior ;  // Indicates behavior of
                                // radio box
    WidgetList      toggles ;   // List of toggles
    ToggleCallback  userCB ;    // User toggle callback
    void            *udata ;    // User data for user
                                // toggle callback

    friend void toggleCB
      (Widget w, XtPointer clientd, XtPointer calld) ;
      // Internal toggle callback handler

public:

    RadioBox(const CString          &name,
          const GraphicalObject *parent    = NULL,
          Behavior               bv        = MANY,
          uint                   columns   = 0) ;
      // Constructor

    ~RadioBox(void) ;
      // Destructor

    void setToggleCallback(ToggleCallback cb,
                        void *udata = NULL) ;
      // Sets toggle callback

    void addToggle(const CString &toggleName) ;
      // Adds a toggle to end of radio box

    uint togglePos(const CString &tname) const ;
```

```
    // Obtains position according to toggle name

CString toggleName(uint pos) const ;
    // Obtains name according to toggle position

inline uint toggleCount(void) const
{ return toggles.length() ; }
    // Obtains number of toggles in box

Boolean changeToggle(uint pos,
                     Boolean val,
                     Boolean invoke = FALSE) ;
    // Changes the state of a toggle, and possibly
    // invokes callback.
    // Returns FALSE if out of range.

void setAllToggles   (Boolean invoke = FALSE) ;
void clearAllToggles (Boolean invoke = FALSE) ;
    // Sets/clears every toggle in box

Boolean isSet(uint pos) const ;
    // Determines if a toggle is set

uint getSelected(void) const ;
    // Obtains position of the first selected toggle
    // encountered
} ;
```

We allow the user to specify the number of toggles that the end user is permitted to set at any one time. This is accomplished by way of the class Behavior type.

- ONE_OR_NONE: Zero or one toggles may be set by the end user.
- ALWAYS_ONE: Exactly one toggle must always be set at any one time.
- MANY: Implements a check box, in which any number of toggles, including 0, may be set by the end user at any one time.

We allow the user to register a callback handler function, which is invoked any time the end user changes the state of a toggle. The prototype for such callback handlers is the `ToggleCallback` class type.

```
class RadioBox : public GraphicalObject
{
  public:

    ...
    // Callback for toggling
    typedef void (* ToggleCallback)(RadioBox    &radioBox,
                                    uint         pos,
                                    void        *udata) ;

    ...
} ;
```

When such a callback is invoked, it is passed the `RadioBox` for which the callback was registered. It is also passed the position of toggle that changed state and any user data that was registered for the callback.

7.10.2 Construction and Destruction

The `RadioBox` constructor is passed the name and parent for the instance. At this point we also set the behavior of and the number of toggle columns for the `RadioBox`.

```
// Includes
extern "C"
{
# include <Xm/ToggleB.h>
# include <Xm/RowColumn.h>
# include <limits.h>
}
#include "RadioBox.h"
#include "CString.h"

// Class static initializations
```

```
const uint RadioBox::NONE_SELECTED = UINT_MAX ;

RadioBox::RadioBox(const CString          &name,
                   const GraphicalObject  *parent,
                   RadioBox::Behavior      bv,
                   uint                    columns) :
                   GraphicalObject()
{
    // Initialize data members
    userCB  = NULL ;
    udata   = NULL ;

    // Get the parent object for the radio box
    Widget wparent = parent ? (Widget) *parent : topLevel ;

    // Figure out the number of columns
    short numCols = columns ? (short) columns : 1 ;

    // Create RowColumn manager for radio box explicitly
    rtr.mrep = XtVaCreateWidget(name,
                                xmRowColumnWidgetClass,
                                wparent,
                                XmNpacking, XmPACK_COLUMN,
                                XmNentryClass,
                                  xmToggleButtonWidgetClass,
                                XmNnumColumns, numCols,
                                XmNradioBehavior, bv !=MANY
                                XmNradioAlwaysOne,
                                  bv ==ALWAYS_ONE,
                                NULL) ;
}
```

For once, we have a real destructor on our hands. This is because when a user adds a toggle to a RadioBox, we add a new Motif ToggleButton widget to the list of widgets represented by data member toggles. Motif will not destroy these ToggleButton widgets automatically. Therefore, we must destroy them explicitly in the destructor.

```
RadioBox::~RadioBox(void)
{
    WidgetListIndex  i ;

    for (toggles.reset(i); toggles.inRange(i);
         toggles.advance(i))
         XtDestroyWidget(toggles[i]) ;
}
```

7.10.3 Adding Toggles

We can add a toggle by passing the label text to the `RadioBox` method
`addToggle()`.

```
void RadioBox::addToggle(const CString &label)
{
    // Create toggle
    Widget togb = XtVaCreateManagedWidget((const char *)
                                          label,
                             xmToggleButtonWidgetClass,
                             rtr.mrep, NULL) ;

    // Add to list
    toggles += togb ;

    // Add callback
    XtAddCallback(togb,
                  XmNvalueChangedCallback,
                  toggleCB,
                  this) ;
}
```

This method creates a Motif `ToggleButton` widget and appends it to the `tog-gles` data member of the `RadioBox` instance. Also, we register the internal callback handler `toggleCB()` for the new widget. See Section 7.10.5 for a discussion on managing toggle callbacks.

7.10.4 Manipulating Toggles

Once we have added all of the toggles to a RadioBox, we can manipulate them in a variety of ways. First, we can obtain the position of the first toggle within a RadioBox that matches a given name (i.e., label) by using the method togglePos().

```
uint RadioBox::togglePos(const CString &name) const
{
    uint              pos = 0 ;
    WidgetListIndex   i ;

      // Find first toggle with name
      for (toggles.reset(i); toggles.inRange(i);
           toggles.advance(i))
      {
        if (name == XtName(toggles[i])) break ;
        pos++ ;
      }

      // Return the position
      return pos < toggles.length() ? pos : NONE_SELECTED ;
}
```

Conversely, we can find the name of a toggle from the position of the toggle within the RadioBox by using the method toggleName().

```
CString RadioBox::toggleName(uint pos) const
{
    CString name ;

    // Check bounds
    if (toggles.length() > 0 and pos < toggles.length())
        name = XtName(toggles[pos]) ;

    return name ;
}
```

We can use the method changeToggle() to explicitly set or clear a toggle and even to trigger the toggle callback.

```
Boolean RadioBox::changeToggle(uint        pos,
                                Boolean    state,
                                Boolean    invoke)
{
    // Check bounds
    if (toggles.length() > 0 and pos < toggles.length())
    {
      XmToggleButtonSetState(toggles[pos],
                             (Bool) state,
                             (Bool) invoke) ;
      return TRUE ;
    }

    return FALSE ;
}
```

We can set or clear all the toggles at once if the behavior of the RadioBox allows for this. The setAllToggles() methods sets every toggle in the RadioBox by invoking changeToggle() for every toggle with the correct values. The clearAllToggles() method clears all of the toggles in a RadioBox and is implemented in a similar fashion.

We can determine whether a toggle at any given position is set by calling the isSet() method.

```
Boolean RadioBox::isSet(uint pos) const
{
    Boolean set = FALSE ;

    // Check bounds
    if (toggles.length() > 0 and pos < (uint) toggles.length())
      set = XmToggleButtonGetState(toggles[pos]) ;

    return set ;
}
```

Finally, we can get the position of the first toggle that is set in a RadioBox.

```
uint RadioBox::getSelected(void) const
{
    uint        i ;

    // Loop until selected button is found
    for (i = 0 ; i < toggles.length() ; i++)
        if (XmToggleButtonGetState(toggles[i])) return i ;

    return NONE_SELECTED ;
}
```

7.10.5 Managing Toggle Callbacks

The RadioBox class declares an internal callback handler called toggleCB(), which is registered with every new Motif ToggleButton widget. Every time the end user changes the state of a toggle, this callback is invoked for the specific toggle in a specific RadioBox.

When invoked, the internal handler in turn invokes the user toggle callback handler for the instance. If any user data has been registered for the callback, it gets passed to the handler as well.

```
void toggleCB(Widget w, XtPointer clientd, XtPointer calld)
{
    RadioBox *radioBox = (RadioBox *) clientd ;

    // See if there is a user callback
    if (radioBox->userCB)
    {
      // Invoke it
      radioBox->userCB(*radioBox,
                        radioBox->togglePos(XtName(w)),
                        radioBox->udata) ;
    }
}
```

The user callback handler may be registered with the `setToggleCall-back()` method.

```
void RadioBox::setToggleCallback(RadioBox::ToggleCallback cb,
                                 void                    *data)
{
    userCB  = cb ;
    udata   = data ;
}
```

7.10.6 Using Radio Boxes

Returning to our geographic mapping example, let's take a look at a code fragment that creates and uses such a RadioBox.

First, let's hypothesize a class called Map, which represents geographic maps. This class provides a nested enumerator called Feature and a public method called setFeatureDisplay().

```
class Map
{
    // Implementation details...

  public:

    ...

    // All of the features in a map
    enum Feature
    {
      Highways, Railroads, Lakes,
      Rivers, Gullies, SideStreets,

      NUM_FEATURES // Counts the literals
    } ;

    ...
```

```
    void setFeatureDisplay(Feature feat, Boolean state) ;
        // Determines whether kind of feature is displayed
        // in map


    ...
} ;
```

Now let's use a `RadioBox` to provide a mechanism for changing which features are displayed in a `Map`.

```
...
#include "RadioBox.h"
#include "CString.h"
#include "Map.h"    // A hypothetical geographic map class

static char *FeatureName[] =
{
    "highways", "railroads", "lakes",
    "rivers", "gullies", "side streets"
} ;

// Defined elsewhere
extern GraphicalObject *parent ;

//Radio box for Feature types
static RadioBox *box = NULL;

// Our toggle callback
static void setDisplayCB(RadioBox      &box,
                         uint          pos,
                         void          *udata)
{
    Map *map = (Map *) udata ;

    map->setFeatureDisplay((Map::Feature) pos, box.isSet(pos)) ;
}

void changeMapFeatureDisplay(Map *map)
```

```
{
    if (box == NULL)
    {
      box = new RadioBox("changeDisplayBox",
                         parent,
                         RadioBox::MANY,
                         2) ;

      // Set toggle callback
      box->setToggleCallback(setDisplayCB, map) ;
    }
    int i ;

    // Add the toggles
    for (i = 0 ; i < Map::NUM_FEATURES ; i++)
        box->addToggle(FeatureName[i]) ;

    // Display the radio box
    box->manage() ;
}
...
```

In Section 8.1.4 we will see how we can place a RadioBox in a dialog for temporary interaction with the end user.

7.11 Scales

Motif Scale widgets present an excellent mechanism for setting numerical values. A scale is a graphical representation of a slide bar that allows for the adjustment of a numerical value between some minimum and maximum. Consider a text editor application in which we want to allow the end user to set the number of blank lines between lines of text. Let's assume that the minimum number of blank lines is 0, and that the maximum is 10. We can accomplish this task by presenting the end user with the Scale widget depicted in Figure 7.22.

The Scale library class is implemented on top of the Motif Scale widget class.

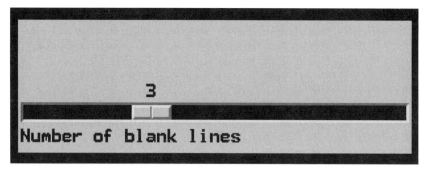

Figure 7.22. A scale for blank lines.

```cpp
#include "GraphicalObject.h"

class CString ;

class Scale : public GraphicalObject
{
  public:

    // Should scale be vertical or horizontal?
    enum Orientation
    {
      HORIZONTAL, VERTICAL
    };

    Scale(const CString          &name,
        const GraphicalObject   *parent     = NULL,
        Boolean                  sensitive  = TRUE,
        Orientation              orient     = HORIZONTAL) ;
      // Constructor

    void setBounds(double maxVal,
                double minVal    = 0.0,
                short decPts      = 0) ;
      // Sets the miniumum, maximum and number of
      // decimal places to display for the scale
```

```
    operator double(void) const ;
      // Obtains current scale value

    double operator =(double d) ;
      // Sets scale value

    void setLabel(const CString &label) ;
      // Sets scale label
} ;
```

We construct a Scale instance by specifying the name and parent, as usual. We also indicate whether we wish to make the Scale available for end user interaction. In some cases, we may want a Scale to display some numerical data for an application without giving the end user the ability to change it. Finally, we can also specify whether we want a Scale to be oriented vertically or horizontally.

```
extern "C"
{
# include <Xm/Scale.h>
}
#include "Scale.h"
#include "CString.h"

Scale::Scale(const CString          &name,
             const GraphicalObject  *parent,
             Boolean                sensitive,
             Scale::Orientation     orient):
             GraphicalObject()
{
    // Get the parent widget for the scale
    Widget wparent = parent ? (Widget) *parent : topLevel ;

    Arg        argv[4] ;
    Cardinal   argc = 0 ;

    // Set arguments
```

```
      XtSetArg(argv[argc], XmNshowValue,   True) ; argc++ ;
      XtSetArg(argv[argc], XmNsensitive,   (Bool) sensitive) ;
         argc++ ;
      XtSetArg(argv[argc], XmNvalue,       0) ; argc++ ;
      XtSetArg(argv[argc], XmNorientation, orient ==
                                           HORIZONTAL ?
                                           XmHORIZONTAL :
                                           XmVERTICAL) ; argc++ ;


      // Create Motif scale widget
      rtr.mrep = XmCreateScale(wparent,
                               (const char *) name,
                               argv, argc) ;
}
```

Once we have created a `Scale`, we must set its boundaries and the number of decimal places it will display. Inside the Motif `Scale` widget, the value is stored as an integer. However, we may want to use the scale to display a floating point value. We can do this by allowing the user to specify the number of decimal places to shift the value. For example, if the `Scale` widget internal value is 3147 and the number of user-specified decimal places is 2, the value is interpreted as 31.47. Fortunately, Motif directly supports the display of the value shifted right by some decimal places. However, we must still convert the internal scale value ourselves before setting it or getting it from the `Scale` widget. In doing so, we will hide the entire value shifting mechanism from the user.

```
// Includes
extern "C"
{
# include <math.h>
}

// Defines
#define shiftLeft(val, places) (val * pow(10, places))

void Scale::setBounds(double maxVal,
                      double minVal,
                      short decPts)
```

```
{
    // Compute integer values for scale
    int smin = (int) shiftLeft(minVal, decPts) ;
    int smax = (int) shiftLeft(maxVal, decPts) ;

    XtVaSetValues(rtr.mrep,
                    XmNminimum,              smin,
                    XmNmaximum,              smax,
                    XmNdecimalPoints,        decPts,
                    NULL) ;
}
```

The Scale class provides the double cast operator, which obtains the current numerical value of the scale. This means that we can use a Scale anywhere a double is expected.

```
#define shiftRight(val,places) (val / pow(10, places))

Scale::operator double(void) const
{
    int     value ;
    short   decPts ;

    // Get the current scale value and number
    // of decimal places
    XtVaGetValues(rtr.mrep,
                    XmNvalue,                &value,
                    XmNdecimalPoints,        &decPts,
                    NULL) ;

    return shiftRight(value, decPts) ;
}
```

We also allow the user to assign a double value directly to a Scale instance by using the double assignment operator.

```
double Scale::operator =(double d)
```

```
{
    short decPts ;

    // Get the number of decimal places
    XtVaGetValues(rtr.mrep,
                XmNdecimalPoints, &decPts,
                NULL) ;

    // Compute the internal scale value
    int value = (int) shiftLeft(d, decPts) ;

    // Set the new value
    XtVaSetValues(rtr.mrep, XmNvalue, value, NULL) ;

    return d ;
}
```

We return the argument to allow for chained assignment.

Finally, a Scale is useless unless the end user knows what it is used for.

```
void Scale::setLabel(const CString &label)
{
    // Build the Motif compound string
    XmString mlabel =
        XmStringCreateSimple((const char *) label) ;

    // Set the new value
    XtVaSetValues(rtr.mrep, XmNtitleString, mlabel, NULL) ;

    // Clean up
    XmStringFree(mlabel) ;
}
```

Let's return to our example concerning setting the number of blank lines between text in a text editor application. First of all, we will hypothesize a class called EditArea, which provides two public methods called set-BlankLines() and getBlankLines().

```
class EditArea
{
public:

    ...
    void setBlankLines (uint num) ;
    uint getBlankLines (void) const ;
    ...
} ;
```

We can now set a "value changed" callback for a Scale, which will change the number of blank lines every time the end user modifies the scale value.

```
// Includes
#include "Scale.h"
#include "CString.h"
#include "EditArea.h" // A hypothetical text editor class

// Defined elsewhere
extern GraphicalObject *parent ;

// Value changed callback for scale
static void changeBlanksCB(GraphicalObject              &gobj,
                           GraphicalObject::CallbackType type,
                           void                          *udata)
{
    EditArea    *edit  = (EditArea *)   udata ;
    Scale       *scale = (Scale *)      &gobj ;

    edit->setBlankLines((uint) ((double) *scale)) ;
}

void changeBlankLines(EditArea *edit)
{
    Scale *scale = new Scale("blankLinesScale", parent) ;
```

```
    // Set scale bounds
    scale->setBounds(10) ;

    // Set initial value for scale
    *scale = (double) edit->getBlankLines() ;

    // Set scale label
    scale->setLabel("Number of blank lines") ;

    // Set value changed callback for scale
    scale->registerCallback(GraphicalObject::CB_VALUE_CHANGED,
                            changeBlanksCB,
                            edit) ;

    // Put scale on screen
    scale->manage() ;
}
```

In the preceding fragment, the value changed callback handler change-BlanksCB() will be invoked any time the end user changes the value of the scale. This callback handler calls the setBlankLines() method on the EditArea instance pointed to by edit.

In Section 8.1.4 we will see how we can place a Scale in a dialog for temporary interaction with the end user.

7.12 Drawing Areas

Motif DrawingArea widgets present an excellent interface tool for communicating shapes and other kinds of nontextual data to or from the end user. Motif DrawingArea widgets are represented in our library by the DrawingArea class.

In presenting the declaration for the DrawingArea class, we again hypothesize some shape classes the method of implementation of which is beyond the scope of this book. These classes were first introduced in the discussion of PixelMaps in Section 5.5.3.

```cpp
// Includes
#include "GraphicalObject.h"

// Forward declarations
class CString ;
class Context ;
class PixelMap ;
class FontString ;    // See PixelMap class
class Vertex ;        // See PixelMap class
class Segment ;       // See PixelMap class
class Line ;          // See PixelMap class
class Polygon ;       // See PixelMap class

class DrawingArea : public GraphicalObject
{
  public:

    DrawingArea(const CString           &name,
              const GraphicalObject   *parent = NULL) ;
      // Constructor

    inline ~DrawingArea(void) {} // NULL
      // Destructor

    void draw(const Context &c, const Vertex       &v) ;
    void draw(const Context &c, const Segment      &s) ;
    void draw(const Context &c, const Line         &l) ;
    void draw(const Context &c, const Polygon      &p) ;
    void draw(const Context &c, const FontString   &f) ;
    void draw(const Context &c, const PixelMap     &pmap,
            int locx = 0, int locy = 0) ;
      // Draws various elements to the drawing area

    void fill(const Context &c, const Polygon &poly) ;
      // Fills polygon

    void capture(const Context &c, PixelMap &pmap,
```

```
                    int locx = 0, int locy = 0) const ;
    // Captures a portion of the drawing area
    // to a pixel map
};
```

The `DrawingArea` class provides a constructor, an empty destructor, and a number of methods for rendering various shapes.

The constructor calls the Motif convenience function `XmCreate-DrawingArea()` to create the widget.

```
// Includes
extern "C"
{
# include <X11/StringDefs.h>
# include <Xm/DrawingA.h>
}
#include "DrawingArea.h"
#include "Context.h"
#include "PixelMap.h"
#include "Vertex.h"
#include "Segment.h"
#include "Line.h"
#include "Polygon.h"
#include "FontString.h"


DrawingArea::DrawingArea(const CString        &name,
                         const GraphicalObject *parent) :
                         GraphicalObject()
{
    // Get the parent widget for the drawing area
    Widget wparent = parent ? (Widget) *parent : topLevel ;

    // Create the widget
    rtr.mrep = XmCreateDrawingArea(wparent,
                                   (const char *) name,
                                   NULL, 0) ;
}
```

Motif does not provide any drawing routines. For this reason, all of the draw() methods are implemented on top of X. For the sake of brevity, we will look only at one of these, namely, the version for the hypothetical Polygon class.

```
void DrawingArea::draw(const Context &context,
                       const Polygon &poly)
{
    // Check for an empty polygon
    if (poly.pointCount() < 3) return ;

    int i ;
    XPoint pts[p.pointCount() + 1] ;

    // Populate array of X points
    for (i = 0 ; i < poly.pointCount() ; i++)
    {
      pts[i].x = (short) poly[i].x ;
      pts[i].y = (short) poly[i].y ;
    }

    // Repeat the first point
    pts[i].x = (short) poly[0].x ;
    pts[i].y = (short) poly[0].y ;

    // Draw the polygon
    XDrawLines(display,
               XtWindow(rtr.mrep),
               (GC) context,
               pts,
               poly.pointCount() + 1,
               CoordModeOrigin);
}
```

Notice that this is almost identical to the draw(...Polygon...) method for the PixelMap class, except that we draw to the window corresponding to the Motif DrawingArea widget instead of to the X pixmap.

This points out an interesting technique that we can use to perform rendering. We can create a `PixelMap` object of exactly the same dimensions as the `DrawingArea` and use the `PixelMap` to "back up" the `DrawingArea`. In other words, we can perform all rendering tasks on the `PixelMap`. When we are ready to display the rendered items we draw the `PixelMap` to the `DrawingArea`. This has a couple of advantages:

1. The end user sees the entire picture almost instantaneously, leaving the impression that the interface is very fast.
2. Refreshing the drawing is as simple as redrawing the `PixelMap` to the `DrawingArea`.

To draw a `PixelMap` to a `DrawingArea`, we can use the `draw(...PixelMap...)` method provided by the `DrawingArea` class.

```
void DrawingArea::draw(const Context    &context,
                       const PixelMap    &pmap,
                       int               locx,
                       int               locy)
{
    XCopyArea(display,
              (Pixmap) pmap,
              XtWindow(rtr.mrep),
              (GC) context,
              0, 0,
              pmap.getWidth(), pmap.getHeight(),
              locx, locy) ;
}
```

Similarly, we can capture part or all of the picture displayed in a `DrawingArea` object by using the `capture()` method.

```
void DrawingArea::capture(const Context    &context,
                          PixelMap         &pmap,
                          int              locx,
                          int              locy) const
```

```
{
    XCopyArea(display,
              XtWindow(rtr.mrep),
              (Pixmap) pmap,
              (GC) context,
              locx, locy,
              pmap.getWidth(), pmap.getHeight(),
              0, 0) ;
}
```

Of course, many other methods can be formulated for the DrawingArea class, based on the needs of specific applications.

The drawing area is a prime candidate for the workspace of a MainWindow, especially when drawing or rendering pictures is the primary purpose of an application. We will see some examples of using DrawingArea objects in Sections 9.1 and 9.2.

## CHAPTER 8

Advanced Graphical Objects

In the preceding chapter, we discussed how to encapsulate some useful representative Motif widgets into library classes. However, this is not all we can do with Motif. We can also formulate some very advanced interface elements using other Motif widgets or various combinations of these widgets.

8.1 Custom Dialogs

In Section 7.9 we introduced the `Dialog` class tree for simple dialogs. These dialogs were described collectively as an essential mode of communication between the application and the end user. However, it would be nice to extend the `Dialog` class so that <u>any</u> `GraphicalObject` could be presented to the end user.

We introduce the `CustomDialog` class to our library for just this purpose. A "custom" dialog means just that: the user is able to customize the dialog to present <u>any</u> `GraphicalObject`.

A custom dialog (like a simple dialog) is divided into two regions. The top region is called the *control area,* and the bottom region is called the *action area* (see Heller, 1992). A control area contains the primary interface element for end user interaction. For simple dialogs, these are Motif `Label` and `TextField` widgets, among others. For custom dialogs, these can be anything. An action area contains the dialog buttons with which the end user indicates the disposition of the dialog. This end user disposition can be approval, cancellation, or, in some cases, application.

The `CustomDialog` class is derived directly from class `Dialog`.

```
// Includes
#include "Dialog.h"

// Forward declarations
class CString ;

// Defines
#define NUM_BUTTONS Dialog::UNKNOWN

class CustomDialog : public Dialog
{
  protected:

    GraphicalObject       *controlArea ;
    Separator             *separator ;
    Form                  *actionArea ;
    TextButton            *button    [NUM_BUTTONS] ;
    CallbackHandler        activate  [NUM_BUTTONS] ;
    void                  *udata     [NUM_BUTTONS] ;

    inline Widget findButton(StandardButton b) const
    { return (Widget) *(button[b]) ; }
        // Finds standard dialog button

    friend void customButtonCB(GraphicalObject &,
                               CallbackType,
                               void *);
    // Updates state of dialog when a button
    // is pressed and invokes any registered user
```

```
    // callback handlers

    TextButton *createButton(int   buttonPos,
                             int &buttonCount) ;
      // Creates buttons for custom dialogs

  public:

    CustomDialog(const CString            &name,
             const GraphicalObject    *parent = NULL) ;
      // Constructor

    ~CustomDialog(void) ;
      // Destructor

    void customize(GraphicalObject &controlArea, ;
                  Boolean           createOK     = TRUE,
                  Boolean           createCancel = TRUE,
                  Boolean           createApply  = FALSE,
                  Boolean           createHelp   = FALSE) ;
      //Customize a custom dialog

    inline void setButtonLabel(StandardButton b,
                             const CString &label) ;
    { button[b]->setLabel(label) ; }
      // Overloaded label set method

    void registerCallback   (CallbackType,
                             CallbackHandler, void *)
    void unregisterCallback (CallbackType) ;
      // Overloaded callback registration methods
} ;
```

The CustomDialog class adds some data members to the Dialog class, which are used to store the various GraphicalObjects for customization.

- controlArea: This is actually a GraphicalObject instance specified by the user as the primary interface element for the dialog.
- separator: This is a Separator that is used to indicate the boundary between the control and action areas of the dialog.
- actionArea: This is a Form that is used to arrange the standard dialog buttons for approval, cancellation, application, and help.
- button: This is an array of TextButton objects representing the standard dialog buttons for approval, cancellation, application, and help.
- activate: This is an array of user activation callbacks, one per button, which the user may have registered with the CustomDialog.
- udata: This is an array of user data, one per button, which the user may have registered with the CustomDialog with an activation callback.

Because we explicitly manage the standard dialog buttons, we must make sure that CustomDialogs behave as any other GraphicalObject.

8.1.1   Construction and Destruction

We create CustomDialog instances by providing the name and parent of the dialog, as usual. The CustomDialog constructor invokes the Dialog constructor with the Motif dialog creation function XmCreateFormDialog().

```
// Includes
#include "CustomDialog.h"
#include "CString.h"

#define ButtonLoop(i) for (i = 0 ; i < NUM_BUTTONS ; i++)

CustomDialog::CustomDialog(const CString          &name,
                           const GraphicalObject   *parent):
                           Dialog(XmCreateFormDialog, name,
                                  parent)
{
  int i ;

  // Invalidate data members
  ButtonLoop(i)
```

```
{
  button[i]       = NULL ;
  activate[i]     = NULL ;
  udata[i]        = NULL ;
}
actionArea        = NULL ;
separator         = NULL ;
controlArea       = NULL ;

  // Hide buttons until explicitly shown
  hideButton(APPLY) ;
  hideButton(HELP) ;
}
```

The body of the `CustomDialog` constructor invalidates the data members and hides the help and application buttons by default.

When destroying a `CustomDialog` instance, we must be sure to destroy all of the data members explicitly. However, the user is responsible for destroying the `controlArea` data member.

```
CustomDialog::~CustomDialog(void)
{
    int i ;

    // Destroy graphical objects
    // NOTE: the controlArea member will be destroyed by
    //       the user
    ButtonLoop(i) if (button[i]) delete button[i] ;
    if (actionArea) delete actionArea ;
    if (separator) delete separator ;
}
```

8.1.2 Customizing

Once we have created a `CustomDialog` instance, we use it as the parent for whatever `GraphicalObject` we will be using as the control area. Once we have created the control area `GraphicalObject` in the application, we must tell the `CustomDialog` about it by calling the `customize()` method.

```
void CustomDialog::customize(GraphicalObject &ctrlArea,
                             Boolean        createOK,
                             Boolean        createCancel,
                             Boolean        createApply,
                             Boolean        createHelp)
{
    int i ;

    // If dialog has already been customized,
    // get rid of the old customization
    ButtonLoop(i) if (button[i]) delete button[i] ;
    if (separator) delete separator ;
    if (actionArea) delete actionArea ;

    // Store the control area
    controlArea = &ctrlArea ;

    // Create the separator
    separator = new Separator("sep", this) ;

    Boolean cflag[Dialog::UNKNOWN] ;
    int     bCnt = 0 ;

    //Initialize create flags
    if (cflag[Dialog::OK]     = createOK)       bCnt++ ;
    if (cflag[Dialog::CANCEL] = createCancel)   bCnt++ ;
    if (cflag[Dialog::APPLY]  = createApply)    bCnt++ ;
    if (cflag[Dialog::HELP]   = createHelp)     bCnt++ ;

    //Create action area
    actionArea = new Form("actionArea", this, TIGHTNESS *
                          bCnt + 1) ;

    //Create the desired buttons
    bCnt = 0
    ButtonLoop(i)
         if (cflag[i]) button[i] = createButton(i, bCnt) ;
```

```
Widget ca = (Widget) *controlArea ;

// Special case for composites which allow scrolling
if (XtClass(XtParent(ca)) == xmScrolledWindowWidgetClass)
    ca = XtParent(ca) ;

// Attach

XtVaSetValues(ca,
                XmNtopAttachment,    XmATTACH_FORM,
                XmNleftAttachment,   XmATTACH_FORM,
                XmNrightAttachment,  XmATTACH_FORM,
                XmNbottomAttachment, XmATTACH_WIDGET,
                XmNbottomWidget,     (Widget) *separator,
                NULL) ;

XtVaSetValues((Widget)            *separator,
                XmNleftAttachment,   XmATTACH_FORM,
                XmNrightAttachment,  XmATTACH_FORM,
                XmNbottomAttachment, XmATTACH_WIDGET,
                XmNbottomWidget,     (Widget)*actionArea,
                NULL) ;

XtVaSetValues((Widget)              *actionArea,
                XmNleftAttachment,   XmATTACH_FORM,
                XmNrightAttachment,  XmATTACH_FORM,
                XmNbottomAttachment, XmATTACH_FORM,
                NULL) ;

// Manage the children
controlArea->manage() ;
separator->manage() ;
actionArea->manage() ;
}
```

This method creates all of the GraphicalObjects that comprise a Custom-Dialog instance and attaches them to each other and to the Motif Form widget created by the Motif dialog creation function XmCreateFormDialog().

Notice that there is a special case for control areas which are represented by Motif ScrolledWindow widgets. This is because such widgets are composite, and we need to use the root of the composite widget tree for form attachment.

The customize() method makes use of the CustomDialog class friend function called createButton() to actually create the button widgets.

```
#define TIGHTNESS 15

TextButton *CustomDialog::createButton(int    buttonPos,
                                       int &buttonCount)
{
    const char *label ;

    // Figure out button label
    if        (buttonPos == 0) label = Dialog::OK_LABEL ;
    else if   (buttonPos == 1) label = Dialog::APPLY_LABEL ;
    else if   (buttonPos == 2) label = Dialog::CANCEL_LABEL ;
    else                       label = Dialog::HELP_LABEL ;

    // Calculate button position
    int lPos = TIGHTNESS * buttonCount++ + 1;
    int rPos = lPos + TIGHTNESS - 1;

    // Create button
    TextButton *button = new TextButton(label, actionArea) ;

    // Set button resources unique to custom dialogs
    actionArea->attachPosition (*button, Form::LEFT,   lPos) ;
    actionArea->attachForm     (*button, Form::TOP) ;
    actionArea->attachForm     (*button, Form::BOTTOM) ;
    actionArea->attachPosition (*button, Form::RIGHT,  rPos) ;

    // Register state callback for button
    button->registerCallback(GraphicalObject::CB_ACTIVE,
                             customButtonCB,
                             this) ;
```

```
    //Manage button
    button->manage() ;

    return button ;
}
```

This function creates a Motif `PushButton` widget and adds it to the `Form` widget for the action area. In doing so, it calculates the correct position of the button within the region. Finally, it adds the internal dialog state callback handler `customButtonCB()` as the activation callback for the given button.

8.1.3 Managing Custom Dialog Buttons

In the declaration of the `Dialog` class, we presented a function called `stateCB()` which was registered as a callback handler for some special Motif callback resources peculiar to simple dialogs. Unfortunately, there are no such resources for Motif `FormDialog` widgets. These resources are:

- `XmNokCallback`

- `XmNapplyCallback`

- `XmNcancelCallback`

- `XmNhelpCallback`

Each of these resources corresponds to a standard dialog button in a simple dialog. Since we are managing the dialog buttons ourselves, we must provide the user with a mechanism for registering these callbacks. Callback registration must be done in such a way that the mechanism is transparent to the user, so that the there is no difference between simple and custom dialogs with respect to the class interface.

We hide the differences between simple and custom dialogs by overriding the `registerCallback()` and `unregisterCallback()` methods provided by the `GraphicalObject` class. The objective is to map each simple dialog Motif callback resource to the activation callback resource for a custom dialog button.

```
void CustomDialog::registerCallback(CallbackType    type,
                                    CallbackHandler  cb,
                                    void             *data)
{
```

```
StandardButton b ;

// See which callback type the user is registering
switch (type)
{
  case CB_OK:
    b = OK ;
    break ;

  case CB_CANCEL:
    b = CANCEL ;
    break ;

  case CB_APPLY:
    b = APPLY ;
    break ;

  case CB_HELP:
    b = HELP ;
    break ;

  // If it is not a button callback, just pass it
  // through to GraphicalObject
  default:
    GraphicalObject::registerCallback(type, cb, data) ;
    return ;
}

activate[b]    = cb ;
udata[b]       = udata ;
}
```

We first figure out which simple dialog button callback the user is requesting. If the user is not requesting any such callback, we pass the user callback and data along to the registerCallback() method for Graphical-Object.

When unregistering a dialog button callback for a CustomDialog, we use the method unregisterCallback().

```
void CustomDialog::unregisterCallback(CallbackType type)
{
    StandardButton b ;

    // See which callback type the user is registering
    switch (type)
    {
      case CB_OK:
        b = OK ;
        break ;

      case CB_CANCEL:
        b = CANCEL ;
        break ;

      case CB_APPLY:
        b = APPLY ;
        break ;

      case CB_HELP:
        b = HELP ;
        break ;

      // If it is not a button callback, just pass it
      // through to GraphicalObject
      default:
        GraphicalObject::unregisterCallback(type) ;
        return ;
    }

    activate[b]  = NULL ;
    udata[b]= NULL ;
}
```

Remember that in the previous section we registered an activation callback handler called `customButtonCB()` when creating each standard dialog button for a `CustomDialog` instance. This handler performs two major tasks:

1. It changes the state of the dialog when a standard dialog button is depressed by the end user.
2. It calls the user callback handler corresponding to the simple dialog button callback resources disussed above.

Every time `customButtonCB()` is invoked for a `CustomDialog` button, we translate the button into a Motif reason code for the simple dialog button callback resource. We then explicitly invoke the internal callback handler `stateCB()`, declared in the `Dialog` class with the modified call data. This will set the appropriate state for the `CustomDialog` instance.

```
static int SimpleReasonLookup[] =
{
    XmCR_OK, XmCR_APPLY, XmCR_CANCEL, XmCR_HELP
} ;


//Lookup for callback reasons
static GraphicalObject::CallbackType CallbackTypeLookup[] =
{
  GraphicalObject::CB_OK,
  GraphicalObject::CB_APPLY,
  GraphicalObject::CB_CANCEL,
  GraphicalObject::CB_HELP
} ;


void customButtonCB(GraphicalObject              &button,
                    GraphicalObject::CallbackType  reason,
                    void                          *udata)


{
    CustomDialog    *dialog = (CustomDialog*) udata ;
    int             i ;

    // Find custom dialog button
    ButtonLoop(i) if (&button == dialog->button[i]) break ;

    XmAnyCallbackStruct cbs ;
```

```
    // Set the reason
    cbs.reason = SimpleReasonLookup[i] ;

    // Explicitly invoke Dialog internal state callback
    stateCB(button, dialog, &cbs) ;

    // Invoke user callback handler, if any
    if (dialog->activate[i])
        dialog->activate[i](*dialog,
                            CallbackTypeLookup[i]
                            dialog->udata[i]) ;
}
```

This handler compares the button for which the callback was triggered to the standard buttons for the dialog passed as user data. It then invokes state-CB() with the appropriate arguments. Finally, it checks to see whether the user has registered an activation callback for the dialog and, if so, invokes it.

8.1.4 Using Custom Dialogs

Let's revisit the RadioBox example we first saw in Section 7.10.6. This fragment allows the end user to pick which features are displayed in a hypothetical Map class object. This time, however, we use a CustomDialog to present the RadioBox to the end user for temporary interaction. We will now allow the end user to set the toggles without affecting the Map, and then change the displayed features all at once when the dialog is approved.

```
...
#include "RadioBox.h"
#include "CustomDialog.h"
#include "CString.h"
#include "Map.h"   // A hypothetical geographic map class

// Feature name strings
extern char *FeatureName[] =
{
    "highways", "railroads", "lakes",
```

```
        "rivers", "gullies", "side streets"
} ;

// Defined elsewhere
extern GraphicalObject *parent ;

void changeMapFeatureDisplay(Map *map)
{
    CustomDialog dialog ("featureDisplayDialog", parent) ;
    RadioBox box          ("changeDisplayBox",
                           &dialog,
                           RadioBox::MANY,
                           2) ;

    uint i ;

    // Add the toggles
    for (i = 0 ; i < Map::NUM_FEATURES ; i++)
        box.addToggle(FeatureName[i]) ;

    // Customize the dialog
    dialog.customize(box) ;

    // Place dialog on screen
    dialog.pose() ;

    // Set the displayed features
    if (not dialog.wasCancelled())
    {
      for (i = 0 ; i < Map::NUM_FEATURES ; i++)
          map->setFeatureDisplay((Map::Feature) i,
                                 box.isSet(i)) ;
    }
}
...
```

Notice that we can accomplish the same thing by using the dialog button call-backs.

```
...
#include "RadioBox.h"
#include "CString.h"
#include "CustomDialog.h"
#include "Map.h"     // A hypothetical geographic map class

// Feature name strings
extern char *FeatureName[] ;

// Defined elsewhere
extern GraphicalObject     *parent ;
extern Map                 *map ;

// Dialog button callback handler
void buttonCB(GraphicalObject                 &gobj,
           GraphicalObject::CallbackType      type,
           RadioBox                           *box)
{
    CustomDialog *dialog = (CustomDialog *) &gobj ;

    // See if we should update the map
    if (type == GraphicalObject::CB_OK)
    {
      int i;

      for (i = 0 ; i < Map::NUM_FEATURES ; i++)
          map->setFeatureDisplay((Map::Feature) i,
                                 box->isSet(i)) ;
    }

    // Clean up
    delete dialog ;
    delete box ;
}

void changeMapFeatureDisplay(void)
```

```
{
    CustomDialog *dialog =
        new CustomDialog ("featureDisplayDialog", parent) ;
    RadioBox *box =
        new RadioBox    ("changeDisplayBox",
                         dialog,
                         RadioBox::MANY,
                         2) ;

    // Register callbacks
    dialog->registerCallback
        (GraphicalObject::CB_OK, buttonCB, box) ;
    dialog->registerCallback
        (GraphicalObject::CB_CANCEL, buttonCB, box) ;

    uint i ;

    // Add the toggles
    for (i = 0 ; i < Map::NUM_FEATURES ; i++)
        box->addToggle(FeatureName[i]) ;

    // Customize the dialog
    dialog->customize(*box) ;

    // Place dialog on screen
    dialog->pose(Dialog::NO_WAIT) ;
}
...
```

The CustomDialog can be seen in Figure 8.1.

A RadioBox is not the only GraphicalObject that can be placed in a CustomDialog. To see this, let's reexamine the code fragment concerning the use of Scale objects, first seen in Section 7.11.1. We will also adapt this fragment to use a CustomDialog for temporary interaction with the end user.

```
// Includes
#include "Scale.h"
```

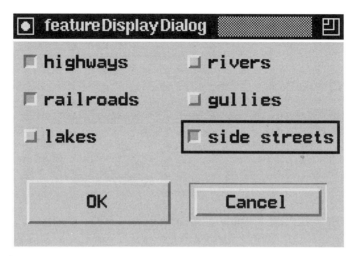

Figure 8.1. A `RadioBox` in a `CustomDialog`.

```
#include "CString.h"
#include "CustomDialog.h"
#include "EditArea.h" // A hypothetical text editor class

// Defined elsewhere
extern GraphicalObject *parent ;

void changeBlankLines(EditArea *edit)
{
    CustomDialog dialog ("blankLinesDialog", parent) ;
    Scale        scale  ("blankLinesScale", &dialog) ;

    // Set scale bounds
    scale.setBounds(10) ;

    // Set initial value for scale
    scale = (double) edit->getBlankLines() ;

    // Set scale label
    scale.setLabel("Number of blank lines") ;
```

```
// Customize the dialog
dialog.customize(scale) ;

// Place dialog on screen
dialog.pose() ;

// Set the number of blank lines
if (not dialog.wasCancelled())
    edit->setBlankLines((uint) ((double) scale)) ;
}
```

Once again, we do not actually perform any updates until the CustomDialog is approved by the end user. This CustomDialog can be seen in Figure 8.2.

8.2 Advanced Text Fields

In Section 7.8 we were introduced to the TextField class, which permitted end users to enter a text string into the application via the GUI. However, we can make text fields much more powerful by extending them in a couple of ways.

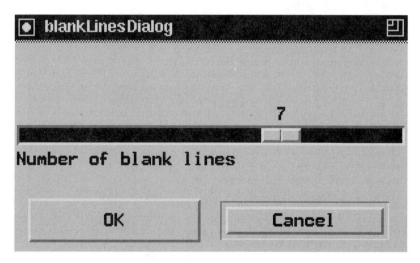

Figure 8.2. A Scale in a CustomDialog.

8.2.1 Self-Validating Text Fields

We can extend the `TextField` class so that instances can validate themselves according to user-specified criteria. For example, we may want to force the end user to enter only numbers into a text field. We can do this by forcing the text field to reject all characters but digit characters and the '+' and '-' characters.

We extend the `TextField` class by deriving a new class called `SVTextField` for "self-validating" text field.

```
// Includes
#include "TextField.h"

// Forward declarations
class CString ;

class SVTextField : public TextField
{
  public:

    // User validation callback handler prototype
    typedef Boolean (* ValidateCallback)(SVTextField &field,
                                         CString   &text,
                                         uint      currIns,
                                         uint      startPos,
                                         uint      endPos,
                                         void      *udata) ;


  protected:

    ValidateCallback      cb ;
    void                  *udata ;

    friend void validateCB(Widget      w,
                           XtPointer   textField,
                           XtPointer   cbs) ;
      // Internal validation callback
```

```
public:

   SVTextField(const CString         &name,
               const GraphicalObject *parent = NULL ,
               uint                   cwidth = DefaultWidth,
               uint                   maxLen = Unlimited) ;
      // Constructor

   inline ~SVTextField(void) {} // NULL
      // Destructor

   inline void setValidateCallback(ValidateCallback   ucb,
                                   void         *data = NULL)
   { cb = ucb ; udata = data ; }
      // Sets verification callback
} ;
```

The key to providing self-validation is the SVTextField nested prototype ValidateCallback. This callback is invoked when the end user modifies the text in a SVTextField. Functions matching the prototype return a Boolean value indicating whether the modification was approved. They are passed the following data every time the text in a SVTextField is modified.

- field: This is the SVTextField instance for which the callback was registered.
- text: This is text representing the portion of the SVTextField contents the end user has attempted to change. This text is about to be placed in the SVTextField. The user callback handler may modify this value!
- currIns: The character position at which newly modified text, if any, was inserted into the SVTextField.
- startPos: The character position at which the modification begins for the SVTextField.
- endPos: The character position at which the modification ends for the SVTextField.
- udata: The user data, if any, registered with the user callback handler for the SVTextField.

A `SVTextField` instance is constructed in exactly the same manner as is a `TextField`.

```
extern "C"
{
#      include <Xm/TextF.h>
}
#include "SVTextField.h"
#include "CString.h"

SVTextField::SVTextField(const CString          &name,
                        const GraphicalObject  *parent,
                        uint                    cwidth,
                        uint                    maxLen) :
                        TextField(name, parent, cwidth,
                                        maxLen)
{
    cb    = NULL ;
    udata = NULL ;

    // Add internal validation callback handler
    XtAddCallback(rtr.mrep,
                XmNmodifyVerifyCallback,
                validateCB, this) ;
}
```

The constructor initializes the new data members and registers a validation callback handler with Xt. This handler is `validateCB()`.

```
void validateCB(Widget w, XtPointer calld, XtPointer clientd)
{
    SVTextField *field = (SVTextField*) calld ;
    XmTextVerifyCallbackStruct *cbs =
        (XmTextVerifyCallbackStruct*) clientd ;

    // If there is no user callback, approve
    if (not field->cb)
```

```
{
  cbs->doit = True ;
  return ;
}

CString                          text ;
int                              i ;

// String in callback data is NOT null-terminated,
// so copy character by character
if (cbs->text->ptr)
{
  for (i = 0 ; i < cbs->text->length ; i++)
      text += cbs->text->ptr[i] ;
}

// Invoke user callback
cbs->doit = field->cb(*field,
                      text,
                      (uint) cbs->currInsert,
                      (uint) cbs->startPos,
                      (uint) cbs->endPos,
                      field->udata) ;

// Re-assign modification string to callback structure,
// because user callback may have changed it
if (cbs->doit)
{
  // First free the existing text
  XtFree(cbs->text->ptr) ;

  // Set the length of the new text
  cbs->text->length = (int) text.length() ;

  // Set the new text
  if (text.length() == 0) cbs->text->ptr = NULL ;
  else
```

```
    {
        cbs->text->ptr = XtMalloc(text.length()) ;
        for (i = 0 ; i < (int) text.length() ; i++)
            cbs->text->ptr[i] = text[i] ;
    }
  }
}
```

This internal handler makes extensive use of the XmTextVerifyCallback-Struct * variable called cbs. This structure is used to communicate modification approval back to Motif. The doit field tells Motif whether the modification was approved. The text field contains the modified text. This itself may have changed within the user callback handler, if the original modification does not satisfy user validation criteria.

Let's take a look at how we would use a SVTextField in a "real" application. The following code fragment creates a SVTextField object within a CustomDialog and sets the validation callback to accept only numbers with no more than the specified number of digits. The dialog is illustrated in Figure 8.3.

```
...
// Includes
extern "C"
{
#  include <ctype.h>
}
```

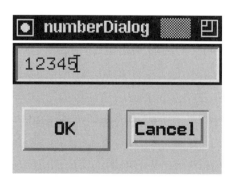

Figure 8.3. A CustomDialog for number entry.

```
#include "SVTextField.h"
#include "CustomDialog.h"

// Defined elsewhere
extern GraphicalObject *parent ;

// Validation callback
static Boolean validateNumber(SVTextField   &field,
                              CString        &text,
                              uint           ci,
                              uint           sp,
                              uint           ep,
                              void          *udata)
{
    uint maxLen = (uint) udata ;

    // See if there is anything to validate
    if (text.isBlank()) return TRUE ;

    // Get contents of field
    CString currText = (CString) field ;

    // See if the new text is over maximum digits
    if (currText.length() + text.length() > maxLen)
        return FALSE ;
    if (ci + text.length() > maxLen) return FALSE ;

    uint    i ;

    // Make sure all of the characters are digits
    for (i = 0 ; i < text.length() ; i++)
        if (not isdigit(text[i])) return FALSE ;

    return TRUE ;
}

// The maximum number of digits in a user number
```

```
#define MAX_USER_NUMBER 10

long getUserNumber(void)
{
    CustomDialog dialog("numberDialog", parent) ;
    SVTextField field("numberField",
                      &dialog,
                      MAX_USER_NUMBER, MAX_USER_NUMBER) ;

    // Set the callback
    field.setValidateCallback(validateNumber, (void *)
                              MAX_USER_NUMBER) ;

    // Customize the dialog
    dialog.customize(field) ;

    // Wait for end user response
    dialog.pose() ;

    // Return the end user value
    return dialog.wasCancelled() ? 0 : (long) ((CString)
                                                field) ;
}
...
```

The next code fragment illustrates a SVTextField contained in a CustomDialog for password validation. The validation callback replaces every character typed by the end user with the '*' character. This can be very useful when entering passwords into the application interface, for example. The dialog is illustrated in Figure 8.4.

```
...
// Includes
#include "SVTextField.h"
#include "CustomDialog.h"
#include "CString.h"
```

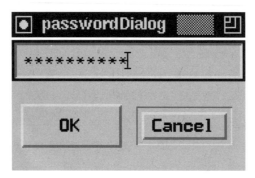

Figure 8.4. A CustomDialog for password entry.

```
// Defined elsewhere
extern GraphicalObject *parent ;

// Validation callback
static Boolean starReplace(SVTextField    &field,
                           CString         &text,
                           uint             ci,
                           uint             sp,
                           uint             ep,
                           void            *udata)
{
    CString *string = (CString *) udata ;

    // Don't forget to change the actual string
    if(sp<ci)
      *string = string->subString (0,String->length()-1);
    else*string +=text ;

    uint    i ;

    // Change all of the characters to '*'
    for (i = 0 ; i < text.length() ; i++) text[i] = '*' ;

    return TRUE ;
}

CString getPassword(void)
{
```

```
CustomDialog  dialog("passwordDialog", parent) ;
SVTextField   field("passwordField", &dialog) ;

CString password;

// Set the callback
field.setValidateCallback(starReplace, &password) ;

// Customize the dialog
dialog.customize(field) ;

// Wait for end user response
dialog.pose() ;

// Return the end user password
return dialog.wasCancelled() ?
    CString::Empty : password ;
}
...
```

Eventually, we could create a library containing only various validation callbacks for SVTextFields. This would allow us to construct various data entry applications in a jiffy!

8.2.2 Labeled Text Fields

In data entry applications it is often the case that we must present a number of SVTextFields grouped together in a Form. However, this presentation may confuse the end user, because the text fields are not labeled appropriately.

To solve this problem, we formulate a new library class called LTextField, for "labeled" text field (Figure 8.5). This class is multiply derived from the Form, SVTextField, and Label classes.

```
#include "Form.h"
#include "Label.h"
#include "SVTextField.h"
```

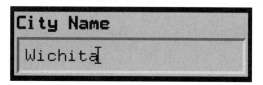

Figure 8.5. A LTextField.

```
// Forward declarations
class CString ;

class LTextField : private Form, public SVTextField,
                   public Label
{
  public:

      LTextField(const CString &name,
      const GraphicalObject    *parent  = NULL,
      uint                      cwidth  =
                                TextField::DefaultWidth,
      uint                      maxLen  =
                                TextField::Unlimited,
      Boolean                   stretch = FALSE) ;
        // Constructor

      inline ~LTextField(void) {} // NULL
        // Destructor

      inline operator Graphical Object *(void) const
      {return (Form*) this;}
        // Cast to graphical object

      inline operator Widget(void) const
      { return Form::operator Widget() ; }
        // Cast to widget

      inline void manage       (void) const
      { Form::manage() ; }
```

```
        inline void unmanage      (void) const
        { Form::unmanage() ; }
        inline void realize       (void) const
        { Form::realize() ; }
        inline void unrealize     (void) const
        { Form::unrealize() ; }
        inline Boolean isRealized (void) const
        { return Form::isRealized() ; }
} ;
```

When dealing with the Motif widget corresponding to a LTextField
instance, we want it to act like a Form. For this reason, we override the Widget cast operator to return the widget corresponding to the Form portion of
the instance. When a LTextField is managed, we want the Form portion to
be managed, so we override the manage() and unmanage() methods as
well. The same goes for the realization methods.

When performing construction on a LTextField object, we must perform
the construction on the Form part of the object first, because we will use the
Form as a parent to both the SVTextField portion and the Label portion
of the object.

```
extern "C"
{
#  include <Xm/TextF.h>
#  include <Xm/Form.h>
#  include <Xm/Label.h>
}
#include "LTextField.h"
#include "CString.h"

LTextField::LTextField(const CString          &name,
                       const GraphicalObject  *parent,
                       uint                   columns,
                       uint                   maxLen,
                       Boolean                stretch) :
    Form(name, parent),
    Label(name + "_label", (Form *) this),
```

```
        SVTextField(name + "_field",
                    (Form *) this, columns, maxLen)
{
  // Don't treat this as a tab group
  XtVaSetValues(Form::rtr.mrep,        XmNnavigationType,
                                       XmNONE, NULL) ;
  XtVaSetValues(SVTextField::rtr.mrep, XmNnavigationType,
                                       XmNONE, NULL) ;

  // When form is placed on screen, label and text field
  // should also appear
  Label::manage() ;
  SVTextField::manage() ;

  // Set up attachments
  attachForm(*((Label *) this),       Form::LEFT) ;
  attachForm(*((Label *) this),       Form::TOP) ;
  attachForm(*((SVTextField *) this), Form::BOTTOM) ;
  attachForm(*((SVTextField *) this), Form::LEFT) ;
  attachObjects(*((SVTextField *) this), *((Label *) this),
                                       Form::TOP, 0) ;

  // Should we allow the text field and label to stretch?
  if (stretch)
  {
    attachForm(*((Label *) this),       Form::RIGHT) ;
    attachForm(*((SVTextField *) this), Form::RIGHT) ;
  }
}
```

When traversing through a group of LTextFields, we do not want each field to act as a *tab group* (see Heller, 1992). A tab group is a major subset of graphical elements within the interface. We can switch between tab groups by pressing the <TAB> key. For example, a ControlPanel instance would act as a tab group, and the PictureButtons contained in the panel would be members of the group.

Under most circumstances we want a `LTextField` to act as a simple graphical element, <u>not</u> as a tab group. Therefore, we must clear the `XmNnavigationType` resource for the `Form` and `SVTextField` portions of a `LTextField` instance.

After dealing with the navigation issue, we attach the `Label` and `SVTextField` to each other and to the `Form`, with the `Label` on top. If we wish to allow the end user to resize the `LTextField`, we must attach the `Label` and `SVTextField` to the right side of the `Form`.

8.2.3 Data Entry with Validation

Let's take a look at a code fragment that illustrates how to build a `Custom-Dialog` for data entry. This dialog is illustrated in Figure 8.6.

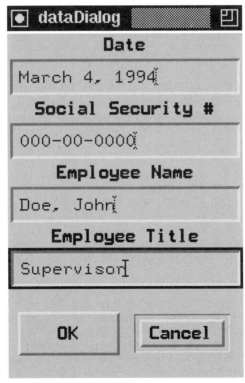

Figure 8.6. A `CustomDialog` for data entry.

```
...
// Includes
#include "CustomDialog.h"
#include "LTextField.h"
#include "UserStruct.h" // A hypothesized class
#define GOBJ(g) *((GraphicalObject*)g)

// Defined elsewhere
extern GraphicalObject *parent ;

// Validation callbacks defined elsewhere
extern SVTextField::ValidateCallback validateDate ;
extern SVTextField::ValidateCallback validateSSNumber ;
extern SVTextField::ValidateCallback validateName ;
extern SVTextField::ValidateCallback validateTitle ;

UserStruct *getData(void)
{
    CustomDialog dialog      ("dataDialog",   parent) ;
    Form         form        ("dataForm",    &dialog) ;
    LTextField   dateField   ("dateField",   &form),
                 ssField     ("ssField",     &form) ,
                 nameField   ("nameField",   &form) ,
                 titleField  ("titleField",  &form) ;

    // Set the labels
    dateField.Label::changeText   ("Date") ;
    ssField.Label::changeText     ("Social Security #") ;
    nameField.Label::changeText   ("Employee Name") ;
    titleField.Label::changeText  ("Employee Title") ;

    // Place fields under management of form
    dateField.manage() ;
    ssField.manage() ;
    nameField.manage() ;
    titleField.manage() ;
```

```
    // Set the validation callbacks
    dateField.setValidateCallback        (validateDate) ;
    ssField.setValidateCallback          (validateSSNumber) ;
    nameField.setValidateCallback        (validateName) ;
    titleField.setValidateCallback       (validateTitle) ;

    // Set up form attachments among fields
    form.attachForm      (GOBJ(dateField), Form::TOP) ;
    form.attachForm      (GOBJ(dateField)  Form::RIGHT) ;
    form.attachForm      (GOBJ(dateField), Form::LEFT) ;
    form.attachObjects   (GOBJ(ssField),
                         (GOBJ(dateField), Form::TOP) ;

    form.attachForm      (GOBJ(ssField),   Form::RIGHT) ;
    form.attachForm      (GOBJ(ssField),   Form::LEFT) ;
    form.attachObjects   (GOBJ(nameField),
                         (GOBJ(ssField),   Form::TOP) ;

    form.attachForm      (GOBJ(nameField), Form::RIGHT) ;
    form.attachForm      (GOBJ(nameField), Form::LEFT) ;
    form.attachObjects   (GOBJ(titleField),
                         (GOBJ(nameField), Form::TOP) ;

    form.attachForm      (GOBJ(titleField),Form::RIGHT) ;
    form.attachForm      (GOBJ(titleField),Form::LEFT) ;
    form.attachForm      (GOBJ(titleField, Form::BOTTOM) ;

    // Customize the dialog
    dialog.customize(form) ;

    // Wait for user response
    dialog.pose() ;

    UserStruct  *ustruct = NULL ;
```

```
    // Populate the user structure
    if (not dialog.wasCancelled())
    {
      ustruct = new UserStruct ;
      // Populate the structure...
    }

    return ustruct ;
}
```

This fragment builds a `Form` full of `LTextField` objects for the current date and some employee information. The `Form` is placed in the dialog and the dialog is posed. While the end user is entering the data, each `LTextField` in the dialog is validating itself. Once the end user dismisses the dialog, we can populate some hypothetical user structure and return it.

8.3 Scrolling Text Windows

Motif `ScrolledText` widgets are used to present the end user with an extremely well-thought-out interface for editing large amounts of text. This widget emulates the EMACS text editor by providing a similar keyboard interface. This widget is represented in our library by the `ScrollingText` class. This class is an excellent candidate for the workspace of a `MainWindow`, as discussed in Section 7.2.

```
// Includes
#include "GraphicalObject.h"
#include "CString.h"

class ScrollingText : public GraphicalObject
{
  public:

    ScrollingText(const  CString            &name,
                  const GraphicalObject   *parent    = NULL,
                  Boolean                  editable   = TRUE,
```

```
            uint                    rows     = 0,
            uint                    columns  = 0) ;
// Constructor

inline ~ScrollingText(void) {} // NULL
  // Destructor

void setText(const CString &text) ;
  // Replaces contents of window

CString getText(void) const ;
  // Obtains currently displayed text

void setSelection(uint first, uint last) ;
  // Sets selected text

CString getSelection(void) const ;
  // Obtains currently selected text

long length(void) const ;
  // Obtains length of text in object

void appendText(const CString   &text,
           Boolean              show = TRUE) ;
  // Appends text to existing text within instance

void insertText(const CString   &text,
           long                 position,
           Boolean              show = TRUE) ;
  // Inserts text at position

void replaceText(long               first,
           long                 last,
           const CString     &newText) ;
  // Replaces text between starting and ending positions
```

Figure 8.7. A ScrollingText object.

```
void clearText(void) ;
   // Clears displayed text

long getCursorPos(void) const ;
   // Obtains current text insertion cursor position

void setCursorPos(long newPos) ;
   // Sets the text insertion cursor position
} ;
```

An example of a ScrollingText object is given in Figure 8.7.

8.3.1   Construction and Destruction

As usual, we pass the name and GraphicalObject parent to the
ScrollingText constructor. However, we also pass a flag indicating whether
the object is read-only, as well as the dimensions. The dimensions are specified
in character widths for columns and lines of text for rows.

```
// Includes
extern "C"
{
# include <Xm/Text.h>
```

```
}
#include "ScrollingText.h"

ScrollingText::ScrollingText(const CString          &name,
                            const GraphicalObject *parent,
                            Boolean               editable,
                            uint                  rows,
                            uint                  columns) :
                            GraphicalObject()
{
    // Figure out the parent
    Widget wparent = (parent ? (Widget) *parent : topLevel) ;

    Arg    argv[5] ;
    Cardinal  argc = 0 ;

    // Set the create arguments
    XtSetArg(argv[argc],    XmNeditable, (Bool) editable) ;
                                        argc++ ;
    XtSetArg(argv[argc],    XmNcursorPositionVisible,
                                        (Bool) editable) ;
                                        argc++ ;
    XtSetArg(argv[argc],    XmNeditMode, XmMULTI_LINE_EDIT) ;
                                        argc++ ;
    if (rows) XtSetArg(argv[argc],     XmNrows,    rows),
                                        argc++ ;
    if (columns) XtSetArg(argv[argc],  XmNcolumns, columns),
                                        argc++ ;

    // Create the widget
    rtr.mrep = XmCreateScrolledText(wparent,
                                    (const char *) name,
                                    argv, argc) ;
}
```

Once again, we let the GraphicalObject destructor handle the destruction of the widget, leaving the ScrollingText destructor empty.

8.3.2 Manipulating Text

The ScrollingText class provides a number of methods to perform various manipulations on any text the end user may have entered into a Scrolling-Text object. All of these are implemented as simple calls to corresponding convenience functions provided by Motif for its ScrolledText widgets.

The setText() method allows the user to place text into a Scrolling-Text object directly, bypassing the end user.

```
void ScrollingText::setText(const CString &text)
{
  XmTextSetString(rtr.mrep, (const char *) text) ;
}
```

The getText() method allows the user to retrieve all of the text from within a ScrollingText instance.

```
CString ScrollingText::getText(void) const
{
    CString text = XmTextGetString(rtr.mrep);
    return text ;
}
```

The setSelection() method allows the user to *select* some text, bypassing the end user. Selected text is any subset of the text which has been highlighted for some special purpose, such as deleting or changing the typeface.

```
void ScrollingText::setSelection(uint first, uint last)
{
    XmTextSetSelection(rtr.mrep, first, last, 0);
}
```

The user can also find out what text has been selected by calling the getSelection() method.

```
CString ScrollingText::getSelection(void) const
{
```

```
    CString text = XmTextGetSelection(rtr.mrep) ;

    return text ;
}
```

The `ScrollingText` class provides a `length()` method, which allows the user to obtain the length of the entire text within a `ScrollingText` instance.

```
long ScrollingText::length(void) const
{
    return (long) XmTextGetLastPosition(rtr.mrep);
}
```

We also allow the user to explicitly insert or append text in/to the existing text, once again bypassing the end user.

```
void ScrollingText::insertText(const CString &text,
                               long pos, Boolean show)
{
    // Insert the text
    XmTextInsert(rtr.mrep, pos, (const char *) text);

    // Conditionally force the inserted text to be displayed
    if (show) XmTextShowPosition(rtr.mrep, pos);
}

void ScrollingText::appendText(const CString &text,
                               Boolean show)
{
    // Append text
    XmTextInsert(rtr.mrep, length(), (const char *) text);

    // Conditionally force the appended text to be displayed
    if (show) XmTextShowPosition(rtr.mrep, length());
}
```

Both the `insertText()` and the `appendText()` methods allow the user to specify whether the changes are to be displayed. This is accomplished by specifying the proper flag value as an argument for the show parameter.

In addition to inserting and appending text, we also provide the replaceText() method, which allows the user to replace some text with new text.

```
void ScrollingText::replaceText(long          first,
                                long          last,
                                const CString &text)
{
    XmTextReplace(rtr.mrep, first, last, (const char *) text);
}
```

The user may also choose to erase all of the text within the ScrollingText instance, by calling the clearText() method.

```
void ScrollingText::clearText(void)
{
    XmTextSetString(rtr.mrep, NULL) ;
}
```

Finally, we allow the user to explicitly bypass the end user when manipulating the position of the insertion cursor for a ScrollingText object.

```
void ScrollingText::setCursorPos(long newPos)
{
    XmTextSetCursorPosition(rtr.mrep, newPos) ;
}

long ScrollingText::getCursorPos(void) const
{
    return (long) XmTextGetCursorPosition(rtr.mrep);
}
```

Of course, many more text manipulation methods can be added to the ScrollingText class. Most of these can be implemented in a fashion similar to the implementation of the above methods. However, whatever methods we choose should reflect the needs of the class users.

8.3.3   Using Scrolling Text Objects

As we mentioned when first introducing the `ScrollingText` class, a `ScrollingText` object is an excellent candidate for the workspace within a `MainWindow`. This is true of applications that require the end user to type large amounts of text, such as text editor or word-processing applications.

Let's take a look at how to place a `ScrollingText` object as the workspace of a `MainWindow` object.

```
// Includes
#include "MainWindow.h"
#include "PixelMap.h"
#include "ControlPanel.h"
#include "PictureButton.h"
#include "ScrollingText.h"

// Functions defined elsewhere
GraphicalObject::CallbackHandler replaceTextCB ;
GraphicalObject::CallbackHandler searchTextCB ;

main(int argc, char **argv)
{
    // Initialize environment
    GraphicalEnv::setEnvironment("stDemo", argc, argv) ;

    // Pixel maps for picture buttons
    PixelMap *pm1    = new PixelMap,
             *ipm1   = new PixelMap,
             *pm2    = new PixelMap,
             *ipm2   = new PixelMap ;

    // Read in the images
    if (not pm1->read   ("replace.pm"))    exit(1) ;
    if (not ipm1->read  ("replace.ipm"))   exit(1) ;
    if (not pm2->read   ("search.pm"))     exit(1) ;
    if (not ipm2->read  ("search.ipm"))    exit(1) ;

    MainWindow    mainWindow ("mainWindow") ;
```

```
ControlPanel   panel     ("panel",    mainWindow) ;
ScrollingText  workSpace ("edit",     &mainWindow) ;
PictureButton  pb1       ("replace",  panel, pm1, ipm1) ;
PictureButton  pb2       ("search",   panel, pm2, ipm2) ;

// Register callbacks
pb1.registerCallback(GraphicalObject::CB_ACTIVE,
                 replaceTextCB, &workSpace) ;
pb2.registerCallback(GraphicalObject::CB_ACTIVE,
                 searchTextCB,  &workSpace) ;

// Set the main window
mainWindow.set(workSpace, NULL, &panel) ;

// Put everything on screen
mainWindow.realizeAll() ;
mainWindow.manage() ; // ... and everthing else

// Start application
GraphicalEnv::startApplication() ;
}
```

In the preceding fragment we create a `MainWindow` object that contains a
`ScrollingText` object as the workspace and a `ControlPanel` containing
two buttons. These buttons invoke callbacks that allow the end user to perform text replacement and search tasks.

8.4 Scrolling Lists

Motif `ScrolledList` widgets provide a wonderful mechanism by which an
end user can select from a (possibly varying) number of named alternatives.
Basically, the end user is presented with a list of alternatives from which he
or she may select. Any time the end user makes a selection, a callback mechanism is triggered from which the selection can be processed. Motif
`ScrolledList` widgets are represented by the `ScrollingList` class in
our library.

```
// Includes
#include "GraphicalObject.h"
#include "CString.h"
#include "List.h"
// Defines
#define UintList        List<uint>
#define UintListIndex   ListIndex<uint>

class ScrollingList : public GraphicalObject
{
  public:

    enum ResizePolicy
    {
      CONSTANT,    // Width remains constant
      VARIABLE     // Resize as needed
    } ;

    enum ModeType
    {
      SINGLE,    // Single item can be selected or deselected
      BROWSE,    // Exactly one item must be selected
      MULTIPLE,  // Any number of items can be selected
      EXTENDED   // Selected items can be non-contiguous
    } ;


    enum SelectType
    {
      SELECT_ERROR,    // Exception
      INITIAL,         // Start of a new selection
      MODIFICATION,    // Modification of existing selection
      ADDITION         // Addition to existing selection
    } ;

    typedef void (* SelectHandler)(ScrollingList    &sl,
                                   SelectType        type,
```

```
                                   const UintList    &pos,
                                   void              *udata) ;
   // User selection callback prototype


   // Names end of list
   static const uint AtEnd ;

private:

   ModeType        mode ;      // Current selection mode
   SelectHandler   selCB ;     // User selection callback
                               // handler
   void            *udata ;    // User data for user selection
                               // callback

   static void handleSelectCB(Widget    w,
                              XtPointer  clientd,
                              XtPointer  calld) ;
      // Handles selection callbacks

public:

   ScrollingList(const CString    &name,
      const GraphicalObject      *parent = NULL,
      ModeType                    mode = SINGLE,
      ResizePolicy                policy = VARIABLE) ;
      // Constructor

   inline ~ScrollingList(void) {} // NULL
      // Destructor

   void setVisible(uint count) ;
      // Sets number of displayed items in list

   void setSelectionMode(ModeType mode) ;
   inline ModeType getSelectionMode(void) const
   { return mode ; }
```

```
    // Sets or obtains selection mode

uint itemCount(void) const ;
  // Obtains a count of all items

CString operator [](uint index) const ;
  // Obtains item at position

void addItem(const CString &item, uint pos = AtEnd) ;
  // Adds an item to list

void selectItem    (unsigned pos = AtEnd) ;
void selectItem    (const CString &item) ;
void selectAl      (void) ;
  // Item selection methods

void deselectItem (uint pos = AtEnd) ;
void deselectItem (const CString &item) ;
void deselectAll  (void) ;
  // Item de-selection methods

void removeItem     (uint pos = AtEnd);
void removeItem     (const CString &iname);
void removeSelected (void) ;
void removeAll      (void) ;
  // Item removal methods

void getSelected    (UintList &sel) const ;
uint selectedCount  (void) const ;
  // Obtains the list and count of selected items

void registerCallback(SelectHandler selectCB,
                      void *udata = NULL) ;
void unregisterCallback   (void) ;
  // Selection callback registration methods
};
```

As you probably have surmised, the items in a `ScrollingList` are plain old strings. A `ScrollingList` object does not attach any semantic meaning to the strings it presents to the end user, as this is outside the scope of the class. It only provides a mechanism by which the end user may communicate a subset of selected strings to the application.

The `ScrollingList` class provides a number of types that allow the user a great deal of flexibility when interacting with the end user.

- `ResizePolicy`: The user may specify whether the width of a `ScrollingList` is to remain constant or whether it is to grow as items are added such that it always remains wider than the longest string it displays.

- `ModeType`: This is an enumerator that allows the user to specify the cardinality of any selection that an end user can make.

  - `SINGLE`: The end user may select at most one item in the `ScrollingList`.

  - `BROWSE`: One and only one item in the `ScrollingList` must always be selected.

  - `MULTIPLE`: The end user may select multiple contiguous items in the `ScrollingList`.

  - `EXTENDED`: The end user may select multiple noncontiguous items in the `ScrollingList`.

- `SelectType`: When the user registers a user callback handler to handle end user selections, we use this class enumerator to communicate how the current selection is to be treated with respect to previous selections. For example, it may be the case that the end user wishes to add more items to currently selected items in the `ScrollingList`.

- `SelectHandler`: This is a prototype for selection callback handlers that the user may register with instances of the `ScrollingList` class. The parameters provide information about the `ScrollingList` in question, what type of selection has occurred, the positions of the items in the selection, and any user data the user may have registered with the callback handler.

When taken together, these types permit the user to perform almost any kind of selection interaction with an end user.

The ScrollingList class adds three new data members to the Graphical Object base class. The mode data member represents the current selection mode for the ScrollingList object. The selCB member is the user selection callback handler, which may be registered with the instance. The udata member stores any user data that may have been registered with the selection callback.

8.4.1 Construction and Destruction

The ScrollingList constructor takes the name and parent of the object, as usual. In addition, we tell the constructor which selection mode we wish the ScrollingList to operate under and whether it can grow to fully display all item strings.

```
// Includes
extern "C"
{
# include <Xm/List.h>
# include <limits.h>
}
#include "ScrollingList.h"

// For translation of class mode type to Motif type
static unsigned char SelModeLookup[] =
{
    XmSINGLE_SELECT,    XmBROWSE_SELECT,
    XmMULTIPLE_SELECT,  XmEXTENDED_SELECT
} ;

// For translation of resize policy to Motif policy
static unsigned char PolicyLookup[] =
{
    XmCONSTANT, XmVARIABLE
} ;
```

```
ScrollingList::ScrollingList(const CString        &name,
                            const GraphicalObject  *parent,
                            ScrollingList::ModeType smode,
                            ScrollingList::ResizePolicy
                                                    policy) :
                            GraphicalObject()
{
    // Figure out the parent
    Widget wparent = parent ? (Widget) *parent :
        topLevel ;

    // Initialize data members
    selCB = NULL;
    udata = NULL;

    Arg            argv[5] ;
    Cardinal       argc = 0 ;

    // Set up create arguments
    XtSetArg(argv[argc], XmNscrollingPolicy,     XmAUTOMATIC)
            argc++ ;
    XtSetArg(argv[argc], XmNautomaticSelection, False) ;
            argc++ ;
    XtSetArg(argv[argc], XmNlistSizePolicy,
                        PolicyLookup [policy]) ; argc++ ;
    XtSetArg(argv[argc], XmNvisualPolicy,
                        PolicyLookup [policy]) ; argc++ ;
    XtSetArg(argv[argc], XmNselectionPolicy,
            SelModeLookup[mode = smode]) ; argc++ ;

    // Create the scrolled list
    rtr.mrep = XmCreateScrolledList(wparent,
                                    (const char *) name,
                                    argv, argc) ;
}
```

The destructor is once again empty, as the GraphicalObject destructor will destroy the widget.

8.4.2 Changing the Number of Visible Items

The number of items in a ScrollingList may be quite large, depending on what it is used for. The user should be very careful to set the number of items the ScrollingList may display at one time to a value that is reasonable for the number of items contained in the ScrollingList. For example, if a ScrollingList contained 100 items, we would want to display a lot more than 2 items at a time. A more reasonable value might be 15 or 20.

Even though the number of visible items for any Motif ScrolledList widget can be specified in a file such as .Xdefaults, we allow the user to override this value by using the setVisible() method. This method explicitly sets the number of visible items for a ScrollingList object.

```
void ScrollingList::setVisible(uint count)
{
    XtVaSetValues(rtr.mrep,
                  XmNvisibleItemCount, (short) count,
                  NULL) ;
}
```

8.4.3 List Ordering

When we insert items into a ScrollingList, we should be careful to take advantage of any "natural" ordering of the items. For example, if we were inserting the names of months (e.g., "January" or "August") into a list, we should do this in the natural progression of months:

"January"
"February"
"March"

. . .

Such a ScrollingList is depicted in Figure 8.8.

Matching the natural order of list items to their position in the list can affect both the friendliness and performance of the interface. For example, it would be quite unfriendly to present the months to the end user in a random fashion:

Figure 8.8. A `ScrollingList`.

"February"
"October"
"April"

.   .   .

In many cases, the position of a list item within its natural ordering acts as a key to some larger set of data. For example, a payroll application may use months to index payroll data. In such a case we can dispense with manipulating the list items by their associated strings, and instead manipulate them by position.

If the natural ordering does not represent some kind of indexing (i.e., is not the key for the list items), then more code is needed to map a list item to what it represents externally. This is why list ordering can affect the performance of the interface.

When the list ordering does not key the external data, we can always fall back to the item string itself, if each string is guaranteed to be unique within a given `ScrollingList`. If this is the case, then we can use the `getKey()` method from the `CString` class to assign a unique numerical value to each string.

Our `ScrollingList` class treats all position values as 0-based, that is, starting from 0. Unfortunately, Motif uses a 1-based positioning system. Therefore, in class methods dealing with item position, we must translate position values for our 0-based system to the 1-based Motif system, and vice versa.

Motif uses the 0 position as a designation for the end of the list. For example, if we add an item to a `ScrolledList` widget at position 0, it would appear at the end of the list. In the `ScrollingList` class, we use the class constant `AtEnd` to denote the end of a list.

```
...
// Class static initializations
```

```
const uint ScrollingList::AtEnd = UINT_MAX ;
...
```

We use the maximum unsigned integer, so that we are guaranteed that a greater position can not be specified.

8.4.4 *Manipulating Items*

The ScrollingList class provides a wealth of methods for manipulating items, both by item string and by item position. First, it is always useful to be able to determine the number of items in a ScrollingList.

```
uint ScrollingList::itemCount(void) const
{
    int count ;

    XtVaGetValues(rtr.mrep, XmNitemCount, &count, NULL);
    return (uint) count;
}
```

It is also extremely useful to be able to obtain an item string if we know the position of the item within a ScrollingList.

```
CString ScrollingList::operator [](uint index) const
{
    uint count = itemCount() ;
    CString item ;

    // Check validity of position
    if (index < count)
    {
      XmStringTable    items ;
      char             *titem ;

      // Get all items
```

```
XtVaGetValues(rtr.mrep, XmNitems, &items, NULL) ;

    // Get item string at specified position
    XmStringGetLtoR(items[index],
                    XmSTRING_DEFAULT_CHARSET, &titem) ;

    // Translate to our string
    item = titem ;

    // Clean up
    XtFree(titem) ;
    }
    return item ;
}
```

The ScrollingList class also provides methods for adding an item to an instance at a specified position.

```
void ScrollingList::addItem(const CString &item, uint pos)
{
    // Translate from 0-based to 1-based position
    uint mpos = pos < itemCount() ? pos + 1 : 0 ;

    // Add the item to the list
    XmString mstring = XmStringCreateSimple
                        ((const char *) item);
    XmListAddItemUnselected(rtr.mrep, mstring, mpos);
    XmStringFree(mstring);
}
```

Of course, if we can add items to a ScrollingList by position, we should be able to remove them by position as well.

```
void ScrollingList::removeItem(uint pos)
{
    // Translate from 0-based to 1-based position
    uint mpos = pos < itemCount() ? pos + 1 : 0 ;
```

```
    // Deselect and remove item
    XmListDeselectPos(rtr.mrep, mpos) ;
    XmListDeletePos(rtr.mrep, mpos) ;
}
```

We deselect an item before deleting it so that the appropriate callback mechanisms, if any, are triggered.

The `ScrollingList` class also allows items to be removed from an instance by name.

```
void ScrollingList::removeItem(const CString &item)
{
    XmString mstring = XmStringCreateSimple((const char *)
                                            item) ;
    XmListDeselectItem(rtr.mrep, mstring) ;
    XmListDeleteItem(rtr.mrep, mstring) ;
    XmStringFree(mstring) ;
}
```

As a convenience to class users, the `ScrollingList` class provides a method that can be used to remove all of the items in an instance at once.

```
void ScrollingList::removeAll(void)
{
  XmListDeselectAllItems(rtr.mrep) ;
  XmListDeleteAllItems(rtr.mrep) ;
}
```

8.4.5 Managing Selection

There are two ways of managing selection for `ScrollingList` objects:

1. Perform no processing on selected items until the end user indicates that changes to the set of selected items are complete. This type of selection management usually occurs when a `ScrollingList` is presented in a custom dialog.
2. Perform processing on each item as it is selected.

The second case is the subject of this discussion, as it is a bit more complicated.

Take as an example the interface of a language-sensitive editor, such as EMACS. Assume that the editor is being used to write C++ code. We may wish to present the end user with a list of all reserved words for C++ and then insert the formal syntax involving a particular reserved word into the work area when it is selected. In such a case, we would need to perform processing upon each item as it is selected.

The ScrollingList class performs this kind of selection management by providing a selection callback mechanism. The user may register a callback matching the class prototype SelectHandler.

```
class ScrollingList : public GraphicalObject
{
  public:

    . . .
    typedef void (* SelectHandler)(ScrollingList    &sl,
                                   SelectType        type,
                                   const UintList   &pos,
                                   void             *udata) ;
      // User selection callback prototype
    . . .
} ;
```

Every time the end user changes the composition of the selected items, the user selection handler will be invoked. The handler receives the ScrollingList for which the change was made and how the selection should be treated with respect to prior selections. It also receives a list containing the positions of all the selected items. Finally, the handler receives any user data that the user may have registered with the handler.

User selection callback handlers are registered using the registerCallback() method provided by the ScrollingList class. This method registers the internal callback function handleSelectCB() with Xt. This callback resource for which handleSelectCB() is registered depends on the mode of selection.

```
static String SelCallbackLookup[] =
```

```
{
    XmNsingleSelectionCallback,
    XmNbrowseSelectionCallback,
    XmNmultipleSelectionCallback,
    XmNextendedSelectionCallback
} ;

void ScrollingList::registerCallback
    (ScrollingList::SelectHandler cb,
     void                          *data)
{
    // Assign data members
    selCB = cb ;
    udata = udata;

    // Add the callback
    XtAddCallback(rtr.mrep,
                    SelCallbackLookup[mode],
                    handleSelectCB,
                    this) ;

    // Add BOTH extended and multiple selection callback,
    // because we switch to extended mode in order to
    // artificially select multiple items
    if (mode == EXTENDED)
    {
        XtAddCallback(rtr.mrep,
                    XmNmultipleSelectionCallback,
                    handleSelectCB,
                    this);
    }
}
```

Notice that we register `handleSelectCB()` <u>twice</u> when the Scroll-ingList is in EXTENDED selection mode. This is because Motif resets the set of selected items when we explicitly select an item from EXTENDED mode (see Heller, 1992).

When invoked, the handleSelectCB() function determines the effect of the current selection on the items previously selected and passes this information along with the position of all selected items.

```
void ScrollingList::handleSelectCB(Widget      w,
                                   XtPointer   clientd,
                                   XtPointer   calld)
{
    XmListCallbackStruct  *lcbs = (XmListCallbackStruct *)
                                   calld ;
    ScrollingList         *list = (ScrollingList *) clientd ;

    SelectType    type ;
    UintList       positions ;
    int            i ;


    // Why was callback invoked?
    switch (lcbs->reason)
    {
        case XmCR_SINGLE_SELECT:
        case XmCR_BROWSE_SELECT:
          {
              type       = INITIAL ;
              positions += (uint) (lcbs->item_position - 1) ;
          }
          break;

        case XmCR_MULTIPLE_SELECT:
        {
            type = INITIAL ;

            // Populate positions
            for (i = 0 ; i < lcbs->selected_item_count ; i++)
              positions += (uint)
                (lcbs->selected_item_positions[i] - 1) ;
        }
```

```
        break;

    case XmCR_EXTENDED_SELECT:
        {
            switch (lcbs->selection_type)
            {
                case XmINITIAL:
                 type = INITIAL ;
                 break ;

                  case XmMODIFICATION:
                   type = MODIFICATION ;
                   break ;

                  case XmADDITION:
                   type = ADDITION ;
                   break ;

                  default:
                   type = SELECT_ERROR ;
                   break ;
            }

            // Populate positions
            for (i = 0 ; i < lcbs->selected_item_count ; i++)
              positions += (uint)
                 (lcbs->selected_item_positions[i] - 1) ;
        }
      break ;

    default:
      break ;
  }

  // Invoke user callback
  list->selCB(*list, type, positions, list->udata);
}
```

Notice that the only mode in which we can have anything other than an INITIAL selection is EXTENDED mode. This is because selections in other modes can't be added to or modified once they have been made.

The ScrollingList class provides the method unregisterCall-back() to complement the registerCallback() method.

```
void ScrollingList::unregisterCallback(void)
{
    // Add the callback
    XtRemoveCallback(rtr.mrep,
                    SelCallbackLookup[mode],
                    handleSelectCB,
                    this) ;

    // If extended mode, then we have registered 2
    if (mode == EXTENDED)
    {
        XtRemoveCallback(rtr.mrep,
                        XmNmultipleSelectionCallback,
                        handleSelectCB,
                        this) ;
    }
}
```

Note that when in EXTENDED mode, we must unregister two callbacks with Xt.

8.4.6 *Item Selection*

The ScrollingList class provides a number of methods which allow the user to bypass the end user and explicitly manipulate the selection and deselection of items. For example, a user may wish to preselect an item as a default before presenting a ScrollingList to the end user.

First, the setSelectionMode() method allows the user to change the mode of selection dynamically for a ScrollingList.

```
void ScrollingList::setSelectionMode(ModeType smode)
{
```

```
    // Set the policy
    XtVaSetValues(rtr.mrep,
                 XmNselectionPolicy, SelModeLookup[smode],
                 NULL) ;

    // Re-register selection callback for new selection mode
    if (selCB)
    {
      unregisterCallback();
      mode = smode ;
      registerCallback(selCB, udata);
    }
    else mode = smode ;
}
```

When changing selection modes, we must reregister the `handleSelectCB()` function according to the new mode of selection.

The `ScrollingList` class also provides a method to explicitly select an item according to the position of the item within a `ScrollingList`.

```
void ScrollingList::selectItem(uint pos)
{
    // Translate from 0-based to 1-based position
    uint mpos = pos < itemCount() ? pos + 1 : 0 ;

    int   selCount ;

    // Get selected item count
    XtVaGetValues(rtr.mrep,
                 XmNselectedItemCount, &selCount,
                 NULL) ;

    // If selection policy is EXTENDED, and there are
    // already items selected, switch to MULTIPLE
    // temporarily to *** add *** to selections
    if (mode == EXTENDED and selCount > 0)
    {
      XtVaSetValues(rtr.mrep,
```

```
                    XmNselectionPolicy, XmMULTIPLE_SELECT,
                    NULL) ;
   }

   // Select item, display at top
   XmListSetPos(rtr.mrep, mpos) ;
   XmListSelectPos(rtr.mrep, mpos, TRUE) ;

   // Change mode back, if necessary
   if (mode == EXTENDED and selCount > 0)
   {
     XtVaSetValues(rtr.mrep,
                   XmNselectionPolicy, XmEXTENDED_SELECT,
                   NULL) ;
   }
}
```

Notice that if the selection mode is EXTENDED, then we temporarily switch to MULTIPLE mode to select the item. We can do this easily because we registered handleSelectCB() with Xt for both EXTENDED and MULTIPLE mode when the selection mode is EXTENDED.

We can also explicitly select an item by name.

```
void ScrollingList::selectItem(const CString &item)
{
   // Get system string
   XmString mstring = XmStringCreateSimple
                      ((const char *) item) ;

   int   selCount ;

   // Get selected item count
   XtVaGetValues(rtr.mrep,
                 XmNselectedItemCount, &selCount,
                 NULL) ;

   // If selection policy is EXTENDED, and items are
   // already selected, switch to MULTIPLE temporarily
```

```
    // to *** add *** to selections
    if (mode == EXTENDED and selCount > 0)
    {
      XtVaSetValues(rtr.mrep,
                    XmNselectionPolicy, XmMULTIPLE_SELECT,
                    NULL) ;
    }

    // Perform selection
    XmListSetItem(rtr.mrep, mstring);
    XmListSelectItem(rtr.mrep, mstring, TRUE);

    // Change mode back, if necessary
    if (mode == EXTENDED and selCount > 0)
    {
      XtVaSetValues(rtr.mrep,
                    XmNselectionPolicy, XmEXTENDED_SELECT,
                    NULL) ;
    }

    // Deallocate system string
    XmStringFree(mstring);
}
```

Once again we temporarily switch to MULTIPLE mode before actually adding the item to the Motif ScrolledList widget.

For convenience, there is also a method that allows us to select all of the items at once.

```
void ScrollingList::selectAll(void)
{
    if (mode < MULTIPLE) return ;

    // NOTE: The code below seems to toggle selection
    // instead of selecting,
    //     Therefore, we deselect all items first.
    XmListDeselectAllItems(rtr.mrep) ;
```

```
    // If selection policy is EXTENDED, and items are
    // already selected, switch to MULTIPLE temporarily
    // to *** add *** to selections
    if (mode == EXTENDED)
    {
      XtVaSetValues(rtr.mrep,
                    XmNselectionPolicy, XmMULTIPLE_SELECT,
                    NULL) ;
    }

    uint count = itemCount(),
                 mpos ;

    // Perform selection on all but the last entry
    for (mpos = 1 ; mpos < count ; mpos++)
        XmListSelectPos(rtr.mrep, mpos, FALSE);

    // Select last item to invoke callback
    XmListSelectPos(rtr.mrep, count, TRUE);

    // Change mode back, if necessary
    if (mode == EXTENDED)
    {
      XtVaSetValues(rtr.mrep,
                    XmNselectionPolicy, XmEXTENDED_SELECT,
                    NULL) ;
    }
}
```

When explicitly selecting all items, we force Motif to wait until the last item in the `ScrolledList` widget is selected before invoking any callbacks.

The `ScrollingList` class also provides a complementary set of methods for deselecting items. These are all implemented as calls to Motif convenience functions for `ScrolledList` widgets, `XmList*()`.

```
void ScrollingList::deselectItem(uint pos)
```

```
{
    // Translate from 0-based to 1-based position
    uint mpos = pos < itemCount() ? pos + 1 : 0 ;

    // Deselect item
    XmListDeselectPos(rtr.mrep, mpos);
}

void ScrollingList::deselectItem(const CString &item)
{
    XmString mstring = XmStringCreateSimple
                            ((const char *) item) ;

    XmListDeselectItem(rtr.mrep, mstring) ;
    XmStringFree(mstring) ;
}

void ScrollingList::deselectAll(void)
{
    XmListDeselectAllItems(rtr.mrep) ;
}
```

The ScrollingList class provides a method called getSelected() that allows the user to obtain the selected items from a ScrollingList at any point in processing.

```
void ScrollingList::getSelected(UintList &sel) const
{
    int selCount, *positions ;

    // Get all selected positions
    if (XmListGetSelectedPos(rtr.mrep, &positions, &selCount))
    {
      uint i ;

      for (i = 0 ; i < selCount ; i++)
```

```
        sel += (uint) (positions[i] - 1) ;
    }
}
```

We must always remember to translate between our 0-based and Motif's 1-based ordering system.

It may be extremely useful for the user to be able to remove all of the selected items from the list. The ScrollingList provides the removeSelected() method to do just that.

```
void ScrollingList::removeSelected(void)
{
    int    count, *positions ;

    // Get all selected positions
    if (XmListGetSelectedPos(rtr.mrep, &positions, &count))
    {
        int pos, remCount ;

        // Delete each item in the list
        for (remCount = 1, pos = 0; pos < count; pos++, remCount++)
            removeItem((uint) positions[pos] - remCount);
    }
}
```

Finally, the ScrollingList class provides a method called selected-Count(), which indicates the number of items currently selected.

```
uint ScrollingList::selectedCount(void) const
{
    int count;

    // Get the count of items selected
    XtVaGetValues(rtr.mrep, XmNselectedItemCount,
                  &count, NULL);
    return (uint) count;
}
```

8.4.7   Using Scrolling Lists

Assume that we need a way to display the total of our household expenses for any subset of months in a given year. We can use a `ScrollingList` to perform this task dynamically.

```
...
#include "CustomDialog.h"
#include "ScrollingList.h"
#include "CString.h"

// Number of months in a year
#define NUMBER_OF_MONTHS 12

// Month strings
static char *MonthName[] =
{
    "January",      "February",      "March",       "April",
    "May",          "June",          "July",        "August",
    "September",    "October",       "November",    "December"
} ;

// Monthly expenses
extern float expenses[NUMBER_OF_MONTHS] ;

// Displays total in the interface, defined elsewhere
extern void displayTotal(float total) ;

// Selection callback
static void expenseCB(ScrollingList              &sl,
                      ScrollingList::SelectType    type,
                      const UintList              &pos,
                      void                        *udata)
{
    static float total = 0.0 ;

    switch (type)
```

```
    {
      case ScrollingList::SELECT_ERROR:
        return ;

      case ScrollingList::INITIAL:
      case ScrollingList::ADDITION:
      case ScrollingList::MODIFICATION:
        {
              UintListIndex uli ;

              total = 0.0 ;
              ListLoop(pos, uli)
                 total += expenses[pos[uli]] ;
        }
        break ;
    }

    // Display the total
    displayTotal(total) ;
}

// Parent object defined elsewhere
extern GraphicalObject *parent ;

void checkExpenses(void)
{
    CustomDialog   dialog   ("expenseDialog", parent) ;
    ScrollingList  list     ("monthList",
                             &dialog,
                             ScrollingList::EXTENDED) ;

    int i ;

    // Add the items to the scrolling list
    for (i = 0 ; i < NUMBER_OF_MONTHS ; i++)
         list.addItem(MonthName[i]) ;
```

```
    // Customize the dialog
    dialog.customize(list) ;

    // Initialize displayed total
    displayTotal(0.0) ;

    // Set visible item count in list
    list.setVisible(NUMBER_OF_MONTHS) ;

    // Register selection callback
    list.registerCallback(expenseCB) ;

    // Place dialog on screen
    dialog.pose() ;
}
...
```

The preceding fragment sets up a ScrollingList that displays all of the months in a year. The end user is free to repeatedly change the selected items. Every time the selected items are changed, a total, presumably displayed in a TextField somewhere, is updated to reflect the currently selected months.

CHAPTER *9*

Putting It All Together

U p to this point we have seen how to use up to three or four Graph-icalObjects in conjunction with one another, but we do not yet have a clear picture of how to structure a large interface. In this chapter we discuss some techniques for managing some of the conceptual complexities associated with large interfaces.

9.1 Application Structure

As we develop more and more interfaces for various applications, we will start to notice that the structure of these interfaces resemble one another quite closely, regardless of the application. This is because of the nature of event-driven programming, which requires us to create the elements, associate handlers with the elements, and start an event loop.

The method of structuring an interface for a typical application will usually consist of the following steps.

1. Initialize the graphical environment by calling the GraphicalEnv method setEnvironment and passing it the application name and command line arguments. This is optional, but friendly, as otherwise the command line arguments will be ignored.

2. Create the main `GraphicalObject` for the application, presumably a `MainWindow` object.

3. Recursively create each `GraphicalObject` in the application, and parent each one appropriately. As soon as each object is created, associate all callback and event handlers for the object.

4. If a `MainWindow` object is the main `GraphicalObject` for the application, call the `set()` method to initialize the regions. This places the `GraphicalObjects` for the regions under management of the `MainWindow`.

5. Call the `realizeAll()` method provided by the `GraphicalObject` class. This is optional and may not be desirable if the interface is large. This is because a call to the `realizeAll()` method will allocate system resources for all `GraphicalObjects`, whether they are actually used or not.

6. Call the `manage()` method for the permanent `GraphicalObjects`. If this is not done, nothing will ever be placed on screen.

7. Call the `static` method `startApplication()` provided by the `GraphicalEnv` class. This starts the main event loop for the application.

These steps are illustrated in the following code fragment, which creates an interface for a drawing application by using a `DrawingArea` as the workspace for a `MainWindow`.

```
// Includes
#include "MainWindow.h"
#include "PixelMap.h"
#include "MenuBar.h"
#include "ControlPanel.h"
#include "DrawingArea.h"

// Functions defined elsewhere
extern DrawingArea   *createWorkSpace (MainWindow &parent) ;
extern ControlPanel  *createMenuBar   (MainWindow &parent) ;
extern MenuBar       *createPanel     (MainWindow &parent) ;

main(int argc, char **argv)
```

```
{
    // STEP 1
    GraphicalEnv::setEnvironment("draw", argc, argv) ;

    // STEP 2
    MainWindow mainWindow("mainWindow") ;

    // STEP 3
    MenuBar      *menuBar   = createMenuBar   (mainWindow) ;
    ControlPanel *panel     = createPanel     (mainWindow) ;
    DrawingArea  *workSpace  = createWorkSpace (mainWindow) ;

    // STEP 4
    mainWindow.set(*workSpace, menuBar, panel) ;

    // STEP 5
    mainWindow.realizeAll() ;

    // STEP 6
    mainWindow.manage() ; // ... and everything else

    // STEP 7
    GraphicalEnv::startApplication() ;
}
```

Of all of the above steps, step 3, in which we recursively create all Graph-icalObjects in the interface, can be the most complex. We hide this complexity in the above fragment by hypothesizing the create*() methods, but in reality this can be quite messy.

A technique for managing the complexities of interface structuring is given in the next section.

9.2 Reentrant Modes

In the previous section, we briefly discussed some of the complexities associated with building the various GraphicalObjects for the interface and registering callbacks for them. Let's take a look at these complexities in some depth.

Consider a drawing application in which we allow the end user to draw various geometric shapes to a `DrawingArea` object using the mouse. In such an application, we must monitor the position and button press data coming from the mouse and invoke various event handlers for these, depending on the shape being drawn.

This means that we must maintain a unique set of event handlers for each shape, and somehow register and unregister them in accordance with the wishes of the end user. We can accomplish this automatically by using *modes*. For the purposes of this discussion, a mode is defined as a unique set of event and callback handlers which together provide a context for performing a specific task within an application, such as allowing the end user to draw a polygon. Furthermore, modes can be *reentrant*. That is, we can suspend a mode and reenter it afresh, as if the mode had not been previously initiated. This suggests the following operations for modes:

- **entry:** The mode is initiated. An existing mode is suspended, and all handlers for the current mode are registered.
- **exit:** The mode is stopped. All event and callback handlers for the current mode are unregistered, and a previous mode is resumed.
- **suspension:** The mode is temporarily stopped. All event and callback handlers for the current mode are temporarily unregistered, and a new mode is entered.
- **resumption:** The mode is resumed after being temporarily stopped. All event and callback handlers for the current mode are reregistered, and the application continues in the mode.

9.2.1 Modes

Modes are represented in our library by the `ModeInfo` class.

```
class ModeInfo
{
    friend class ModeStack ;

  public:
```

```
  // Default mode
  static const uint Empty ;

  // Mode operation
  enum Operation
  {

    ENTER,        // Enter mode
    LEAVE,        // Leave mode
    RESUME,       // Resume suspended mode
    SUSPEND,      // Suspend mode
    OP_COUNT      // Counts the literals
  } ;

  typedef void (* OpCB)(Operation op, void *udata) ;
      // Prototype for mode operation callback handlers

private:

  OpCB   callback  [OP_COUNT] ;
  void *udata      [OP_COUNT] ;

public:

  inline ModeInfo(void)
  {
    int i ;

    for (i = 0 ; i < OP_COUNT ; i++)
    {
      callback[i] = NULL ;
      udata[i]    = NULL ;
    }
  }
      // Constructor

  inline ~ModeInfo(void) {} // NULL
```

```
        // Destructor

    inline void registerCallback(Operation    op,
                                 OpCB          cb,
                                 void         *data = NULL)
    { callback[op] = cb ; udata[op] = data ; }
        // Registers user callback handler for when
        // operation occurs

    inline void unregisterCallback(Operation op)
    { callback[op] = NULL ; udata[op] = NULL ; }
        // Un-registers user callback handler for when
        // operation occurs
} ;
```

The `ModeInfo` class provides two data members called `callbacks` and `udata`. The `callbacks` member is an array of callback handlers that are triggered for the appropriate mode operation. The `udata` member is an array of user data for the corresponding mode operation callbacks.

9.2.2 *Mode Stacks*

The mode operations discussed above imply that we can store modes in a stack (see Hopcroft et al., 1982), and push and pop them as needed. The mode operations are ultimately controlled by the end user. When a mode is pushed, we suspend the previous mode and enter the new mode. When a mode is popped, we exit the current mode and resume the previous mode.

The `ModeStack` class implements a reentrant stack of application modes.

```
// Include
extern "C"
{
# include <sys/types.h>
}
#include "ModeStack.h"
#include "List.h"
```

```
// Defines
#define UintList         List<uint>
#define UintListIndex    ListIndex<uint>
#define ModeList         List<ModeInfo *>
#define ModeListIndex    ListIndex<ModeInfo *>

class ModeStack : private ModeList
{
  private:

    UintList     stack ;    // Actual mode stack

  public:

    inline ModeStack(void) {} // NULL
      // Constructor

    inline ~ModeStack(void) { zap() ; }
      // Destructor

    inline uint modeCount(void) const { return length() ; }
      // Obtains total number of supported modes

    inline uint size(void) const { return stack.length() ; }
      // Obtains number of modes on stack

    inline void addSupport(ModeInfo *mode) { *this += mode ; }
      // Adds support for a mode to the stack

    void push(uint mode) ;
      // Pushes a new mode onto the stack

    uint pop(void) ;
      // Pops a mode from the stack

    inline uint head(void) const
    {
```

```
        return stack.inRange(stack.first()) ?
            stack[stack.first()] : ModeInfo::Empty ;
    }
    // Obtains current mode
} ;
```

The ModeStack class is derived from List<ModeInfo *>. This list is used to store information about any supported modes for a given application. The user is responsible for building ModeInfo objects, registering the appropriate callbacks for each one, and adding support for them in the user-defined order.

The push() method in the ModeStack class is implemented as follows:

```
void ModeStack::push(uint mode)
{
    uint        oldMode = head() ;
    ModeInfo *oldInfo = operator []((long) oldMode) ;

    // Suspend the previous mode
    if (oldInfo and oldInfo->callback[ModeInfo::SUSPEND])
        oldInfo->callback[ModeInfo::SUSPEND]
            (ModeInfo::SUSPEND, oldInfo->udata)

    // Push the new mode
    stack += mode ;

    ModeInfo *info = operator[]((long) mode) ;

    // Invoke the entry callback
    if (info and info->callback [ModeInfo::ENTER])
        info->callback [ModeInfo::ENTER]
            (ModeInfo::ENTER, info->udata)
}
```

Since the ModeStack class is a friend of the ModeInfo class, the push() method can directly access the data members of ModeInfo objects.

The pop() method provided by the ModeStack class is implemented as follows:

```
uint ModeStack::pop(void)
{
    uint        oldMode = head() ;

    // Do we have an empty stack?
    if (oldMode == ModeInfo::Empty) return ModeInfo::Empty ;

    ModeInfo *oldInfo = operator []((long) oldMode) ;

    // Leave the current mode
    if (oldInfo and oldInfo->callback[ModeInfo::LEAVE])
        oldInfo->callback[ModeInfo::LEAVE]
            (ModeInfo::LEAVE, oldInfo->udata) ;

    // Actually pop the stack
    stack.eliminate(stack.first()) ;

    uint mode = head() ;
    ModeInfo *info = operator []((long) mode) ;

    // Resume the previous mode
    if (info and info->callback[ModeInfo::RESUME])
        info->callback[ModelInfo::RESUME]
            (ModelInfo::RESUME, info->udata) ;

    return oldMode ;
}
```

9.2.3   Using Modes

Let's revisit our drawing application example. Assume we have an enumerator called AppMode, which imposes an order on all modes in our drawing application:

```
...
enum AppMode
{
    VERTEX,
    SEGMENT,
```

```
    LINE,
    POLYGON,

    NUMBER_OF_MODES // Counts the literals
} ;
...
```

The following code fragment illustrates how we can build a POLYGON mode for our application.

```
...
// Includes
#include "ModeInfo.h"
#include "DrawingArea.h"
#include "LEvent.h"

// Handles all mouse events for polygon mode
extern GraphicalObject::EventHandler polyEH ;

// Handles mode entry and resumption
static void polygonModeHandler(ModeInfo::Operation   op,
                               DrawingArea          *da)
{
    switch (op)
    {
      case ModeInfo::ENTER:
      case ModeInfo::RESUME:
          da->registerEventHandler
             (LEvent::MotionEvent, polyEH) ;
          da->registerEventHandler
             (LEvent::ButtonPressEvent, polyEH) ;
          break ;

      case ModeInfo::LEAVE:
      case ModeInfo::SUSPEND:
          da->unregisterEventHandler(LEvent::MotionEvent) ;
```

```
            da->unregisterEventHandler(LEvent::ButtonPressEvent) ;
            break ;

    default:
            break;
    }
}


ModeInfo *createPolygonMode(DrawingArea *da)
{
    ModeInfo *mode = new ModeInfo ;
    int i ;

    // Register callbacks
    for (i = 0 ; i < ModeInfo::OP_COUNT ; i++)
        mode->registerCallback(i, polygonModeHandler, da) ;

        return mode ;
}
...
```

We can define similar `ModeInfo` creation functions for all of the other modes in our drawing application. Once we do this we can add support for them to a global `ModeStack` for the application.

```
...
// Includes
extern "C"
{
  #include <stdlib.h>
}
#include "PixelMap.h"
#include "AppMode.h" // Declares AppMode
#include "ModeInfo.h"
#include "ModeStack.h"
#include "DrawingArea.h"
```

```
// Types
typedef ModeInfo *(* ModeCreateFunction)(DrawingArea *) ;

// Mode creation functions
extern ModeCreateFunction createVertexMode ;
extern ModeCreateFunction createSegmentMode ;
extern ModeCreateFunction createLineMode ;
extern ModeCreateFunction createPolygonMode ;

// Global mode stack
extern ModeStack *mstack ;

// Lookup for create functions
static ModeCreateFunction CreateLookup[] =
{
    createVertexMode,
    createSegmentMode,
    createLineMode,
    createPolygonMode
} ;

// Add support for all application modes
void initModeStack(DrawingArea *da)
{
    int i ;

    for (i = 0 ; i < NUMBER_OF_MODES ; i++)
        mstack->addSupport(CreateLookup[i](da)) ;
}
...
```

Now that the all of the modes for the drawing application are supported, we can push and pop them at will. For example, we can push a mode any time a PictureButton representing the mode in the application ControlPanel is depressed by the end user. We can assume that a mode pops itself when the end user generates a specific event within the mode. For example, if the application is in POLYGON mode and the user "closes" a polygon by pressing a certain mouse button, the mode event handler (poly-EH()) pops the mode.

The following code fragment implements the createPanel() function from the previous section. It shows how to build a ControlPanel that pushes each mode.

```
...
// Includes #include "AppMode.h" // Declares AppMode
#include "ModeStack.h"
#include "PictureButton.h"
#include "ControlPanel.h"
#include "DrawingArea.h"

// Global mode stack
extern ModeStack *mstack ;

// Pixel map lookup
static char *ModeStringLookup[] =
{
    "vertex", "segment",
    "line", "polygon"
} ;

// Panel buttons
static PictureButton *button[] =
{
    NULL, NULL, NULL, NULL
} ;

// Pushes a mode
static void pushModeCB(GraphicalObject                &gobj,
                    GraphicalObject::CallbackType  type,
                    void                           *udata)
{
    mstack->push((AppMode) udata) ;
}
```

```
ControlPanel *createPanel(MainWindow &parent)
{
    // Create control panel
    ControlPanel *panel = new ControlPanel("panel", parent) ;

    // Pixel maps for picture buttons
    PixelMap *pm, *ipm ;

    int i ;

    // Populate the panel
    for (i = 0 ; i < NUMBER_OF_MODES ; i++)
    {
      // Create pixel maps for a picture button
      pm  = new PixelMap ;
      ipm = new PixelMap ;

      CString   pmName  = (CString) ModeStringLookup[i] +
                            ".pm",
              ipmName = (CString) ModeStringLookup[i] +
                            ".ipm" ;

      // Read in the images
      if (not pm->read (pmName))   exit(1) ;
      if (not ipm->read (ipmName))  exit(1) ;

      // Create the button
      button[i] = new PictureButton(ModeStringLookup[i],
                                *panel,
                                 pm, ipm) ;

      // Register callbacks
      button[i]->registerCallback(GraphicalObject::CB_ACTIVE,
                                pushModeCB,
                                (void *) i) ;
    }
```

```
    return panel ;
}
...
```

This fragment loops through the application modes and builds a `Picture-Button` for each mode. We then register the callback handler `pushModeCB()` with each button. When one of these `PictureButtons` is activated, the mode will be pushed.

9.2.4 *Application Structure Revisited*

Now that we have mode stacks in our library, we can slightly modify the steps undertaken to build the interface structure of an application, as introduced in Section 9.1.

1. Initialize the graphical environment by calling the `GraphicalEnv` method `setEnvironment` and passing it the application name and command line arguments. This is optional, but friendly, as otherwise the command line arguments will be ignored.
2. Create the main `GraphicalObject` for the application, presumably a `MainWindow` object.
3. Create a global mode stack for the application, and add support for all application modes.
4. Recursively create each `GraphicalObject` in the application, and parent each one appropriately. As soon as each object is created, associate all callback and event handlers for the object.
5. If activation of a `GraphicalObject` is supposed to trigger mode entry, add a callback that pushes the mode onto the global mode stack when the object is activated.
6. If a `MainWindow` object is the main `GraphicalObject` for the application, call the `set()` method to initialize the regions. This places the `GraphicalObjects` for the regions under management of the `Main-Window`.
7. Call the `realizeAll()` method provided by the `GraphicalObject` class. This is optional and may not be desirable if the interface is large. This is because a call to the `realizeAll()` method will allocate sys-

tem resources for all GraphicalObjects, whether they are actually used or not.

8. Call the manage() method for the permanent GraphicalObjects. This must be done or nothing will ever be placed on screen.

9. Call the static method startApplication() provided by the GraphicalEnv class. This starts the main event loop for the application.

Our steps now include support for a global mode stack. These changes are illustrated in the following code fragment.

```
// Includes
#include "MainWindow.h"
#include "PixelMap.h"
#include "MenuBar.h"
#include "ControlPanel.h"
#include "DrawingArea.h"
#include "ModeStack.h"

// Functions defined elsewhere
extern void          initModeStack      (DrawingArea *da) ;
extern DrawingArea   *createWorkSpace   (MainWindow &parent) ;
extern ControlPanel  *createMenuBar     (MainWindow &parent) ;
extern MenuBar       *createPanel       (MainWindow &parent) ;

// Globals
ModeStack *mstack = NULL ;

main(int argc, char **argv)
{
    // STEP 1
    GraphicalEnv::setEnvironment("draw", argc, argv) ;

    // STEP 2
    MainWindow mainWindow("mainWindow") ;

    // STEP 3
    mstack = new ModeStack ;
```

```
    // STEP 4
    MenuBar *menuBar = createMenuBar(mainWindow) ;
    DrawingArea *workSpace = createWorkSpace(mainWindow) ;

    // STEP 4 and 5
    ControlPanel *panel = createPanel (mainWindow) ;

    // STEP 6
    mainWindow.set(*workSpace, panel,menuBar) ;

    // STEP 7
    mainWindow.realizeAll() ;

    // STEP 8
    mainWindow.manage() ; // ... and everything else

    // STEP 9
    GraphicalEnv::startApplication() ;
}
```

Bibliography

Booch, Grady. *Object Oriented Design with Applications,* 2nd ed., Redwood City, CA: Benjamin/Cummings, 1994.

Ellis, Margaret A., and Bjarne Stroustrup. *The Annotated C++ Reference Manual.* Reading, MA: Addison-Wesley, 1990.

Jacobson, Ivar, et al. *Object Oriented Software Engineering, A Use Case Driven Approach.* Reading, MA: Addison-Wesley, 1992.

Flanagan, David, ed. *XToolkit Intrinsics Reference Manual,* 3rd ed. Sebastopol, CA: O'Reilly and Associates, 1993.

Heller, Dan. *Motif Programming Manual.* Sebastopol, CA: O'Reilly and Associates, 1992.

Hopcroft, J. E., A. V. Aho, and J. D. Ullman. *Data Structures and Algorithms.* Reading, MA: Addison-Wesley, 1982.

Motif 1.2 Style Guide, Mountain View, Ca: Sun Microsystems, Inc., 1992.

Lippman, Stanley B. *C++ Primer,* 2nd ed. Reading, MA: Addison-Wesley, 1993.

Nelson, Michael L. An Object-Oriented Tower of Babel. Technical report. Monterey, CA: Department of Computer Science, Naval Postgraduate School, 1991.

Nye, Adrian. *Xlib Programming Manual,* 3rd ed. Sebastopol, CA: O'Reilly and Associates, 1993a.

Nye, Adrian, ed. *Xlib Reference Manual,* 3rd ed. Sebastopol, CA: O'Reilly and Associates, 1993b.

Nye, Adrian, and Tim O'Reilly. *XToolkit Intrinsics Programming Manual,* 2nd ed. Sebastopol, CA: O'Reilly and Associates, 1992.

Rumbaugh, James. Disinherited! Examples of misuse of inheritance. *Journal of Object Oriented Programming,* 5(9):22 (1993).

Stroustrup, Bjarne. Multiple Inheritance for C++. *Computing Systems,* 2(4):367 (1989).

White, Iseult. *Using the Booch Method: A Rational Approach.* Redwood City, CA: Benjamin/Cummings, 1994.

Index

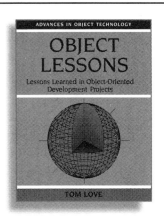

Explore the leading methodologies

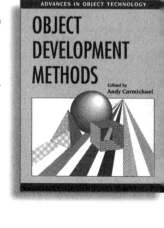

Also available from SIGS BOOKS...

SIGS BOOKS ORDER COUPON

YES! Please rush me the following books:

☐ ___copy(ies) of **Inside the Object Model** (ISBN: 1-884842-05-4)
at the low price of $39 per copy.

☐ ___copy(ies) of **Object Lessons** (ISBN: 0-9627477-3-4)
at the low price of $29 per copy.

☐ ___copy(ies) of **Using CRC Cards** (ISBN: 1-884842-07-0, April 1995)
at the low price of $24 per copy, upon publication.

☐ ___copy(ies) of **Directory of Object Technology** (ISBN: 1-884842-08-9)
at ☐ $69 (Individual Rate) per copy.
☐ $169 (Corporate Library Rate) per copy.

☐ ___copy(ies) of **The Dictionary of Object Technology** (ISBN: 1-884842-09-7, April 1995)
at the low price of $35 per copy, upon publication.

☐ ___copy(ies) of **Object Development Methods** (ISBN: 0-9627477-9-3)
at the low price of $39 per copy.

☐ ___copy(ies) of **Objectifying Real-Time Systems** (ISBN: 0-9627477-8-5)
at the low price of $44 per copy (including diskette).

RISK-FREE OFFER! *If you are not completely satisfied with your purchase, simply return the book within 14 days and receive a full refund.*

Total Purchase

Inside the Object Model	$_____
Object Lessons	$_____
Using CRC Cards	$_____
Directory of Object Technology	$_____
The Dictionary of Object Technology	$_____
Object Development Methods	$_____
Objectifying Real-Time Systems	$_____
Postage	$_____
NY Resident Sales Tax	$_____
TOTAL	$_____

Risk-Free Offer!

METHOD OF PAYMENT
☐ Check enclosed (Payable to SIGS Books)
☐ Charge my: ☐ Visa ☐ MasterCard ☐ AmEx

Card#:_____Exp. date: _____

Signature: _____

SEND TO:

Name _____

Company _____

Address_____

City/State _____

Country_____Postal Code_____

Phone _____

Fax _____

Postage and handling per Item: U.S. orders add $5.00; Canada and Mexico add $10.00; Outside North America add $15.00. Note: New York State residents must add applicable sales tax. Please allow 4-6 weeks from publication date for delivery.
Note: Non-U.S. orders must be prepaid. Checks must be in U.S. dollars and drawn on a U.S. bank.
PBA1

Distributed by Prentice Hall. Available at selected book stores.

RETURN ORDER TO: SIGS Books, P.O. Box 99425, Collingswood, NJ, 08108-9970, USA.
Fax: 609-488-6188 Phone: 609.488.9602